Social Work with Young People

Social Work in Theory and Practice Series

Forthcoming titles

Social Work with Young People

ROGER SMITH

polity

First published in 2008 by Polity Press

Polity Press
65 Bridge Street
Cambridge CB2 1UR, UK

Polity Press
350 Main Street
Malden, MA 02148, USA

ISBN-13: 978-0-7456-3912-3
ISBN-13: 978-0-7456-3913-0 (pb)

A catalogue record for this book is available from the British
Library.

Typeset in 9.5 on 12pt Utopia
by Servis Filmsetting Ltd, Stockport, Cheshire
Printed and bound in Great Britain by
MPG Books Ltd, Bodmin, Cornwall

For further information on Polity, visit our website:
www.polity.co.uk

Contents

Dedication and Acknowledgements

I think it is appropriate to dedicate this book in particular to my young people: Emma, Claire and Daniel; and of course, to Maggie.

Thanks to all the young people who, in their various ways, have made this book possible. I hope no one feels that I have misrepresented or exploited them, and that it does them justice.

Thanks, too, to Emma Longstaff whose original idea this was, and to Fiona and Neil and their colleagues who have helped with all the practicalities, as well as those academic colleagues who have read and commented so helpfully on some or all of the text.

Introduction: Difficult transitions and the role of social work

Recognizing the challenge

The idea of doing social work with young people immediately raises a series of significant questions. Our understanding of youth and its problems, on the one hand, is complex and constantly evolving. On the other, social work itself is a profession in flux, characterized by continuing debates about its core aims and functions. Bringing these two contested subjects together inevitably generates further questions about the nature of their relationship.

As we shall see, the shape of practice in the present era is affected by a number of implicit assumptions about the organization and objectives of social work, but these cannot be taken as given, and alternative constructions of the profession itself may lead to quite different conclusions about the nature of the practice task and its proper objectives. At the same time, adolescence has been the subject of intense inquiry and speculation which reveals considerable diversity of experience and development. Much remains unknown, of course, and yet youth is a life stage which is the subject of considerable public concern, policy change and practice intervention.

Who are we talking about?
Young people and their 'problems'

Firstly, it may be helpful to be as specific as we can be about the constituency which is the subject of this book. Even at this point, some necessary but arbitrary assumptions are incorporated into the discussion, for instance about the age range which encompasses youth or adolescence, or how we apply significant labels such as 'disability'. Nevertheless, some brief headline 'facts' will provide useful contextual material.

The number of young people (age range 12–19) in the UK in 2005 was 6.3 million, some 10.5 per cent of the total population. Of these, 3.2 million were male and 3.1 million female. Although most children and young people continue to live in 'couple families' (around 76 per cent; Self and Zealey, 2007), there has been a rapid increase in the numbers being brought up in lone-parent households, and there is considerable evidence that a substantial proportion of young people will have experienced family change over their lifespan (Smith, M., 2007). In 2006, there were 37,400 children in the care of local authorities in England, although not all of this group would have been living away from home. Significantly, non-white children are over-represented in this figure (23 per cent) relative to their number as a proportion of the general population.

Up to the age of 16, young people are legally required to be in full-time education, and most go on to further education, employment or training after that age; around one in ten, however, are 'not in any form of education, employment or training (NEET)', and this may have longer-term negative consequences for their future employment and health status (DCFS, 2007, p. 22).

In terms of other groups who may be thought likely to become involved with social workers in some way, around 19 per cent of boys and 17 per cent of girls up to the age of 19 are reported to have a 'mild disability', whereas the numbers identified as being 'severely disabled' are much smaller (3 per 10,000 boys aged 15–19 and 2 per 10,000 girls in this age range, for example; Nessa, 2004, p. 12). In 2003, the government estimated that there were 149,942 young people under the age of 18 who were carrying out 'caring' responsibilities for another family or household member (Hansard, 2 June 2003, Col. WA124). In 2004, over 10 per cent of 11–16 year olds 'had a clinically diagnosed mental dis-order' (DCFS, 2007, p. 12), and mental health problems are especially prevalent amongst children and young people with learning difficulties (Foundation for People with Learning Difficulties, 2007). Around a quarter of young people report committing anti-social or criminal acts in the previous year (DCFS, 2007, p. 21), and 7 per cent are regarded as 'frequent offenders', although even of these, it is only a minority who come to the attention of the criminal justice system. Once again, we know that some ethnic groups are significantly over-represented in the population of formally processed young offenders (Smith, R., 2007).

Other aspects of young people's behaviour are also identified as problematic, and it is reported that around 15 per cent of young people (aged 16–24) say they have used drugs in the previous month (DCFS, 2007, p. 10), whilst rates of alcohol consumption for 11–15 year olds in the previous week are around 20 per cent for boys and girls (11–15 year olds), and teenage pregnancy rates are 'high compared to other European countries' (p. 7).

Whilst young people's behaviour may be one trigger for social work intervention, and is often the focal point of public concern, they are also identified as being vulnerable in a number of respects. Thus, around a third of young people will have been 'victimised' in some form or other over the preceding three years (DCFS, 2007, p. 13), and a quarter of 11–15 year olds say they have been 'bullied' in the previous year. According to the NSPCC (2006a), one in six children are likely to have experienced 'serious maltreatment' within the family at some time in their childhood, although these terms themselves are somewhat impre-cise. Similarly, the NSPCC (2006b) has found that roughly 11 per cent of children under the age of 16 'run away from home or are forced to leave, and stay away overnight' at least once. Other groups of young people, too, are demonstrably 'in need', such as children who are asylum seekers (Creighton, 2004), of whom 16,720 were identified in 2001.

This indicates not only that the circumstances of young people are diverse and frequently problematic, but also that we should recognize the cumulative nature of some of the difficulties they encounter, whether these are the multiplier effects of different aspects of social exclusion (SEU, 2005) or the impact of unequal and discriminatory treatment, as seems to be the case in the context of mental health (DCFS, 2007), care (Barn et al., 2005) and youth justice (Smith, R., 2007).

This snapshot thus offers some indication of the present-day circumstances of young people and the kind of difficulties which might bring them into the ambit of social work and other public and independent welfare services. It is immediately apparent that the kinds of issues likely to arise for young people where social work has a role are many and varied, and that understanding young people's problems and developing the capacity to intervene appropriately and effectively is, itself, a significant challenge. This, however, is where social work must start, because a proper appreciation of how young people's lives and experiences are shaped is a necessary prerequisite for getting to know them and then working alongside them.

A dangerous age? Youth as a subject of concern

Not only do young people encounter identifiable problems such as those outlined above, but also youth is a time of life which generates massive worry and apprehension, focusing on both future aspirations and possible negative outcomes. Young people are a source of concern in a number of quarters, including their families, the wider community, educational providers, employers, law-enforcement and other state agencies, the media and politicians. This is partly a reflection of the uncertainty of their status, 'in between' childhood and adulthood. Young people occupy an ambiguous terrain between dependence and autonomy, where they are often viewed simultaneously as responsible for their own actions and necessarily reliant on others for guidance and support. As a result both personal and public responses often seem to be contradictory or confused. For instance, young people are increasingly encouraged to express themselves and to articulate their wishes and feelings, and this has been an explicit element of a range of recent policy initiatives. However, their behaviour has been and remains the subject of continued anxiety, and this is evidenced by the variety of measures introduced specifically to prevent or control youthful transgressions, notably in the form of the Anti-social Behaviour Order in recent years.

Social work by its nature focuses on 'problems', especially at the interface between the individual and society. Thus, it is seen as having a distinctive role in addressing the difficulties experienced by the young as they seek to negotiate their personal and social changes. For some young people, these problems are likely to be more acute and pressing than for others, and it might seem self-evident that social work professionals will have a part to play in helping to deal with these. However, the place of the social worker as mediator between the individual and others (such as family, community and wider social systems) generates substantial uncertainty as to how these responsibilities can be met. The social worker has to make sense of the complex relationships, needs and expectations of young people; but she or he also has to respond to these in the light of her or his wider obligations, to the employing agency, legal requirements, 'public opinion' and professional codes. This may partly account for the ambivalence with which social workers are viewed, not least by young people themselves. Research has indicated that relationships between the two are variable, and on many occasions young people feel that they are not properly supported by someone who they feel should be acting unequivocally in their interests. Practitioners, by contrast, may feel that they have to represent wider interests, too, for instance where young people's behaviour is giving cause for concern. Practitioners may also encounter practical problems such as the need to balance competing demands on their time, which may not always be appreciated by service users whose problems are immediate. Developing ideas about appropriate roles and interventions will not be straightforward, therefore. None the less, social work does have a distinctive contribution to make to the project of tackling the problems faced by young people, not least because its underlying rationale is based on resolving complex personal and social issues. The task facing us here is to unpack some of these complexities in order to develop a framework for effective practice.

The relationship between the young person and the practitioner will incorporate these ambiguities implicitly, and the social work process itself will involve the key task of identifying, addressing and resolving mutual expectations, sometimes common, sometimes differing and sometimes conflicting. The task of building, sustaining and renegotiating an effective basis for working together is constant and continuing.

Social work with young people:
Knowledge, roles and tasks

What, then, are the essential ingredients of social work thinking and practice with young people? Clearly, there is a need to explore the nature of adolescence and young people's experiences, in order to shape interventions in difficult circumstances. At the same time, practice must be founded on a set of distinctive and well-grounded operating principles, knowledge and skills, and it must establish and sustain strong working relationships based on a spirit of mutuality and cooperation.

Firstly, then, we will consider existing ideas and knowledge about youth and its 'problems'. Increasingly, the idea of 'transitions' has come to inform our understanding of this phase of development. A number of key changes can be identified across different aspects of young people's lives, such as leaving school, moving out of the family home, becoming sexually active, establishing new relationships and starting work. Interacting with these experiences are the processes of learning and personal and social development which are features of all young people's lives.

The first part of the book ('Young people: Who are they and what are they like?') seeks to explore the experiences of youth in more detail, both in general terms and in relation to the specific populations with which social work is, or should be, concerned. The transitions undergone by young people are, in the main, seen as 'normal', and as a predictable, if turbulent, part of the process of 'growing up'. These changes are conceptualized in a number of ways, according to whether they are primarily *internal* (genetic, biological, physiological or psychological, for example) or *external* (social, structural, economic, educational); that is, whether they originate within the individual or are the product of wider social systems. It will thus be helpful to consider initially some of the implications of this kind of distinction, and the consequences in terms of the interrelationships between different aspects of 'development'. It can be seen even at this point that the diverse aspects of change in adolescence necessarily lead to a considerable degree of complexity and uncertainty, both for young people, and for those working with them, as teachers, youth workers and health workers, for instance, as well as social workers.

This initial exploration will also consider some of the potential influences on these transitions which make them easier or more difficult to negotiate. Individual pathways will differ, and it is important to recognize that even the more obvious manifestations of adolescence, such as physical growth and sexual maturation, are experienced in many different ways, some of which may be clear, such as gender and cultural differences, whereas other variations may be less apparent or straightforward. Youth transitions are complicated still further to the extent that they interact, and for some groups the consequences of exclusion and disadvantage can be seen to have a substantial, and potentially damaging, effect. Social work by its nature is likely to encounter many of the problems arising from disrupted and uncertain transitions, with complexity and disadvantage being central themes.

Chapter 2 goes on to consider some of the ways in which the 'problems' of youth are constructed. Sometimes it seems that the challenges faced by young people recede into the background and the spotlight is shifted onto the challenges that they present in isolation. This is particularly noteworthy in the context of youth offending, especially in the contemporary era, when young people's criminality takes centre stage, and their welfare needs, whether or not connected to this, are given less attention. However, similar processes can be identified to the extent that young people from the care system or those with disabilities are seen primarily in terms of these characteristics. Interventions can thus be unhelpfully shaped in terms of the negative assumptions made about young people in particular circumstances, rather than in terms of the hopes and expectations they share with their peers. This chapter concludes with a discussion of the appropriate orientation of social work practitioners to the perceived problems of young people, and the importance of recognizing and questioning inbuilt assumptions which we may all hold, in order to provide a strong foundation for constructive practice.

Chapter 3 takes this further, drawing attention to the increasing emphasis, in rhetoric at least, on working alongside service users, and promoting a participative model of intervention. Both nationally and internationally, policy initiatives have recently contributed to a clear emphasis on including young people in decision-making processes and taking account of their views in planning services, both individually and collectively. The practical implications for these developments are discussed, and the chapter stresses the importance for social workers of engaging with young people on their own terms, which may, of course, mean challenging some of the problem definitions imposed on them from above.

The second part of the book ('Social work and young people: Contexts and practice') moves from considering how the problems of young people are experienced and constructed to address the associated challenges for social work practice. Chapter 4 seeks to explore the nature of the relationship between practitioners and young people who are service users. It identifies a number of distinct ideological perspectives on which social workers have typically drawn, suggesting that shifts in the relationship between these can be shown to have influenced the changing shape of practice. Focusing particularly on the 'careers' of looked after young people, this chapter considers the difficulties which arise from the application of specific and fixed classifications. Inflexible and sometimes discriminatory systems appear ill-suited to the breadth and diversity of young people's experiences, and sometimes initial disadvantages are compounded as a result. Poor educational outcomes, for example, may be related to the practical consequences of multiple moves in care rather than reflecting true levels of ability. However, the consequences are almost certain to be felt in terms of limited job or training opportunities, and a curtailment of life chances for those affected.

Social workers, however, face the task of working to deliver effective services, despite system constraints and contradictory expectations. In particular, Chapter 5 explores the ambiguous view of risk which is embedded in the professional codes of practice and has significant implications for the process of engaging with young people. Young people may be 'at risk', or they may pose a threat, to themselves or others. This distinction may fundamentally shape the approach taken by practitioners; yet at the same time they need to take account of the underlying social work aim of assessing and meeting need, as well as the inevitable fact that many young people will fall into both categories simultaneously. Social work must not eschew its core task of helping young people in need simply because their behaviour is unacceptable. The necessity of bridging this divide is underlined here, as is the importance of seeking and reinforcing positives even in the face of undesirable or antagonistic actions.

Following this, Chapter 6 reflects on the experiences and expectations of young people themselves. As the importance of participation has become more strongly emphasized, it is appropriate to give more weight to their views of what social work should offer them. Unfortunately, past experience has not always been positive, and failures, especially within the care system, have resulted in negative expectations of practice. A number of recent initiatives, such as 'Quality Protects', have been put in place to promote improvements, and to engage young people more effectively. This, it is suggested, is bound up with the wider aim of achieving an ethos of mutual respect and moving away from approaches which have 'problematized' young people. Social workers are well placed to incorporate participative principles into many aspects of their day-to-day practice, and the chapter concludes with a number of suggestions as to how this might be achieved in a meaningful fashion.

The third part of the book ('Meeting the challenge: Working effectively with young people') turns to consider the task of putting the principles of effective participatory work into practice. The importance of working alongside young people should be recognized from the start, especially in view of the fact that they are likely to come to the attention of social work practitioners because of problems which have been identified by other people or agencies. Thus, as Chapter 7 underlines, the first task of the assessment process is to enable young people to reclaim or redefine the matter of concern in their own terms. It has been found, for example, that in some circumstances agency priorities dominate at the expense of young people's needs, such as when those who run away are denied assessments because of the resource implications. It also seems to be the case that institutional structures which separate assessment and service provision are perceived as unhelpful. Young people living disrupted lives may wish for the continuity and certainty of dealing with the same practitioner over time, and indeed they may wish to have a degree of choice over who works with them. Time and space to create effective working relationships are thus identified as crucial aspects of good practice.

Chapter 8 goes on to explore the implementation phase, revisiting the issue of 'risk' and how this shapes practice. The distinction is made between three different forms of risk (self-directed, other-directed and other-originated). Although it is clear that young people may fall into more than one of these categories, responses may well be shaped by which one is seen as determinative. However, as the chapter illustrates, the nature of the risk identified should not detract from the need to look beyond that. Social work must avoid becoming purely reactive in these circumstances, and must seek to engage with the stories and perceptions of young people themselves, in order to provide them with the tools to resolve the difficulties they are experiencing. Once again, the pace and timing of interventions are important as practitioners seek to resist the pressure to judge young people and impose quick-fix solutions, whilst finding space and time to enable the young people to express themselves and set their own goals.

In Chapter 9, these participative principles are taken a stage further to address the question of how social work should engage with the problems of young people as they define them. We are reminded that social work does not always offer the breadth or extent of help that young people want or need. Some are socially excluded and simply do not come to the attention of service providers, whilst others, for instance care leavers, find that the support available is limited and inflexible. This chapter argues that a fully inclusive social work needs to find ways of working alongside young people to design and develop services which are valued by young people and enable them to make use of them in their own terms. This challenge can be met in part by promoting and supporting young people in developing collective arguments for different ways of working and more inclusive services; but there is also a need to utilize existing opportunities proactively to enable service users to set and pursue their own priorities.

In conclusion, the book returns to the recurrent themes of tension between the aims and purposes of social work, on the one hand, and the problematic transitions of youth on the other. Social work almost inevitably encounters young people as problematic, and there is thus a significant risk that from the start the emphasis is placed on negative qualities, challenging behaviour and limited expectations. By contrast, positive practice needs to reframe the 'problems' of young people to recognize that these largely stem from processes of discrimination, disadvantage and exclusion. It is therefore the task of progressive practitioners to work alongside young people, so that they can reframe the issues of concern, tell their own stories, take charge of the decision-making process and arrive at their own solutions. By facilitating this approach, social work will make a significant contribution to the objective of empowering young people and promoting positive outcomes, for themselves and for others.

The complex and situated nature of this task militates against a crudely prescriptive approach, so this book incorporates a variety of examples and illustrations to prompt the reader to seek means of engaging constructively with young people, to start 'where they are', and to work creatively with them to achieve personal benefits and socially beneficial outcomes. Thus, the emphasis is on the importance of building and maintaining effective, honest and collaborative relationships and this is woven into the text throughout; in this spirit, it will not be over-directive or offer a false degree of certainty about the right or wrong ways to achieve good practice.

PART I

YOUNG PEOPLE: WHO ARE THEY AND
WHAT ARE THEY LIKE?

1 Who are we talking about? Young people and their changing lives

Why do we see youth as a matter of concern?

As I began writing this chapter, yet another report (Margo and Dixon, 2006) was issued demonstrating the problematic nature of the relationship between our society and its young people. According to the report, there is a widespread fear 'that British youth are on the verge of mental breakdown, at risk from antisocial behaviour, self-harm, drug and alcohol abuse' (p. vii), and it is also suggested that some of these concerns are 'borne out' by the available evidence. Persistent social inequalities and patterns of social organization are likely to be reflected in problematic behaviour and attitudes amongst young people, it seems. At the same time, misunderstanding and fear are common features of the way in which young people are perceived by others. The uneasy nature of the relationship between society and its youth appears to indicate a deep and substantial rift between generations based on conflicting ideas, experiences and values. Of particular significance in this study was the observation that the level of mistrust is higher in Britain than amongst its mainland European counterparts, suggesting both that there is a distinctive aspect to the way in which this country problematizes its young people, and, at the same time, that there is the potential to change and do things differently as far as they are concerned. For those involved in working directly with young people, these messages are significant, as we shall see, because they form a powerful context for the interactive processes which determine the extent to which practitioners are able to intervene constructively.

Of course, there is nothing new in the observation that adolescence is problematic. One of Shakespeare's characters bemoans the irresponsibilities of youth (*The Winter's Tale*, Act 3, Scene 3), and similar depictions are widespread amongst works of fiction through the ages, such as those of Dickens in Victorian England. Apart from what we find in literature, recurrent historical concerns about the behaviour of young people are documented elsewhere (see Pearson, 2002).

In the light of this, we might be tempted to conclude that there is a persistent and consistent quality to the problems experienced by, and indeed caused by, the young. If this is the case, we would need to seek explanations in the fixed and determinate features of this particular life stage. For example, developmental characteristics might be sought out to explain the perennial nature of the behavioural and emotional problems specific to adolescence.

On the other hand, if we take note of historical, cultural and even geographical variations, as the report already cited suggests (Margo and Dixon, 2006, p. ix), we may need to consider the impact of more specific and 'situated' factors as key influences on the shape of young people's lives. Depending on the core assumptions we might make of this kind, rather different lessons might be drawn for the most appropriate way to make policy and intervene with them.

Following on from this, it is also important at the outset to emphasize the need to make a clear conceptual distinction between the way in which young people are perceived and categorized by others, and their own experiences and perceptions. It will become increasingly clear throughout this book that practice with young people is unlikely to be effective unless it seeks to bring about an accommodation between these often divergent and contradictory perspectives. The fact that the wider society harbours a considerable degree of apprehension and uncertainty about its younger members should not, of itself, lead us to believe that this is based on a fair or accurate portrayal of the underlying reality of their lives. On the other hand, these very (mis)perceptions may themselves generate a range of anticipatory actions which impact on young people, shaping their experiences and influencing their actions in turn. Our fearful reactions may both be a response to specific grounds for concern and yet at the same time play a part in giving rise to further misunderstanding and conflict. In order both to understand and to intervene effectively, there is a clear need to distinguish between the 'construction' of youth and the way in which it is actually experienced, whilst recognizing that these remain inextricably intertwined, as well.

However, in order to avoid getting ahead of ourselves, and rushing to the conclusion that the problems of youth are simply the consequences of a clash of interests, we must also ask a number of broader questions, such as why these conflicts should arise in the first place. What makes adolescence distinctive, for instance? How, in fact, is the experience of 'being a young person' constituted? What is it about 'youth' that gives rise to the perennial concerns of society at large?

We will start here by considering some of the ways in which youth and adolescence have been defined before moving on to consider some of the contextual factors which shape the modern-day experience of being a young person. Subsequent discussion will address the issues of the relationship between these observable attributes of the phenomenon and the way in which youth itself is constructed, particularly those aspects which are seen as problematic, whether to young people, or to society at large.

Defining characteristics?

Whilst the terms 'adolescent', 'youth' or 'young person' may convey a picture about which there is a degree of consensus, attempts to agree a precise definition of these terms will prove somewhat more problematic. The common view would probably characterize youth in terms of the life stage falling between childhood and adulthood, covering most or all of the teenage years, and incorporating a series of biological, social, emotional and economic transitions, perhaps best encapsulated in the phrase 'growing up'. Further scrutiny, however, will demonstrate that these assumptions are not entirely unproblematic, and that we should be cautious about using our defining terminology too prescriptively. What about these conventional understandings, then?

Age

Age is clearly of considerable practical use as a determinant of expected attributes and achievements. It is an effective external marker of the progression of individuals through various phases and past key mile-stones on the journey from childhood to adulthood. For example, schooling is explicitly structured in these terms, with increasing num-bers of formal transition points, between 'key stages' and curriculum levels. At the same time, significant markers of changing status and assumed maturity are specified in law, with the range of ages at which children are assumed to acquire 'adult' responsibilities and are treated accordingly. Thus, in England and Wales, the age of criminal responsi-bility is set at 10, the minimum age for employment is 13 (but this is highly restricted), and the minimum age of sexual consent is 16; on the other hand, the minimum driving age is 17, and 18 is the lowest age for watching adult-rated films, or voting in elections. Indeed, the 'end of childhood' is signified quite differently according to a variety of legisla-tive provision and depending on the context of the activity (for instance, where you drink alcohol). We should also note here that these variations are compounded by changes over time, across geographical boundaries,[1] and according to other factors, such as faith groups or family expectations. Other 'systems', such as the education sector, also have a range of explicit milestones at which children and young people make transitions, which are not seen as complete in some cases until their early twenties.

Thus, the use of 'age' as a precise determinant of the phases of youth is potentially problematic. These phases are not coterminous, and clearly imply much greater expectations in terms of autonomy and personal responsibility in some areas than others – with significant implications for those working with young people in specific settings, such as criminal justice, on the one hand, and services for people with learning difficulties, on the other. As indicated previously, the formal definitions of age and the expected points of 'transition' need also be seen in the light of the variations of lived experience amongst young people themselves. For most, for instance, the age at which they leave the family home may be their early twenties; whereas for young people brought up in the care of local authorities, and ironically with less recourse to informal means of support, the age at which they leave home is likely to be much earlier (Wade, 2003). Thus, the 'age of independence' is highly variable.

Developmental stages

Rather than relying on the relatively crude measure of chronological age alone, it may be helpful to modify this by applying the idea of 'developmental stages' to the equation. Indeed, there have been a considerable number of attempts to develop classificatory systems to distinguish life stages and describe the characteristics associated with each of these. It has been suggested that the 'dominant discipline providing knowledge about childhood – developmental psychology – has proposed childhood as a series of stages, linked to age, with each successive stage bearing distinctive cognitive features' (Mayall, 2002, p. 87). This kind of perspective is perhaps most commonly associated with the work of Piaget (1959, for example) whose detailed studies of children's linguistic achievements suggested this kind of progressive mechanism in operation. Similar frameworks have been generated to account for the development of children across other dimensions, as well, including physical, emotional and moral 'growth' (Erikson, 1963; Fahlberg, 1994).

Assessing children's progress usually draws on assumptions that this can be measured against a range of accepted benchmarks which establish 'normal' developmental expectations. Thus, the concept of 'adolescence' as a distinct life stage incorporates a series of more or less agreed norms against which to judge young people's development (Bailey, 2006).

It is suggested that adolescence can be defined in terms of a group of distinctive attributes and behaviours. These include a 'questioning attitude'; a search for moral certainty; and a range of behaviours and characteristics associated with the idea of 'transition' between childhood and adulthood (Coleman and Hendry, 1999). Growing sexual awareness and experimentation, for example, are assumed to be a feature of this phase of someone's life (Bailey, 2006). In summary: 'Adolescence is a transitional stage of development between childhood and adulthood. The developmental tasks of adolescence centre on autonomy and connection with others, rebellion and the development of independence, development of identity and distinction from and continuity with others' (Bailey, 2006, p. 208). Whilst it might appear at first glance as if there are clearly identifiable features of youth as a life stage, underlying this is a considerable degree of uncertainty about the nature and timing of adolescence.

Like 'age' alone, the notion of developmental stages incorporates a number of problems when utilized in an attempt to determine the key characteristics of a particular phase of life, such as youth. Firstly, it is difficult to assign stages of development to fixed points in time with any real accuracy. Key life changes such as puberty and significant physical growth can occur at variable ages, for example. In addition, once we distinguish the modes of development, it becomes clear that there may be a degree of inconsistency between them. Thus, if we think in terms of biological, psychological, social, emotional and intellectual development as distinct categories, it is immediately obvious that these may not progress in parallel. As Coleman and Hendry (1999, p. 39) observe, indeed, it may be the case that many people never achieve the highest levels of cognitive development identified by theorists such as Piaget. Equally, subdividing the idea of development in this way demonstrates the clear differences in the kind of pathways individuals will follow through different aspects of the maturation process.

The variability of progress is further illustrated when we consider biographical and cultural differences based, for example, on gender, ethnicity or disability. These, in turn, are likely to impact on the personal life trajectories followed by young people, in ways which are of major significance. Adolescence is thus a far more complex experience than we might expect from a pure developmental model. It is also important here to recognize that some of the 'stages' that we have identified are determined not by a natural process of progression, but through changes which may be socially constructed or determined. External expectations and forms of regulation may play a significant part in determining the way in which young people experience their own individual life changes.

Turning points and transitions

The interplay between individual developmental biographies and the changes which result from external influences may better be captured in terms of a series of key 'turning points' which shape adolescence and determine the nature of the pathway between childhood and adulthood. It is suggested, for example, that 'the stage of youth' is becoming a longer and more distinctive phase (Coleman and Hendry, 1999, p. 8), and that this is common across international boundaries. Importantly, this indicates that both the concept and experience of adolescence may be socially determined at least as much as being dependent on individual growth and development. Thus, adolescence can be captured in terms of a number of key transitions, which reflect significant changes in personal and social status. In particular, three changes are seen as central to the experience of growing up:

1   the move from education to work or training;
2   the achievement of independence from family or carers; and
3   leaving the 'family' home.

These three transitions themselves clearly do not occur at fixed points, but are variable depending on a variety of personal and social factors. They all, however, represent aspects of the wider movement from a dependent childhood to what is seen as a distinctive and fully respon-sible independent adulthood.

The recognition of these externally defined and significant social indicators of transition is important because it enables us to make the connection between these global aspects of youth and development and those which are located more at the personal level. Youth is thus characterized by a series of significant changes, both those which are specific to the individual ('turning points') and those which are more generalized features of a particular life stage, being socially determined ('transitions'). The important point here is that these different dimen-sions of development and change will inevitably interact:

> The premise underlying integrating notions of transitions and turning points is that transitional periods are characterized by developmental challenges that are relatively universal; that is, most individuals navigate transitional periods, and these periods require new modes of adaptation to biological, psychological or social changes. By definition, then, turning points occurring in the context of transitional periods may be particularly salient to individuals or to subsets of individuals.   (Graber and Brooks-Gunn, 1996, p. 769)

This sense of an interlocking and interactive set of changes, both internal and external, appears to capture the experience of adolescence quite well schematically. These observations lead Coleman and Hendry (1999, p. 11) to identify a number of theoretical principles which should inform a perspective identified as 'developmental contextualism':

1 Human development must be viewed within an 'ecological' context.
2 Human development is continuous – adolescence is connected to other life stages.
3 Individuals and families/carers influence each other (it is not a one-way process).
4 A multi-disciplinary perspective is necessary to understand human growth and development.
5 Individuals play an active part in shaping their own development (see also Smith, R., 2000).
6 Explanations of 'person–context' interactions must consider the 'goodness of fit' between these aspects of development.
                    (adapted from Coleman and Hendry, 1999, pp. 12–13)

Although we shall return to consider these issues in more detail in the practice setting, it is important here to emphasize the significance of these ideas both for our understanding of youth as a life stage and for the development of effective ways of intervening in complex and prob-lematic situations affecting young people. They cannot be dealt with either as purely abstract entities or simply as the products of social circumstances; it is the interaction between the two which is crucial in determining the nature of their experience, their characteristics and the possibilities for change: 'No longer can we consider only one side of the picture; the person and the context are inseparable. What is also important is that developmental contextualism allows us to look at the role of the individual in shaping his or her own world' (Coleman and Hendry, 1999, p. 13)

Youth transitions: Context and consequences

What the preceding discussion has illustrated is the importance of taking account of the factors which shape the individual experiences of young people and set the terms within which their own changes and challenges will be played out. It is the interaction between circumstances and personal characteristics which is significant, and this is clearly very distinctive in the case of some young people. It is thus important to move on at this point to consider some of the ways in which context is determined for them.

Notably, young people have been considered as both having and causing problems over a considerable period of time (Pearson, 1983), and for some (for example, Margo and Dixon, 2006), this is the backdrop against which we must seek to reach understanding and determine policy and practice. However, the picture is not entirely bleak, and it will be of interest to consider the relationship between positive and negative indicators, since this helps to establish the context within which specific decisions are made about how to intervene and provide services for young people.

Positive outcomes

It is possible to draw the broad conclusion that for many young people, life has been continually improving for a number of years. 'There is much to celebrate' (Margo and Dixon, 2006, p. 23), with life expectancy continually increasing, and a rapid reduction in the incidence of childhood diseases, largely thanks to immunization. Young people are reported as saying that they feel well, and that they are in 'good' or 'very good' health.

At the same time, reports suggest that there has been a significant recent increase in educational achievement, as children and young people progress through school. This is reflected in achievements in public examinations, with a substantial increase in the proportion of young people achieving A–C grades at GCSE, for example (from 44.5 per cent in 1995/6 to 57.1 per cent in 2004/5; Margo and Dixon, 2006, p. 43). There have also been very substantial increases over time in the numbers of young people participating in further and higher education: 'These trends suggest that most young people have never had it so good. A greater proportion participates in higher education for longer and receives greater wage premiums later in life' (Margo and Dixon, 2006, p. 45). These improvements may be linked to longer-established changes, such as the move to comprehensive education and the raising of the school leaving age to 16 in the early 1970s. Levels of participation have increased at all stages of the education process over this extended period, and these increases are reported to be 'quite dramatic' (Furlong and Cartmel, 2001, p. 14).

Improvements in education and health for young people have been paralleled by reductions in child poverty, too, which have been the result of improved employment rates, higher benefit levels and the implementation of the tax credits system. We may observe, then, a general picture of enhanced material well-being across a range of indicators for the broad population of young people.

Inequality

At the same time as there is increasing evidence of improvements in living standards for young people overall, there have been worrying signs that deep-seated inequalities have not been addressed and that, if anything, the situation is becoming more intractable. Thus, for example, child poverty has not fallen as quickly as government intended, and the UK has far higher child poverty rates than those of other comparably affluent European countries. The impact on young people of poverty is particularly acute because of their position in the labour market and limited benefit entitlements. The withdrawal of benefits from 16 and 17 year olds in 1988 meant that for those out of work and with limited or no support from families, the 'transition' from education to the labour market interacted highly unfavourably with the 'turning point' of finding themselves without a job or training place (Furlong and Cartmel, 2001, p. 43).

Income inequality also appears to be having a substantive impact on the nature and quality of life experience of children and young people. Children from poorer families are more likely than their better-off peers to live in households where someone is taking Class A drugs, and are more likely to be exposed to tobacco smoke and then to take up smoking themselves. Class and disadvantage are significant factors in relation to other outcomes, too, including personal safety, health and educational attainment. International comparisons suggest that inequity in educational outcomes is much more deeply entrenched in the UK than in other countries (Margo and Dixon, 2006, p. 42).

The upshot of these influences is that social mobility (or lack of it) is strongly associated with family circumstances, and this is increasingly the case. Not only are there observable material differences in outcomes which appear to persist over time, but also these are associated with other 'softer' personal attributes, according to these authors. Material factors appear to have an influence on social and psychological development, too, which is an important observation for those involved in the delivery of welfare services, in general, and social workers, in particular:

> The point is that people's decisions are profoundly affected by their environment and experiences, as well as the way alternatives are presented or 'framed'. Therefore, young people's actual capacity to take up opportunities may be severely constrained by their background and softer skills such as their ability, their motivation or confidence in their own abilities.   (Margo and Dixon, 2006, p. 56)

Thus 'learned responses' appear to be significant in predicting the concrete life chances of young people; whilst, at the same time, their beliefs about their own abilities and capacity to influence change are also likely to be self-fulfilling, at least to an extent. Poorer children are more likely to be concerned about having insufficient money to spend, and to aspire to improvements in their economic circumstances. At the same time, poverty, mediated by a range of intra-familial influences, is likely to impact on the extent to which they feel able to influence events and relationships around them. This interconnected series of findings leads to a view that inequality may be becoming more entrenched, to the extent that there may be a sense of inevitability about future prospects and outcomes, and a corresponding feeling of detachment from the entitlements and obligations of the mainstream society: 'The danger is that eroding young people's social rights of citizenship may also corrode their sense of responsibility as citizens of the future' (Dean, 1997, p. 69). For those who are socially excluded, their material hardships are mirrored by an increasing sense of impotence, and inability to change things for the better. Clearly, this cannot be generalized to all young people in difficult circumstances; nor can it justify a defeatist view that nothing will work in seeking to achieve change. However, the links between material, social and psychological exclusion and their consequences are clearly factors to be taken into account by those who are working with young people experiencing problematic transitions.

Problematic behaviours

The transitions of youth are also associated with concerns about the emergence of problematic behaviours. It is obviously unhelpful to see these as conceptually or practically distinct from related concerns about social exclusion and disadvantage, but it is instructive to consider the implications of viewing this aspect of youth and adolescence through a different lens. In this context, we appear to be more concerned about the problems created *by* young people, rather than problems *for* them. Typically, these issues have been captured under the broad heading of social exclusion over recent years and they have formed the focus of a range of government-inspired policy initiatives, although it seems that many of these areas of concern arise independently of any direct link with disadvantage. Thus, for example, teenage pregnancy is 'a serious problem' in Britain (Margo and Dixon, 2006, p. 26), especially as compared to other European countries, including those which are not as affluent. Sexual health is also worsening, and these problems are reportedly linked with other emerging trends such as deteriorating mental health amongst the young and increasing drug and alcohol use.

In a sense, it is the visible and expressive nature of these 'problem' behaviours that captures a key issue concerning the nature of youth transitions, both from their own perspective and from that of the wider (adult) society. The kinds of changes and developments going on in young people's lives are difficult for them, but also difficult for others, precisely because young people's behaviour is becoming less subject to the formal control of families, schools and other institutions. Just as this is expected and encouraged in the sense that greater independence is seen as desirable, so it leaves open the possibility that the specific manifestations of this will veer off in unexpected and undesirable directions from these institutional perspectives: 'Adolescence, then, represents what could be called a cultural "hot spot". It is presented as a region requiring careful supervision – yet at exactly the point when, we are told, direct adult supervision is becoming increasingly inappropriate' (Marshall and Stenner, 2004, p. 184). 'Health-related behaviours', for example, are significant partly because of what is already known about their long-term consequences, which may not always be apparent or known or of any interest to those engaged in particular activities.

Aside from sexual behaviour, considerable concern is currently expressed about alcohol consumption, as well, not least because of the implications for young people's health in the short and longer term. For those between 11 and 15, there appears to have been a very substantial increase in average alcohol consumption since the early 1990s (NCSR/NFER, 2006), and binge drinking has also seen a substantial increase, especially among young women (Margo and Dixon, 2006, p. 30).

As has been observed, the interplay between the wider culture and the transitional nature of youth is significant in this context. For most young people, the acceptance and even encouragement of alcohol consumption is something which they will have encountered during the course of their lives, through media representations and the behaviour of those around them: 'Young people are brought up within a "wet" culture' (Furlong and Cartmel, 2001, p. 74). It should therefore be no surprise that, with increasing independence, young people should also indulge in 'social drinking'. Indeed, this might be seen as an important 'rite of passage'. On the other hand, extreme levels of drink consumption are recorded amongst a minority of young people, both male and female. Associations of drinking with 'sociability and maturity' may lead young people to accept a certain level of alcohol consumption as 'normal', and even to see excess drinking as relatively unproblematic. Indeed, heavy drinking is sometimes seen as heroic (Box 1.1).

Young people's drinking does cause concern, however, with 'binge drinking' amongst young women being seen as particularly problematic (Margo and Dixon, 2006, p. 30). Indeed, it is suggested that a

Box 1.1

You are the social worker for a 15-year-old young woman who is currently 'looked after' by your agency. You are concerned that since she has moved into her present accommodation, a children's home, she has begun to drink excessively. Staff at the home tell you that she comes in drunk several nights a week, and it is affecting her behaviour and school attendance. When you challenge her about this, she replies: 'Everybody does it, it's not a problem. I bet you drink, too.'

How do you begin to work with her on this issue without appearing either hypocritical or 'out of touch'?
Who is she most likely to listen to on this subject?

common feature of young people's involvement with alcohol is an associated mood of disapproval and alarm from elsewhere: 'Despite the normality of alcohol use among young people, their drinking patterns frequently cause concern among the adult population and have been the focus of numerous moral panics' (Furlong and Cartmel, 2001, p. 75). This observation highlights the importance of taking account of the relationship between young people's behaviour, their changing status and identities, the nature of peer relationships and influences, and the climate of opinion which determines how they are seen from 'the outside'.

Other aspects of their behaviour which give rise to particular concern are those which collectively come to be characterized as 'anti-social'. Whilst some investigators suggest that 'anti-social behaviours' and the tendency to become involved in them can be grouped together, with certain young people being more prone to these, formal definitions tend to restrict the term to cover criminal or quasi-criminal activity. Thus, for example, there is considerable contemporary concern about large-scale increases in young people's criminality over the second half of the twentieth century (Rutter et al., 1998). This has been compounded even more recently by the increasingly close attention being paid to 'anti-social behaviour' which is not necessarily criminal but is socially disruptive none the less. Young people appear to be a particularly central target for the imposition of Anti-Social Behaviour Orders, for example, with over 54 per cent of these orders being imposed on those under the age of 18 in their first two years of operation (Brogan, 2005).

Other evidence suggests that involvement in criminal behaviour of one kind or another is comparatively normal for young people, with more than half of young men and nearly a third of young women admitting to having committed an offence at some time in their lives, in one extensive survey (Graham and Bowling, 1995). Other self-report studies confirm the widespread nature of young people's criminal activities (Smith, R., 2003). Interestingly, however, this evidence also shows that young people from black and ethnic minority groups are no more likely to offend than their white counterparts in general, despite their greater likelihood of coming to the attention of and being processed by the justice system (Coleman and Hendry, 1999, p. 181).

Despite the widespread nature of criminal activity amongst the young, it has also been suggested that a relatively small proportion of young people are responsible for the bulk of crimes coming to the notice of official agencies (Audit Commission, 1996, for example). This has led to the development of typologies of 'anti-social behaviour' careers (Coleman and Henry, 1999), which are said to differ depending on their time of onset and trajectory. Nonetheless, most of the behaviour which causes concern arises specifically in adolescence, leading to a specific interest in the possible reasons for this. However, precise explanations for this pattern have been hard to identify, although it has been speculated that it is associated with normal processes of biological and social development (Coleman and Hendry, 1999, p. 182).

Difficult transitions

Whilst some aspects of our concerns about young people focus on their behaviour and the threat this represents, in other respects their transitions are marked by a number of threats to their well-being, and these are areas of particular relevance to those involved in social work practice.

Young people are not always thought of as potential 'victims', but there is increasingly clear evidence that they are particularly susceptible to victimization of one sort or another (Margo and Dixon, 2006). Recent studies have shown high levels of offending against young people, and that these forms of behaviour often overlap and interact with other aspects of disadvantage (Wood, 2005). It is also of note that there is a strong association between the likelihood of being a victim of crime and committing offences (Smith, R., 2007), which suggests that the effective recent separation of youth justice and social welfare interventions in England and Wales may be problematic, an issue to which we shall return.

In other respects, too, it seems that adolescence is experienced as a problematic time by young people themselves. There has been a gradual growth in awareness of the extent to which young people experience mental health problems, with evidence that the incidence of 'feeling low' increases with age, affecting as many as 40 per cent of 15-year-old females in England and Wales, according to one survey (Quilgars, 2002, p. 360).

Self-harm and attempted suicide are significant problems, with a significant gender bias towards girls and young women (Coleman and Hendry, 1999, p. 132); whilst young men are more likely to take their own lives (Margo and Dixon, 2006, p. 35). Recent trends suggest an increase in these figures since the 1970s, and that this has been disproportionately greater in the UK than other European countries. Attempts

Box 1.2

As a relatively young unqualified residential worker in the late 1970s, I worked for some time with a young woman who had been taken into care and who used to cut herself on the arms. Not only was it the first time I had encountered this, but also, due to my own lack of experience and training, I did not appreciate the likely complexities of trying to 'help' her as a male worker with no knowledge of her past experiences.

Do you expect that our ideas of good practice in these circumstances will have changed substantially over time?
How can our knowledge of the social aspects of inequalities of power, gender and age help us to recognize the challenges for practitioners in this context?

to explain these patterns focus on social causes associated with youth transitions: 'Possible explanations for the general rise [in suicide] include unemployment, alcohol and drug abuse, increased availability of methods for suicide, AIDS, marital breakdown, media influences and social changes' (Coleman and Hendry, 1999, p. 132). Gender differences in rates of self-harm may be attributed to other factors, however, such as earlier puberty for girls, sexual abuse or the gendered nature of their emotional problems. In other words, different outcomes may be attributable not only to different causes, but also to different types of causes, ranging from the biological to the social (Box 1.2).

As well as self-inflicted forms of harm, young people may also be harmed by others in a number of ways specific to their time of life. Whilst 'child abuse' is often associated with younger children (Corby, 2004), there are a number of cases and categories of harm to which young people are equally susceptible. It is noted, for example, that in some cases, such as that of Stephen Menheniott (Reder et al., 1993, p. 37), it is precisely *because* of their age that action is not taken to protect young people. It is assumed that they are capable of fending for themselves (Corby, 2004, p. 208). Forty per cent of those cases where children are registered on grounds of sexual abuse concern young people between the ages of 10 and 16, and nearly two thirds of these are female (p. 209).

There are particular forms of exploitation and abuse to which young people are more susceptible, perhaps partly because they have the capacity to make independent decisions and partly because of societal assumptions that they are able to cope, which are not always justified. There is thus now a significant body of evidence to show that young people who are marginalized face very substantial risks of coming to harm in a number of ways. Young people may take risks in order to assert their independence and control: 'Those who feel powerless may assert themselves through action – for instance, leaving home – even when this involves risk . . . Whatever the risk, young people may leave home as a means of testing, and hopefully proving, their ability to be independent individuals' (Jones, G., 1997, p. 110).

Box 1.3

Young people who run away from home are sometimes perceived to have based this decision on a romanticized vision of their destination. However, they are often found to be more concerned with trying to escape substantial problems at home, including violence and neglect.

Do you think it helps to think of running away as a very visible way of expressing hurt and need rather than as a random act of bravado?
Does this raise issues for the kind of intervention needed, in both the short and longer term?

Some young people leave home by 'running away', and for this quite substantial group (77,000 each year) there are other associated risks. It is acknowledged that running away is most common amongst teenagers, and the peak age is between 13 and 15 (SEU, 2002, p. 7). The young people concerned are likely already to have experienced serious problems, with drugs and alcohol, for example, or because of previous abuse. Family problems are most often cited by young people as their reasons for running away, and these may be related to other difficulties which are a particular feature of adolescence. In turn, the consequences may be equally or even more problematic. One in seven of those who run away from home are physically or sexually assaulted, and a similar number are likely to be sexually exploited (SEU, 2002, p. 18) (Box 1.3).

Thus we are able to conclude that young people are not only a source of concern to the wider society in terms of their behaviour, but also may be 'at risk' themselves in a number of ways which are either distinctively associated with this particular life stage, or are more likely to be prevalent for this group. Once again, links are made by commentators between the intensely personal nature of some of the problems encountered, and the social origins of many of the stress factors involved. It is noted, for example, that financial insecurity associated with unemployment or uncertain work prospects may be linked with mental health problems. Equally important for those out of work may be the loss of social meaning associated with this – status, networks and a sense of purpose may all be threatened for those in insecure jobs or out of work (Coleman and Hendry, 1999, p. 131). This also helps to illustrate the possibility that problematic transitions may be interrelated, so that difficulties in one area of one's life may be compounded by other adverse circumstances.

Young people and state care

For one group of young people in particular, the nature of their 'transitions' appears to be qualitatively different from many others; and, at the same time, it is clearly of direct interest to those involved in social work practice. There are likely to be about 60,000 children and young people 'looked after' by statutory agencies at any one time (DfES, 2006b), and there has been much evidence generated to highlight their specific circumstances and needs. It is clear that this is not a fixed population, with up to 85,000 children experiencing the care system each year, and a very rapid turnover amongst this number. There is thus a sense in which the expected transitions of youth are further complicated by these abrupt changes of living arrangements and personal circumstances. Roughly half of all those who are 'looked after' at any point in their lives will 'spend at least two separate periods in care during their lives' (DfES, 2006b, p. 14). Most children who spend time in care do not stay for long unbroken periods, although 13 per cent will stay for over five years.

A number of different care 'careers' have been identified over a period of time (Packman, 1981, for example), with the largest group (40 per cent) coming into the system for the first time in the 10–15 age range. This group is more likely than younger children to be referred to children's services departments by police or schools, presumably because of concerns about their behaviour. At the same time, there are a number of common features to the experience of children in care, with 63 per cent likely to have been placed there due to prior abuse or neglect (DfES, 2006b, p. 16). Indeed, detailed analysis of the 'in care' population suggests that the profile of this group is distinctive (Bebbington and Miles, 1989), reflecting broader patterns of inequality and social disadvantage.

Once in the care system, too, there is evidence of specific circumstances which may be problematic. Very substantial numbers of young people 'looked after' by local authorities have been reported as having mental disorders (45 per cent, according to one survey: Office for National Statistics, 2003); young people in care are particularly susceptible to changes or interruption in schooling; and other services such as health care are not always available to them (DfES, 2006b, p. 18). In other respects, too, young people who have been in care may be more prone to outcomes which are seen as potentially problematic, such as becoming parents at an early age. One young woman's story captures the experiences and emotions leading to her decision to become a parent (Coleman and Hendry, 1999, p. 113). Having been sexually abused, and 'missing out' on her own childhood because of parental rejection, she was taken into local authority care. Still feeling that 'no one loved me, no one ever loved me, no one would ever love me', she made the decision to have 'her own family', and became a parent at the age of 16.

On leaving care and moving to independence (another important point of transition for young people), the experience of those who have been looked after differs significantly from the population in general. For most young people, the average age at which they leave home is 24, whilst 28 per cent of those leaving care in 2005 were aged 16 (DfES, 2006b, p. 18).

Whilst there is evidence that young people in and leaving care may have had to negotiate a number of adverse life experiences prior to being 'looked after', there is also some evidence to suggest that the quality of statutory care provided has not always served them well (Ward, A., 2004). A series of major inquiries over the years has demonstrated shortcomings in the quality of service provided (e.g., Utting, 1997), and sometimes life in care has been a negative experience.

As is well recognized, young people who enter the care system may have encountered mistreatment or rejection previously, and they may have felt unable to resist or prevent major upheavals in their lives (see Seligman, 1975, on 'learned helplessness'). Once in care, they may similarly be unable to exercise choice and control over key decisions affecting them:

> The painful reality of young people's situation in residential care, then, is that at times they can feel extremely powerless. For many of these young people, important decisions about their present and future life have been taken without their being properly involved and consulted. For example, they may have been required to move away from their previous setting without giving their consent . . . They may be disaffected from and mistrust adult society and be emotionally vulnerable and volatile as a result of loss or other trauma experienced prior to coming into care. (Ward, A., 2004, p. 238)

It is important to avoid creating the impression that being 'looked after' by the state involves a completely separate kind of life experience, or that the population of children in care has nothing in common with other young people; however, there is clearly a greater likelihood that certain problems will be experienced by children in care. At the same time, some aspects of the transitions that all young people are expected to make are distinctively different for young people from care, such as the probability that they will have to 'fend for themselves' at an earlier point in their lives than others who may well have better networks of support (Box 1.4).

Ironically, it seems that it is those who are least well placed to make the transition to independence who will be expected to make this leap

Box 1.4

Young people who are 'looked after' will often have experienced many adverse circumstances as well as repeated disruptions in their lives. Yet interventions are structured according to organizational and professional rules and systems which limit the ability to establish secure and sustained relationships and provide the consistency and stability the young people may need.

What are the responsibilities of practitioners in this context?
Is it important to avoid promising what you can't deliver in terms of personal relationships?

earlier in their lives and with much more limited resources to back them up should things go wrong. Whether or not young people from care are potential candidates for membership of a distinctively separate category, such as those in Williamson's (1997) 'Status Zer0', we should acknowledge the increasing difficulty they are likely to encounter in making several key transitions in parallel, against a backdrop of limited support and prior disruption.

Development, life changes and transitions: An interactive process?

The evidence considered here suggests that it is difficult to conceptualize youth as a clear and distinctive life stage because of the variety of different trajectories followed by young people. For a variety of reasons, it is unrealistic to think in terms of uniform and predictable processes of progression and development. Clearly, opportunities and pathways through adolescence are distributed unevenly, and this is more sharply evident if we also take account of the implications of other factors such as ethnicity, culture, disability, gender or sexuality. These aspects of young people's 'identity' mediate their experiences of transitions, and interact with other developmental dimensions, as Coleman and Hendry (1999) demonstrate.

Recent theories of contemporary society have focused on difference and fragmentation (e.g., Beck, 1992), leading some to suggest that the 'transitions' of young people are increasingly 'individualised' (MacDonald and Marsh, 2005). These observations have led to further questions about the concepts of development and transitions, which seem to imply fixed and specific starting and end points, and which also carry connotations of what are 'normal' or desirable models of a 'better', 'successful' path to adulthood that all should follow (MacDonald and Marsh, 2005, p. 35). Interestingly, for these authors, the evidence that transitions are diverse and not in any sense unilinear does not mean that we should dispense with the notion itself: 'Discovering *empirically* that the transitions that some young people make are messy and complicated, and that the steps taken sometimes lead sideways or backwards, does not require that we jettison the *concept* of transition' (MacDonald and Marsh, 2005, p. 35).

Adolescence is indeed a time of change, and this involves a complex and often highly personalized series of interactions, between social factors, personal circumstances and individual characteristics. However, to be a young person is not necessarily to be beset by uncertainty and turmoil. The demands of adjusting to changes in circumstances and expectations are not always experienced as problematic, and to think of youth purely as something to be survived is to miss out on the positive strengths and achievements which are associated with this life stage.

Perhaps inevitably, however, those young people whom social work practitioners encounter professionally are likely to face specific challenges in terms of one or more aspects of their physical, emotional and social development. The interplay between these features of their lives and those changes which are socially determined, such as leaving school and becoming independent economic actors, suggests that the task of intervening with them is complex. It may be helpful to think in terms of working on a number of levels. For example, the ability to think and act independently may be less well developed for those who have continually experienced uncertainty and a loss of control over crucial aspects of their lives, such as where they live and with whom. Practitioners will need to start from where young people *are* in their lives, rather than where we think they *should be*.

Chapter summary

This chapter has focused on the relationship between the 'transitions' associated with youth in general and the specific issues arising for those young people for whom life changes are unusual, complex or problematic in some way. Key points are:

- Transitions can be defined in a number of ways, such as by age, developmental stage or personal circumstances.
- Youth is a time of life when certain changes are expected, and so a degree of turbulence and uncertainty is accepted as the norm.
- For some young people, these changes are rendered highly problematic because of specific factors affecting them.
- These factors may be rooted in social difference, individual experience or personal characteristics, but they are likely to lead to adverse outcomes
- Interactions between different aspects of disadvantage may compound young people's difficulties.
- Social workers are likely to become involved with young people who are experiencing significant problems, defined sometimes in terms of their behaviour and sometimes in terms of their needs.
- The fact that young people are seen as having (or posing) problems should not lead to assumptions which devalue them or treat their views and wishes as less important in any way.

Further reading

The Nature of Adolescence (Coleman and Hendry, 1999) is a thorough and detailed account of the different aspects of youth development and transitions. It makes effective links between these two concepts and helps us to understand the interplay between social and personal factors as they affect young people.

Freedom's Orphans (Margo and Dixon, 2006) is a policy-oriented analysis of the impact of a 'changing world' on young people, their interactions and experiences. It is suggested that increasing social complexity inevitably has adverse consequences for socially excluded young people, and that policies and services need to adapt to change in order to remain relevant and effective.

Disconnected Youth? (MacDonald and Marsh, 2005) reflects on the experiences of socially excluded young people, and draws attention to the very substantial challenges facing young people who grow up in poor communities. The associated structural problems of 'disconnection' are inevitably significant for social work practice, given its primary focus on those who are socially disadvantaged.

2 Why are young people seen as a social problem?

The problems of young people are not predetermined

In one sense we should not be surprised that the focal point of social work with young people should be their 'problems'. This is, after all, the rationale for the profession's existence and activities across a range of human and social difficulties. However, for a number of reasons we should not take the 'problems' of young people as simply given, or unproblematic in themselves. The processes by which some young people experience adolescence and transitions as difficult have been touched upon in the previous chapter, although by no means exhaustively. However, the ways in which these problems are defined and addressed also incorporate a range of assumptions and, indeed, prejudgements. This is not to suggest that young people do not experience or even present challenges in their lives, but it is to draw attention to the important observation that there is an interactive process involved, influencing the ways in which young people, their risks, needs and behaviours, are problematized. This process needs to be unpicked, in order to help us to understand the ways in which practitioners themselves are involved in making judgements and choices which help to define the specific 'social work issue' which then forms the basis for assessment and intervention. In other words, we need to consider how we and others construct our knowledge about young people, the difficulties they face, and preferred solutions, in order to be better prepared for the complexities and uncertainties which we are likely to encounter. This may be an uncomfortable journey because it involves eschewing certainty and precision in favour of recognizing and dealing with ambiguity and contradiction in analysis and in practice.

Social constructions of youth and its challenges

To begin with, then, it may be helpful to consider some of the ways in which social problems in general, and those concerning youth, in particular, are conceptualized. As we have already seen, concerns about the behaviour and status of the young have been expressed for a very long time. However, it is also suggested that the nature and content of these concerns have shifted over the years (Stainton Rogers, 2004, for example). Thus, the period of reform in nineteenth-century Britain saw the emergence of an 'army of regulators' and moral entrepreneurs who saw it as their role to educate and discipline young people according to the expectations of decent society. Notions of conformity and clean living were important drivers in constructing an understanding of what was acceptable and unacceptable in terms of young people's behaviour and their welfare. As 'childhood' became increasingly understood and investigated as a distinctive life stage, so, too, did aspects of it become problematized. For younger children, these discourses coalesced around concerns about vulnerability, neglect and ill-treatment; whilst for older children and young people, it was their behaviour which became much more central to the priorities of public bodies and welfare practitioners.

Thus, for example, the late nineteenth century saw an emergent moral crusade over the issue of 'juvenile prostitution' (Hendrick, 2003, p. 34). Fears for the welfare of a particular group of adolescents who were apparently in need of 'protection' coincided with a more authoritarian urge to control female sexuality, it seems. Legislation introduced at this time was not just about protecting girls and young women: 'It expressed a fear of sexual precocity among the female children of the non-respectable poor and of working-class childhood itself . . . The objectives of purity campaigners, like their anxieties, were mixed and confused' (Hendrick, 2003, p. 37). In a pattern which has become increasingly familiar across a range of welfare policies and interventions, the measures introduced ostensibly to promote young people's well-being also sought to circumscribe undesirable behaviour on their part.

As Hendrick notes, the ambiguities about the manner and purpose of state interventions with children and young people were further crystallized in the first major piece of child welfare legislation, the Children Act 1908. Whilst the act attempted to deal with child protection and the prevention of cruelty, it also contained measures relating to youth offending and the punishment of criminal behaviour. The establishment of juvenile courts with both criminal and 'care and protection' powers achieved a number of important changes. It seemed to mark out a distinctive age range which would be subject to judicial intervention, but not the full force of the adult criminal law. At the same time, it effectively blurred the distinction between unacceptable behaviour and issues of vulnerability and child protection by bringing both within the remit of the juvenile court. The range of circumstances under which children and young people could be deemed to be 'at risk' was both widened and confused by this legislation:

> The important point . . . is that in extending the categories of non-offenders the 1908 Children Act considerably broadened the scope of the 'at risk' classification for children under 14. Such legislation served to enlarge the role played by care proceedings, thereby making it possible for adults to further limit the freedom of young people.
>
> (Hendrick, 2003, p. 8)

The importance of this emergent confusion over whether to treat young people as vulnerable or dangerous (or both) is that it has become a consistent feature of both welfare and judicial measures addressing them. The extent to which action to deal with their problems should emphasize one or other has become a persistent area of tension, notably, but by no means exclusively, in relation to offending behaviour.

Indeed, we can trace the debates between these perspectives through the subsequent development of strategies to deal with the crimes of the young. Thus, during the 1920s there were a number of moves to reframe youth offending in terms of the social and emotional problems of young people. Psychologists and practitioners began to promote the argument that juvenile delinquency was just an extension of 'naughtiness', and that it should be addressed as part of the wider task of meeting welfare needs. One such authority is reported as commenting that offending behaviour 'should not . . . be solely the concern of the police and the law, since it touched "every side of social work" ' (Hendrick, 2003, p. 113). As a result, legislation began to take a more explicit welfarist turn, in the form of the Children and Young Persons Act 1933. This consensus became institutionalized over the ensuing years, and has only come into question to any significant degree relatively recently.

The focus on the specific welfare needs of young offenders also helped to determine the form that interventions would take, with the development of more sophisticated machinery for assessing need and tailoring interventions accordingly. Reform and rehabilitation became seen as acceptable objectives for the youth justice system, and punishment became relatively less important as a way of dealing with the crimes of the young. Delinquency was seen as inextricably linked with the social, family and psychological antecedents of the offender, and this in turn helped to generate a consensual view of the appropriate forms of intervention needed.

In the same way that these early reforms prefigured subsequent debates about the best way of dealing with the 'risks' associated with young people's needs and behaviour, so, too, did they anticipate later ideas about bringing together a range of expertise to address the interconnected problems identified:

> Around the juvenile court, new powers of judgement and scrutiny were brought to bear upon the families of troubled and troublesome children, utilizing the legal process as a kind of case conference or diagnostic forum and deploying social workers and probation officers to scrutinize and report on the homes of their cases, and to undertake at least a part of the normative assessment and reformation of children and their families. (Rose, 1999, p. 131)

It is clear from this that the way in which youth is 'constructed' by influential sources of ideas and knowledge will have a direct and discernible impact on the form(s) that intervention will take. The conflation of delinquency with underlying personal and social determinants led to the organization of institutional responses of the kind described, somewhat reminiscent of Foucault's (1979) 'army of experts'. The important point to acknowledge here is that this consensus has (and had) specific historical roots and influences, which means that it is also subject to revision and change. In other words, what we 'know' about young people and the determinants of their circumstances is not fixed and may be modified by experience and the emergence of new evidence and ideas. This, in turn, is likely to result in changing views as to what constitutes 'best practice' at any given point in time.

Criminalizing young people?

Considering the issue of crime and delinquency in more detail, we will be able to identify different strands of thinking as to the determinants of young people's behaviour; at the same time, it will be seen that these are likely to have conflicting implications for the way in which formal systems and state agencies ought to respond. The particularly problematic nature of this issue helps to illuminate some major challenges for practitioners.

For Griffin (1993), the most important aspect of this subject is not the 'true' nature of delinquency, but the implications of the various different 'stories' about its origins. Thus, for example, she identifies biological determinism as perhaps the longest-standing, but still influential, explanation for youth crime. The tradition of seeking genetic causes can be traced back to relatively simplistic theories such as those of Lombroso (see Newburn, 2007, for example), but their subsequent developments became more sophisticated, and introduced ideas such as the possibility of ethnic differences in the predisposition towards crime. Griffin draws attention to the inherent racism of such arguments, but suggests that there are traces of such ideas still evident in some academic quarters. Equally, it is possible that popular perceptions of youth may continue to be influenced by these beliefs.

Indeed, there is said to be a 'current vogue' within psychiatric research for identifying biological and genetic causes for certain types of aggressive and anti-social behaviour (Timimi, 2005). There remains a persistent belief that 'there is a clear genetic influence' but that at the same time it can only be seen to act 'indirectly' as a trigger for criminogenic behaviours such as 'hyperactivity' and 'impulsivity' (Kurtz, 2002). Increasingly sophisticated studies appear to have isolated distinct aspects of brain size and functioning which may be linked to specific outcomes. Thus, for example: 'There are interesting differences between the developing male and female brain, possible attributable to hormonal variations that may account for differences in the susceptibility of males to many of the childhood psychopathologies' (Perkins, 2006, p. 65). The offending behaviour of young men may therefore be at least partly attributable to differences in brain structure and chemistry, according to this line of argument.

Other explanations of delinquency have sought to combine factors, suggesting that the causes may involve an interactive process between physiological, psychological and social influences. Susceptible individuals would be more likely to resort to criminal behaviour if other predisposing factors were also present, such as 'inadequate' parenting (Griffin, 1993, p. 104). Thus, the emergence of deviant personalities could be seen to operate 'at the interface between biological and social/cultural' causes. Importantly, as Griffin notes, delinquency in these terms comes to be seen as the result of a '*failure*' of the mechanisms of social and psychological development. As in other areas of concern regarding young people, this can be seen as a 'deficit' model, which focuses on shortcomings at the individual and/or familial level, and suggests that the causes and remedies of young people's problems can be located with them or their immediate social circle (family, carers and peers, usually). Significantly, there is little scope here for making sense of young people's behaviour and beliefs in terms of their own 'agency' and the rational choices they might make in difficult or challenging circumstances.

Nevertheless, such models have continued to exercise a strong influence on research and debate about the origins and dynamics of youth crime. Increasing attention has been focused on trying to capture those key factors which might be responsible, such as disrupted home lives and parenting difficulties (Griffin, 1993, p. 106). As a result, detailed analysis has enabled researchers to identify a list of 'risk factors' which are demonstrably associated with the likelihood of young people committing crimes:

- early child-bearing
- impulsiveness, hyperactivity and restlessness
- low intelligence and poor school performance
- harsh or erratic parental discipline and cold or rejecting parental attitudes
- parental conflict or separation
- social and economic deprivation
- delinquent friends
- school influences
- community influences, such as disorganised inner city areas

(Farrington, 2002, p. 426)

Clearly, the focus on the causes of young people's 'criminality' is not only concerned with explaining certain forms of behaviour, but equally importantly, it also defines the object of concern in a particular way. This is a point to which we shall return, but it is important to consider the extent to which our perspective on intervention is shaped not just by the way in which we understand and account for young people's behaviour, but also by the ways in which it comes to be defined as a social problem.

Young people, teenage pregnancy and parenthood: A matter of norms?

There are other areas, too, in which behaviours and outcomes for young people are seen as inherently problematic, such as the case of teenage pregnancy and parenthood. Indeed, this is a phenomenon which has come to be characterized almost exclusively in negative terms. Problems are perceived in terms of the purportedly 'irresponsible' behaviour of the young parents concerned (both mothers and fathers), the consequences for their children in terms of quality of care and life chances, the impact on their own prospects, increased dependency on family and state welfare and the longer-term disruption of conventional standards of family life.

Teenage pregnancy, in particular, has been the focus of intense policy activity and practice development in recent years, certainly stimulated by the UK government's concern to tackle 'social exclusion' (SEU, 1999). At this level, it was determined that teenage pregnancy was, indeed, a 'problem' and government set targets for improvements in the life chances of young people in order to achieve a substantial reduction in teenage conception rates (Swann et al., 2003).

It should be acknowledged that the drivers of this initial policy concern were varied and complex, and this itself is likely to have contributed to the way in which intervention strategies and objectives subsequently emerged. It has been demonstrated, for example, that investigations into the subject have adopted a variety of perspectives (Bonell, 2004). Some have addressed the issues of the impact on young people themselves, such as health outcomes or poverty, whilst others appear to have been more interested in the social consequences, in terms of welfare expenditure and the 'intergenerational transmission' of socially undesirable lifestyles and patterns of behaviour. There has, therefore, been a consistent trend amongst those researching teenage pregnancy and parenthood to associate it with a range of other aspects of social exclusion, which are seen as collectively problematic both for the individuals concerned and for the wider community: 'Teenage pregnancy has been identified as a mechanism for the intergenerational transmission of poverty and patterns of family deprivation. More recently it has been associated with the general phenomenon of social exclusion, both as "a cause and a consequence"' (Wiggins et al., 2005, p. 1) (Box 2.1).

More detailed examination of the subject has found evidence of a number of factors associated with higher rates of teenage pregnancy, such as have been identified in the UK in particular. Thus, greater social inequality seems to be one underlying issue, whilst other, more localized, influences on behaviour and outcomes in this context appear to include access (or lack of it) to useful sources of information and sex education, experiences of childhood abuse, or limited opportunities in the areas of education and training. In other words, there appears to be

Box 2.1

One study carried out by The Children's Society (Norman and Wilks, 1993) found that the most annoying aspect of their treatment by professionals for young parents was the strong sense of moral disapproval they experienced. They felt that their strengths and abilities were not acknowledged, and nor was it recognized that they were capable of demonstrating appropriate care and affection for their own children.

As a practitioner, do you believe that teenage pregnancy is inherently problematic? For what reasons? Do you think your assumptions are likely to influence your own practice with young people who are pregnant or are already parents? In what ways?

a group of interlinked factors which combine to increase the likelihood of young people becoming parents in the course of their teenage years:

> Teenage pregnancy is a result of many factors including lack of education, poor perceived outlook and ingrained local culture . . . Young people in care, those who are homeless, those involved in crime, those who have been excluded from school, children of teenage mothers and members of some minority ethnic groups are particularly vulnerable to becoming teenage parents.   (Goyder et al., 2003, p. 3)

It has thus been concluded that 'teenage parenthood continues to be a marker for general disadvantage' (Berrington et al., 2005, p. 5).

Partly because the range of factors associated with teenage pregnancy and parenthood is so diverse, attempts to arrive at causal explanations are also fairly eclectic. Some, for example, have sought to ground the origins of teenage parenthood in earlier experiences of abuse and neglect, and low self-esteem (Herrenkohl et al., 1998). Other attempts to classify possible links are rather more generalized, and refer to 'risk factors' rather than causes, in a similar approach to that adopted in relation to youth offending. These include:

- early onset of sexual activity
- poor contraceptive use
- mental health/conduct disorder/involvement in crime
- alcohol and substance misuse
- teenage motherhood [already being a parent]
- repeat abortions
- low educational attainment
- disengagement from school
- leaving school at 16 with no qualifications
- living in care
- daughter of a teenage mother
- ethnicity [some groups proportionally over-represented]
- [low] parental aspirations.   (DfES, 2006a, p. 6)

The way in which these factors are framed suggests a focus on the behavioural, educational and family characteristics of the group identified as most at risk, and this is reflected in the priorities set for intervention. The government's intended strategy (DfES, 2006a) concentrates on 'tackling risky behaviour', 'improving emotional health and well-being', 'improving [educational] attainment, behaviour and attendance', and 'supporting parents and carers to reduce the risk of early pregnancy'.

Overall, then, the characterization of those who experience teenage pregnancy or who become young parents (male and female) is one which appears to make two basic assumptions, both of which could be called into question. Firstly, it seems that the starting point is one of treating the phenomenon as a 'bad thing', which is inherently and unquestionably problematic. It is assumed, for instance, that the 'high' rate of teenage pregnancy in the UK is necessarily an indicator of poorer outcomes than amongst our mainland European counterparts (DfES, 2006c). Secondly, despite the array of evidence, structural, contextual and personal (see Thompson, 2003), the main orientation of intervention strategies is towards securing individual changes in attitudes, competence and behaviour. The difficulty for those seeking to understand and intervene with young people under these terms is that this monolithic view both narrows the scope of interventions, and contributes to the perception of young people who become parents as failures and inadequate in some way. Partly in response to these concerns, more recent discussions of the subject have sought to provide a more balanced view. Thus: 'Much of the research and policy literature emphasizes the negative aspects of teenage parenthood and presumes that the children of teenage mothers are unintended and unwanted. A related clear omission from much of the literature is the voices of teenage parents themselves' (Wiggins et al., 2005, p. 1). This point highlights what will become a continuing theme, which is that the ways in which 'problems' are constructed need to be taken into account in responding to them, as do the perspectives of all those affected, especially those in the 'problem' group, who may be accorded little opportunity to challenge the ways in which they are seen, and the dominant assumptions made about them.

Griffin (1993, p. 164) links the predominantly negative views of teenage pregnancy to essentially public and political dynamics associated with 'moral panics' on the subject. Even though research interest in the issue appears to be 'benevolent', she argues, there is a problem because it effectively constructs young people themselves as the source of the problem, and overlooks deeper-seated problems such as poverty and inequality. The consequence, as Coleman and Hendry (1999, p. 112) argue, is that too often teenage pregnancy and parenthood are viewed against the backdrop of a 'deficit model'. These authors point out that the problem of generalization leads almost to a caricature. There is, for example, in reality a considerable difference between the circumstances and experience of a 19-year-old parent and those of a 14 or 15 year old in a similar situation. Coleman and Hendry note, too, the associated risk of 'stereotyping', which tends to be both negative and superficial, with the result that it becomes 'difficult to consider the needs of young parents in a rational and constructive manner'. They observe, for example, that the apparent deficiency in the parenting skills of young parents may result as much as anything else from comparisons with older parents who could be expected to be more experienced and knowledgeable in any case. Any shortcomings observed, however, are attributed to personal inadequacies rather than simply the passage of time and the relative levels of familiarity with the parental role.

As Coleman and Hendry point out, there have been relatively few studies which have sought to present a more balanced view. It is possible to interpret '*Pathways into Parenthood*' (Hirst et al., 2006) for young people in a positive light, too. Thus, pregnancy at an early age may be 'unplanned', but this does not mean that the child concerned is 'unwanted', or that young parents will have a negative view of their new role. Becoming a parent is identified as one possible route to adulthood, with advantages and disadvantages, just like any other. Benefits might include the ability to have closer intergenerational links, more active grandparental involvement, and more time 'after children', as well. Other authors have suggested that the 'problem' is at least partly the consequence of imposing a dominant and inappropriate model of acceptable behaviour onto groups which, in fact, make rational choices about the risks and consequences of their actions, specific to their own circumstances:

> Thus . . . teenage motherhood in the USA often made sense in the world inhabited by the mothers, in terms of local constitutions of opportunity, constraint and social practice. Similarly . . . early motherhood in London was common in the social networks inhabited by the mothers, was more supported than censured, and . . . most had expected early motherhood in a few years anyway, like their friends, their own mothers and relatives.   (Duncan, 2005, p. 5)

As this author also points out, similar observations could be made about 'young fathers', in that they are not necessarily 'feckless' and irresponsible, but may also have a positive view of parenthood; they are often observed to be 'keen to be better fathers than their own had been', as well as being 'actively involved in childcare'. In fact: 'it was an invisibility to professionals, as well as housing problems, which often excluded them from the parenting they desired. Again, like teen mothers, fathers may be less of a social threat, more of a social possibility' (Duncan, 2005, p. 5).

The important point here for those involved in practice with young people is that there is a key distinction to be made between 'young people *as* problems' and the problems *of* young people. Depending on the perspective adopted, the approach taken to working with young people may differ significantly. Assuming that teenagers who become pregnant, or go on to be parents, are inadequate or irresponsible may be inappropriate, not least because it is likely to lead to forms of intervention which are directive, controlling or patronizing. Duncan (2005, p. 6) notes that 'directing teen mothers towards education and training' may be unacceptable to them to the extent that it treats them as 'inadequate victims, rather than coping agents'. This again underlines the importance of understanding the perspective of young people, and their views of the ways in which their 'problems' are defined, because an effective working relationship will depend on finding some common ground. Neither the status nor the experience of young people themselves should be devalued.

Defining young people's problems: Learning from the deficit and social models of disability

The processes by which young people and their experiences are categorized in other areas are also highly informative. For some young people, it is not so much their behaviour which is problematized as their developmental status. In other words, they are assigned 'abnormal' identities, which require distinctive categorization and treatment. Thus, for example, the way in which notions of disability are applied to young people is important not only in shaping their sense of identity, but also in framing the approach taken to them by agencies and service providers. Where children and young people are identified as being 'disabled', then different rules apply, it seems:

> If a disability is identified, then the [developmental] milestones for that child would have to be carefully redefined . . . Taking such an approach maximises the possibilities of achieving optimal outcomes for individual children with impairments, recognising that some may reach different levels of development along different dimensions.
>
> (Aldgate, 2006, p. 22)

However well intentioned, approaches reflecting an underlying rationale based on 'difference' may be part of a wider process which passes on 'stereotyped ideas about disability which affect adversely the young person's self-image and self-confidence' (French and Swain, 2004, p. 199). Indeed, one-dimensional caricatures appear to be the norm for disabled young people, when they are not simply absent from the picture. The role of institutional forces such as the media, public perceptions and public bodies is seen as being of central importance in creating a conventional view of disability. Disabled people are often portrayed in a passive or 'needy' frame of reference, conveying a sense of dependence on others. The consequence may be that young people find themselves being 'forced' to adopt a 'disabled role' (French and Swain, 2004, p. 201). This both sets them apart as different and ironically at the same time places enormous pressure on them to be 'normal', and to deny the disabled identity which is assigned to them.

In many ways, these contradictory pressures are most strongly encapsulated in the experience disabled young people have of the education system, which simultaneously seeks to segregate and 'normalize' them. Thus, there has been persistent evidence of the impact of segregated educational provision on the lives of disabled young people (Middleton, 1999). The processes involved appear to have resulted in a number of unintended and negative consequences, with the result that the educational experience is 'bleak, oppressive and woefully inadequate' (French and Swain, 2004, p. 200). It is not just the case that educational outcomes appear to be affected, but also that there are implications in terms of personal and social impacts. This is not simply a result of decisions about whether or not disabled children and young people should be educated at mainstream or special schools, but appears more likely to be related to the expectations placed on them. Thus, Middleton (1999, p. 14) notes that anticipated outcomes and performance levels were highly significant in setting limits to the achievements of disabled young people. The young people in her study were all degree students, but most had been told at one time or another that they would never achieve much educationally.

Equally, in this context, the young people involved encountered the personal and social impacts of being defined in terms solely of their disabilities. This might result in their being separated from friends in order to attend a special school, or, by contrast, being treated as a 'guinea pig' (Middleton, 1999, p. 17) by a mainstream school.

Other sources also describe the way in which assumptions about certain groups of young people shape expectations and the provision of services. One investigation of South Asian young disabled people and their families (Hussain et al., 2002) notes a pattern of attitudes extending from family members into social networks and into service settings. The young people's 'difference' was emphasized, and they and their families 'felt excluded from services because of cultural insensitivity and by stereotypes of both culture and disability which did not take account of their real life needs' (Hussain et al., 2002, p. 3). Perhaps as a result, these young people also tended to experience their parents as 'over-protective' and having low expectations for them. The perception of the young people was that they were missing out on 'social opportunities' as compared to their non-disabled siblings.

Further studies have focused on the way in which 'transitions' are conceptualized and experienced by specific groups of young people whose circumstances or developmental pathways are not 'normal' (Morris, 2002; Stalker, 2002; Valentine and Skelton, 2007;). As in the previous illustration, for instance, 'low expectations' are a feature of the attitudes of teachers and service providers in mainstream settings towards 'D/deaf[1] pupils', which is reflected in professionals' 'limited efforts at effective communication, and inappropriate decision-making on behalf of their D/deaf young people' (Valentine and Skelton,

2007, p. 110). Some young people in this study reported being with-drawn from 'academic' settings and redirected towards unsuitable work experience placements or practical courses 'such as art'. As a result of this process, career options are narrowed and young people find themselves 'pigeonholed into stereotypical work such as catering and warehouse work'. This is described as the consequence of a process of 'marginalization', which is partly attributable to choices being made for 'D/deaf young people . . . without their understanding or consulta-tion'. Whilst these authors are at pains to stress the 'resilience' often demonstrated by young people making 'transitions', the authors also recognize the capacity of the world around the young people to impose restrictive assumptions on them.

Other work on transitions, specifically in relation to young disabled people, also identifies specific consequences of the prevailing attitudes which they are likely to encounter. For example, blanket assumptions about the stages and rates at which young disabled people develop in all aspects of their lives may lead to some unhelpful misperceptions: 'Sex and sexuality figure as important issues in the transition to adult-hood for non-disabled young people but adults do not always recog-nise that disabled young people will have the same sexual feelings as others of their age' (Morris, 2002, p. 7). Such problems may arise partic-ularly for young people with learning difficulties, where an undue focus on intellectual development may spill over into other areas. Young people may find that 'others make decisions for them'. Young people with learning difficulties are believed to be 'passive and accepting' and unwilling to challenge adults' opinions (Stalker, 2002, p. 3).

The issue of disability therefore highlights some important chal-lenges for those engaging with young people as professional practi-tioners, both specific and general. Key concepts such as 'development' and 'transitions' are thrown into sharp relief to the extent that they play a part in shaping young people's lives. This is especially so in the case of disability, which is a subject imbued with its own underlying assump-tions and debates (Marchant, 2001). Thus, impairments affecting chil-dren and young people come to be their distinguishing characteristics, according to which all aspects of their lives and experience are defined and played out. This, it is noted, is a problem not just for children and young people, but also for family and carers: 'The pressures of parent-ing a child with complex needs can be very demanding. The more complex the child's needs the higher the risk of skewed expectations and standards' (Marchant, 2001, p. 212).

The consequences may be problematic in specific practice contexts, such as the assessment process, where 'untangling' the child's develop-mental needs from other aspects of her or his life is a challenging task. The continuing focus in the assessment process on the impairment, and on what the individual child or young person *cannot* do, is likely to concentrate attention unduly on this one issue, at the expense of other wishes and needs. Young disabled people are likely to have had:

extensive previous experiences of assessment, as will their families. At least some of these experiences are likely to have been within a pathologising, deficit model where the child was tested against some concept of normality. Some children are very clear about the focus of this kind of assessment: 'it's always about what's wrong with me'.

(Marchant, 2001, p. 215)

For disabled young people who are experiencing transitions, problems may arise due to the interaction of relatively 'fixed' assumptions about the nature of their impairments, which may be seen as permanent and intractable, generalized ideas about developmental progression, and the specific changes in their lives determined by chronological factors. Views of young people with learning difficulties as not fully competent or capable of exercising choice in their own right may thus lead to their exclusion from the 'transition planning process' (Ward, L., et al., 2003, p. 134), and the rather restricted range of issues discussed in this process (Box 2.2).

The continuing absence of young people's 'voices' in the decision-making process is attributed to 'a continuance of the unquestioning assumption that the voice and reason of the professional (and other adults) is truth. The principle of including the child's voice continues to be undermined' by assumptions embedded in professional culture (Gibson, 2006, p. 322). As a consequence of this, perhaps: 'transition services do not pay any or adequate attention to the things that are most important to (disabled) young people, such as friendships, social life and leisure' (Beresford, B., 2004, p. 583).

Associated with this issue, the low expectations held equally by young people and relevant staff lead to an absence of positive outcomes for many. The overwhelming impression created is that the young disabled person is 'constructed' as a problem to be managed (Gibson, 2006, p. 320) rather than as a free-standing individual with her or his own (probably quite conventional) hopes and dreams (see Prime Minister's Strategy Unit, 2005, p. 126). The persistence of what are termed 'disabling attitudes' is well documented, and this has significant implications for the way in which young people who are

Box 2.2

One group of young people with learning difficulties I met were very outspoken about the importance of controlling their own money and making financial decisions (right or wrong) on their own (Allard et al., 1995). They felt that their parents and other adults were reluctant to give them this responsibility.

Do you think the principle of financial independence should apply to young people with learning difficulties in the same way as it does to everyone else?
How would you go about resolving tensions and disagreements between young people and parents who may be reluctant to give up control over money and allow them to make their own mistakes?

disabled are able to negotiate transitions to 'independence and social inclusion'.

The significance of discourse and 'representations'

The key concern arising from these examples is the way in which young people in specific circumstances are problematized, especially given that social work as a form of practice is necessarily geared to assessing and responding to the problems of individuals in their social setting. It will thus be helpful to consider in a little more detail some of the dynamics involved in identifying particular young people and their characteristics and behaviour as a matter of concern, drawing on the concepts of 'discourse' (Howarth, 2000) and 'representation' (Griffin, 1993).

Although it is a complex and contested term, the idea of 'discourse' is particularly helpful in illustrating some of the ways in which conventional understandings of social phenomena emerge. In essence, the term is used to characterize a coherent set of ideas, processes and outputs which encapsulate a specific way of thinking about a given subject. Thus, for example: 'The discourse of development lays out the path from childhood through adolescence to "mature" adulthood, heterosexuality, marriage, parenthood, and (hopefully) a full-time job. This series of transitions marks out the "normal" and "ideal" pattern' (Griffin, 1993, p. 171). The idea of 'normality' operates in two ways here: deriving from the standardized models of growth and change associated with biological and psychological sciences, and also acting to determine what is desirable and acceptable. The importance of this elision is that it accords a degree of authority to our 'common sense' assumptions and practices (Griffin, 1993, p. 9). This, in turn, leads to the reproduction of power relationships as if they are obvious and natural. As Howarth (2000, p. 9) points out, discourses are not just interconnected sets of ideas or productions, they also represent 'concrete systems of social relations and practices', which incorporate the capacity to define the dividing line between 'insiders' and 'outsiders'. This theme is echoed by Garland (2001) in his discussion of criminology and crime control. He suggests that a powerful element in contemporary thought and practice is the 'criminology of the other', initially encapsulated in the call of a previous prime minister 'to condemn more and to understand less' (p. 184). For him, this is an important symbolic shift, as it enables those involved in tackling crime simply to categorize offenders and their behaviour as unacceptable, and thus for them to be made subject to measures of control, irrespective of their social circumstances or welfare needs.

Importantly, too, the way in which normality and difference are defined helps to focus our attention on specific groups and individuals, rather than other factors which might contribute to setting them apart. As Griffin (1993, p. 173) notes, perhaps somewhat presciently, the association of 'teenage pregnancy' with other patterns of behaviour, such as alcohol and drug use, school problems, and crime, enables it to be defined as part of a broader pattern of 'deviance', captured more recently under the umbrella term of 'social exclusion', but still largely explained in terms of individual or family shortcomings. For Griffin, these connections are not accidental, and derive from the close association between a series of 'mainstream' discourses: those of 'education and training' and 'criminality' and the 'clinical discourse'. The focus in each case is on the inadequacies of the individual concerned, sometimes extending to her or his family, and as a result, programmes of intervention are likely to be targeted at these deficiencies and framed in terms of 'remedial' action on an individualized basis. This represents a partial, victim-blaming approach to tackling the problems of young people, and also works to 'conceal forms of opposition and oppression' (p. 208).

Not only does the dominant discourse serve to conceal certain aspects of the 'problem', in this way, but also it may contribute to the processes of oppression and exclusion experienced by certain groups of young people. As we have already observed, for example, the depiction of teenage pregnancy and teenage parenthood as the consequence of irresponsibility (and sometimes poor parenting) may have a significant effect on the subsequent treatment of young people in this position.

We also know that when it comes to questions of sexuality, young people often encounter exclusion and oppression when they do not conform (Logan, 2001; Hind, 2004). As in the broader population, young people who are Lesbian, Gay or Bisexual find themselves to be marginalized and often ostracized by a society which does not understand them or take their needs seriously. Pressures to be normal are felt particularly strongly at a time of change, and especially where other aspects of their lives may be problematic. The problems of establishing open and honest relationships between social workers and young people become even more challenging in a context where dominant expectations constrain practitioners and service users alike:

> Lesbians and gay men would be in an ideal position to provide young people with positive self-images, however the risks associated with being open about their sexuality may deny social workers, residential workers in particular, the opportunity to be the positive role models these young people so badly need.   (Logan, 2001, p. 567)

In this context, the discourse of 'normality' may thus help to close down an important avenue for collaborative and relationship-based practice.

Equally, in the context of disability and learning difficulties, the dominant ('clinical') discourse has certain consequences in terms of the ways in which young people's social competence is viewed. Gibson (2006), for instance, graphically illustrates this point through her depiction of a 'culture of silence' in special educational settings. She suggests that special education has been characterized by a process of both conceptual and (often) physical separation, whereby children and young people became objectified and in need of 'normalisation through scientific formulas of teaching and healthcare' (Gibson, 2006, p. 318). The voice of the child or young person is not considered relevant because the experience and knowledge she or he holds has no value in the face of objective, professional understandings of her or his needs. Even though recent shifts at the level of policy have seen greater emphasis placed on the principle of participation, this has not been observed in practice: 'The professional remains in control, the dominator, the one with the authoritative, legitimate voice, who stands on the platform of valued knowledge' (Gibson, 2006, p. 322). In effect what Gibson is describing here is the outcome of a collision between two competing discourses: the 'pathological' model of need and the (emergent) emphasis on participation and service user control. In her view, however, the latter continues to be subsumed under the persistent belief in the principle that 'the professional knows best' (p. 322).

In a sense, this captures the circularity of the process. 'Problems' are defined in terms of dominant assumptions, which are supported by legitimized sources of scientific knowledge and professional expertise. These are located at the level of individual young people and their families, who are 'othered' by this process, and therefore their own knowledge and experience become suspect and potentially invalid. For young people in particular, these effects are compounded by the overarching presumption that they are still 'developing' and undergoing transitions leading to a mature and competent adulthood. In the light of this, emergent ideas of participation and inclusion appear to offer a distinctive and user-centred form of legitimacy. However, the forms and processes of participation remain dependent on dominant sources of power (such as state authority and professional expertise) which determine the context and content of any input from young people. At the same time, the terrain for any such dialogue is established by the way in which the original 'problem' was formulated in the first place. Crucially, the power and authority to determine the underlying nature of the problem, and to locate it firmly at the level of the individual young person, remain in place: 'The exercise of power itself is influential in the production of specific form of knowledge; there is no "disinterested knowledge" – there are those who know the answers and those who do not!' (Tucker, 2004, p. 85).

The Youth Offender Panel is a helpful illustration of this kind of dynamic. This mechanism has been proclaimed as a significant development in bringing restorative principles to the youth justice arena, allowing for a participative approach to dealing with young offenders outside the court process, and promoting dialogue and problem-solving between offender and victim. To this extent, it appears to have created space for the young person to articulate her or his (usually his) own perspective on the offence. At the same time, however, the focus for the intervention remains the actions of the young person (a prior admission of guilt is necessary); the central problem is identified with her or him, and intervention concentrates essentially on dealing with the offence rather than any other significant issues of concern. The young person's perspective comes into play, but the power to define the 'problem' and the form of intervention remains elsewhere.

Whilst the power and influence of dominant discourses of young people and their problems remains highly significant, however, Tucker (2004, p. 86) also helpfully reminds us that this position is not inviolate, and that practitioners have the capacity to 'challenge and resist it' in order to 'deproblematise the young'.

The challenge for practitioners: Retaining a critical perspective

For those engaged in practice, the relevance of the preceding discussion may not be immediately clear, but there are a number of important points arising which can be summarized in terms of one's 'orientation' towards interventions.

Firstly, it is of course in the nature of social work in general, and with young people in particular, that the starting point will take the form of a requirement to deal with a matter of concern about a particular individual. In addition, the issue is likely to revolve around some aspect of the relationship between the individual and her or his family or community (Box 2.3).

As we have seen, the issue may be framed in terms of the individual's deviation from the norm, in relation to her or his developmental progress or 'transitions'. For the social worker, especially where she or he has statutory responsibilities, there is the potential to play a part in assessing and (re)defining the initial problem. In this context, it is therefore important to be aware of the processes and dynamics which have led to the construction of the matter of concern in the form that it takes, particularly in terms of the power relations involved, and the possible competing definitions brought to bear on the issue. Marchant (2001, p. 217) offers a number of helpful suggestions in relation to work

Box 2.3

We have heard of a number of recent cases where Anti-social Behaviour Orders have been sought and sometimes obtained where young people with acknowledged behavioural problems are seen by community members as acting unacceptably (*BBC News*, 23 February 2007).

What do you think are the potential consequences of criminalizing young people in this way?

What is the role of social work in mediating between young people with behavioural problems, their families and communities?

with children and young people with disabilities, which also apply more broadly:

- *'Think about your own understanding.'* Professionals are bound to have been influenced at some level by prevailing discourses and assumptions, or even through their own direct experience, and it is important to 'factor this in' to the intervention process.
- *'Be clear about the position of your service.'* Practitioners operate within a network of organizational and structural relationships which, in themselves, play a significant part in defining the nature of the problem.
- *'Take responsibility for communicating.'* In the context of disability, this advice has clear practical implications, but equally important is the principle that the young person's 'voice' should be incorporated into the process of assessment and intervention.
- *'Try to take the* [young person's] *perspective.'* It may not be possible to start from her or his definition of the 'problem', but try to ensure that this is incorporated into the intervention process, and influences the outcome.

We should therefore see dialogue as being at the very heart of practice, and by incorporating the perspective of young people who use services in their own right, we may find that the key focus of intervention is fundamentally reformulated. Thus whilst an impairment may have been the reason for an initial referral, this may well not be the most important issue from the young person's point of view. Her or his most pressing issues may be to do with friendships and relationships, as they often are for young people in general. If her or his concerns are not identified and explored actively, it is unlikely that the intervention will be effective, at least from the service user's own perspective.

Chapter summary

This chapter has focused on the processes by which young people, their characteristics and behaviour, become defined as problematic for communities and agencies. In doing so it has sought to illustrate some of the anomalies and arbitrary aspects of this process. Key points are:

- There is a tendency to take a negative view of youth and young people in general.
- This is heightened in relation to specific groups because of their behaviour or identified needs.
- As a result, the 'problems' of young people are often defined in a one-dimensional manner and a 'deficit' model of youth is applied.
- The challenge for social work is to adopt a critical view of conventional understandings, to recognize the validity of young people's own views, and to promote a positive view of their strengths and potential.

Further reading

Representations of Youth (Griffin, 1993) provides a detailed historical account of the social processes by which young people and their behaviour have been problematized. It concludes that a proper sense of the experience of youth and transitions depends on involving young people themselves in investigating and researching their lives.

Disabled Children: Challenging Social Exclusion (Middleton, 1999) draws on the experiences of young disabled people, offering a critical view of the ways in which their upbringing may be shaped by the label applied to them. Alternative, inclusive approaches to policy and practice are identified here.

Naughty Boys (Timimi, 2005) is an interesting critical account from within the psychiatric profession of the way in which specific diagnoses such as ADHD (Attention Deficit Hyperactivity Disorder) are both culturally grounded and self-justifying. Timimi argues that powerful definitions such as this are often misleading and counter-productive, and that medicalized problems need to be 'reframed' from the perspective of children and young people.

3 Looking at things from young people's perspective

Taking young people's views seriously

The previous chapters have largely focused on the externally defined processes of youth transitions, and the ways in which these are both shaped and constrained by external circumstances, and, in some cases, problematized. This is, in one sense, quite reasonable, because for present purposes we need to be able to understand the origin and dynamics of the issues likely to be encountered by social workers in the course of their practice. However, it is also a reflection of a wider pattern, which is increasingly coming into question, and which accords primacy to the 'adult' perspective and devalues the views, aspirations and concerns of young people themselves. Indeed, this is linked with notions of youth as a transitional phase, between the naïve and irresponsible state of childhood and the fully formed and competent status assigned to adult citizenship. Adolescence is seen as an unfinished life phase, which has implications for the validity and weight given to the views of young people themselves. In combination with other problems which may be ascribed to them, this means that the perspective of young people themselves may not always be taken properly into account. Whilst the picture appears to be changing, with an increasing recognition that young people's voices have not always been heard, or taken into account, in the past, the extent to which their needs and aspirations are now becoming more influential or decisive is still open to question.

In what follows, we will consider the process by which young people's participation has increasingly become seen as important. A combination of factors, including research evidence, active lobbying by children's organizations, and policy initiatives, has generated much greater emphasis on the importance of taking young people's views seriously. As a consequence, it is now possible to identify a number of measures in policy and practice which have sought to achieve greater influence for young people, such as the establishment of the Children and Young People's Unit by government in 2001, and the eventual establishment of the office of Children's Commissioner for England in 2004, which complemented similar appointments already made for the other countries of the UK.[1] Although the extent and impact of this cultural shift may be open to question, it is important to consider its implications. Following on from this, the chapter will explore some of the ways in which this greater openness to the views of young people has produced concrete results in terms of a better understanding of their perspective, both in general and in relation to the interests of specific marginalized groups. Finally, this will enable us to consider in more detail areas where the policy and practice 'agendas' identified by young people themselves differ widely from those determined for them by other interests. Of course, there may be significant implications of this analysis for both the style and substance of welfare interventions with young people, and the chapter will conclude by considering what these are.

Young people's rights: A (relatively) new agenda?

It has been suggested that historically perspectives on children and young people can be identified with a number of distinctive 'positions' (Fox Harding, 1997). Four approaches to welfare provision and policy relating to children and young people can be identified as exerting significant influence over time:

- '*laissez-faire*': the family is the best place to bring up children and state intervention should be avoided unless absolutely necessary;
- '*state paternalism*': the role of the state is to ensure that children and young people are safeguarded and protected, and intervention should be determined accordingly;
- '*birth family defender*': welfare provision should proactively seek to promote children and young people's well-being through supporting families;
- '*children's rights*': the primary determinant of their interests should be children and young people themselves, and intervention should be based on this principle.

Fox Harding suggests that the first three of these can be viewed as exerting dominance over policy and practice concerning the young at different points in time, with, for example, the Victorian era being associated with a belief in the primacy of the patriarchal family. At other points in time, alternative perspectives have tended to become more influential; for instance, the 'birth family defender' position became influential in the aftermath of the Second World War where there was a particular concern with social reconstruction and family stability. This assumed that even young people in trouble could best be helped by providing strong forms of support to their families: 'Juvenile offending was a field where there had long been work on rehabilitating children with their original family. As indicated, a belief now grew that neglect and juvenile delinquency were rooted in similar causes, factors to do with a malfunctioning of the family' (Fox Harding, 1997, p. 104).

The state paternalist perspective takes the most positive view of state intervention, holding that it is right to take proactive measures to safeguard children, and to provide alternative forms of care to the family of origin where this is in the individual's best interests. This position often appears to gain prominence following major inquiries into cases where children are seriously harmed or killed in family settings. It may be associated with an increased use of mandatory powers and an increase in the numbers of children 'looked after' by the state.

It is the fourth perspective, that which prioritizes the rights of children and young people, however, which has been given least prominence in the context of service provision and decision-making about key aspects of their lives. The other perspectives all, to some degree at least, share a view that someone other than the child or young person knows best, whether that is parents, carers or the state welfare agencies.

Fox Harding suggests that it is only comparatively recently that more emphasis has been given to the distinctive rights of children and young people. Whilst internationally, countries such as Norway had taken the lead in promoting the rights of the young, changes in the UK were somewhat slower to take place. It was only with the landmark *Gillick* case in 1986, the subsequent ratification of the United Nations Convention on the Rights of the Child in 1989, and the almost simultaneous passage of the Children Act (in England and Wales) that there began to be established the principle that children and young people should have a say in key aspects of their lives. In different ways, both the legislative instruments set out a series of both substantive and participation rights, to which the young should have access. However, they also both fell short in certain respects, given that the UN Convention is not enforceable, and the Children Act essentially only applies to those under 18 with identified welfare needs, and not to the population in general. Subsequent research also suggested that there was a reluctance on the part of public bodies and the legal establishment to give substance to these notional rights in formal decision-making processes. Roche (2002), for example, suggests that the priority given to the 'paramountcy principle' means that courts may continue to pre-empt young people's own wishes 'for their own good', citing the case of a High Court decision which 'bypassed' the right of a 15-year-old girl to refuse a psychiatric assessment: 'So the "mature minor" enjoys the right under the Children Act to refuse to submit to a court-ordered assessment but this right can be "trumped" in "appropriate cases" [by the High Court]' (Roche, 2002, p. 68). Roche goes on to cite other examples of the ways in which limits to young people's rights are imposed in formal settings, such as the failure to provide them with appropriate information. Whilst the Children Act provided for a much more active process of identifying the 'wishes and feelings' of children and young people, it did not necessarily challenge underlying assumptions about professional expertise or the way in which power is distributed within decision-making systems. Roche concludes that the promotion of the rights of the young is a 'fragile project' which is a continuing process, necessitating cultural and structural change as well as formal procedural advances.

Despite this element of pessimism, there is a general acknowledgement that the rights of young people have become increasingly prominent in public and academic agendas. Thus, for example, Franklin (Franklin, B., 2002a) notes that there has been a burgeoning of research activity in this subject area, as well as the emergence of a distinctive political agenda focusing on the interests of the young. By 2001, for instance, the Liberal Democrats had included a commitment to giving young people (over 16) the vote, and the New Labour government initiated a number of measures specifically targeted at promoting the interests and involvement of young people.

Promoting participation

A range of measures, both general and targeted, have been implemented in recent years to promote the active participation of young people across differing aspects of their lives. Some of these measures have focused on enfranchisement, in both conventional and broader political senses, whilst others have been directed towards giving young people a greater say over what happens to them in specific circumstances. Taken together, though, these steps appear to be indicative of a general change of mood, although of course we should be wary of reading too much into 'good intentions'.

Nonetheless, it has been suggested that there is a systematic move towards promoting participation of the young which can be traced back to the 1990s: 'The UK government's commitment . . . has led to a series of legislative and policy measures to ensure that children have a say about their neighbourhoods, education, health and social services' (Spicer and Evans, 2006, p. 177). These developments are attributed, at least in part, to the work of the Social Exclusion Unit (SEU), which focused on a range of areas identified as key social problems by the incoming New Labour government in 1997.

Unsurprisingly, perhaps, young people as a group became a focal point of concern for the government, and the SEU set up an investigative team (Policy Action Team (PAT) 12) to investigate the problems of the young and how they might be addressed. As we saw in the previous chapter, this focus may have had the unintended result of problematizing young people as a group, and specific categories in particular. Key concerns were identified as 'illiteracy, homelessness, mental illness, drug addiction and serial offending' (PAT 12, 2000, p. 7). Importantly, too, though, the report suggested that young people were also losing out because of 'gaps in services'. It was stated that prior to that point in time:

- there has not been enough emphasis on prevention, particularly through work with families
- services have been poorly designed to meet the real circumstances of the poorest young people
- services have been provided haphazardly or on a restricted basis . . .
- Services have failed to adapt to new problems experienced by young people such as poor mental health, drug abuse and family conflict.

(PAT 12, 2000, p. 9)

But in addition, the report observed, policies and services had previously failed to listen to young people's views or to involve them in deciding what services should be provided and how. This 'makes young people feel alienated'. Young people should therefore be involved to a much greater extent at all levels, from the design and prioritization of services, through to direct work with individuals. The aim of the report was to promote a new 'inclusive' approach to policy and practice with young people. A national framework should be established to deliver this, it was argued, but equally importantly, local systems and practices should reflect the same philosophy. Key tasks would therefore include: 'identifying the local needs of young people; promoting a common assessment framework for young people; sharing information between agencies; identifying public, private and voluntary resources which could help young people; and developing a local youth strategy based on effective consultation' (PAT 12, 2000, p. 10).

This indicated a wish to see practitioners working in more collaborative and integrated ways to support the needs which young people identify for themselves. For social work practitioners, this would mean having to address the challenges of engaging more proactively on young people's behalf with mainstream providers such as schools and health services; whilst at the same time having to consider the implications of a more open approach to the use of (potentially sensitive) information.

In concluding that services should be 'designed around the needs of young people', PAT 12 did not resolve the ambiguity as to who should define those 'needs', but it did argue for a much more clearly defined 'consultative' approach to working with them. Whilst accepting that approaches to consultation would necessarily vary depending on the setting, a number of core principles were identified:

Consultation:

- should be a process, not a one-off event;
- should involve dialogue . . .
- should be sensitive to young people's expectations about how they want to be treated and how they wish to respond, not based on adult procedures and timescales; and
- . . . should adapt the process to what works with new groups.

(PAT 12, 2000, p. 82)

This eminently sensible statement of intent provided the basis for subsequent more detailed initiatives to bring participation to the centre of work with young people, collectively and individually.

Following this exercise, the government initiated a drive to promote young people's participation, and the Children and Young People's Unit (CYPU) was established with this aim in mind. The unit very quickly set out what it saw as the 'core principles' of participation, to be pursued at all levels of intervention. The underlying rationale for improving participation was explained in terms of the potential for better services, promoting social inclusion, and personal and social education and development. Thus, benefits would arise both through the process of involving young people and through improved outcomes. Core principles of participation for children and young people should include:

- a visible commitment to involving them;
- appropriate resources to enable participation to take place;
- their involvement should be valued;
- they should have 'equal opportunity' to get involved; and
- a commitment should be made to evaluation and improvement of participation practices.   (CYPU, 2001, p. 11)

Certain concrete expectations follow from this, such as the importance of providing appropriate opportunities for young people to express their views, by 'targeting' those facing barriers to involvement, such as travellers, those from minority ethnic groups, and disabled or disadvantaged young people. At the same time, it is incumbent on those agencies and individuals engaging with young people to ensure that they are 'treated honestly', so that they understand the constraints and potential consequences of their involvement. Of course, this is highly problematic, since if this information is presented in an unhelpful way, it will be received by young people as a deterrent to expressing their own wishes and feelings, rather than as a form of encouragement.

Contributions from children and young people should be demonstrably taken seriously and acted upon, according to the CYPU (2001), and clear and appropriate feedback ought to be provided to them. Again, the point is made that being 'listened to' is only a positive experience if there is evidence of change being achieved as a result. In setting out these principles, the CYPU drew attention to the existing example of the government's 'Quality Protects' initiative, which was designed to improve outcomes for children in need, and its incorporation of a consultative approach into the development of changes in policy and practice. Again, the point is made that: 'children and young people's improved involvement in discussions, for example about their care arrangements, [is] an important means to provide better protection and more responsive care arrangements for children being looked after' (CYPU, 2001, p. 22).

Having established the value of participation, government policy has subsequently built on this idea in more detail. The Green Paper, *Youth Matters* (DfES, 2005a), set out a vision of young people as participating citizens, with complementary rights and responsibilities. It was observed, for example, that: 'Life for teenagers is full of opportunities' (Kelly, 2005, p. 1). Whilst most young people could and would make use of these, some would be unable to for reasons of disadvantage, whilst others would 'choose' not to take up what was on offer, with the result that they might get into a 'downward spiral' of unacceptable behaviour. Participation for young people is framed in this context as a 'responsibility' as well as being a 'right'. Failure to act responsibly in this respect would thereby exclude young people from their entitlements: 'with new opportunities will come a new emphasis on young people's responsibilities'. The new agenda for young people was set out in the Green Paper in terms of a 'balance', with young people being entitled to expect greater opportunities and more responsive services, so long as they meet their responsibilities to those around them and the wider society.

The key challenges identified by *Youth Matters* included: 'engaging' young people to shape their own services; 'encouraging' them to play a fuller part in communities; 'providing' better information and advice to enable them to make informed choices; and offering 'personalized intensive support' to those experiencing serious problems (DfES, 2005a, p. 5). The idea of giving them a greater voice in the construction of these services was also explicit: 'We want young people to have more influence over what is being provided in each locality. They should have more opportunities to be involved in the planning and delivery of services and more opportunities to express their views during local inspections' (DfES, 2005a, p. 7). Further support for participation was offered by the recognition that the 'system' in place does not take sufficient notice of the perspective of young people about when, where and how they want services to be provided (p. 16), although at the same time it was again suggested that 'services should not be an unconditional benefit'. Nevertheless, the paper made an important statement of intent in proposing on behalf of government that: 'We want young people to have more direct involvement in all stages of service design, development, delivery and evaluation. By involving them, we can help to ensure that they will share ownership of decisions and use facilities and services responsibly' (DfES, 2005a, p. 37). Thus, participation and involvement should not be seen as a 'one-off' activity, taking place at a specified point in the process, but should be integrated into the entire spectrum of service activity. This is clearly significant, not just as a general principle, but also as an operational guideline, prompting agencies and practitioners to consider whether they, too, are treating consultation and shared decision-making as a continuous feature of intervention.

The Green Paper also points up a number of practical options for promoting participation, both individually and collectively, including the creation of roles for young people as active contributors, rather than just passive recipients of services. In order to participate fully and effectively, though, young people need the right practical tools and opportunities. In *Youth Matters*, these are framed in terms of 'Information, Advice and Guidance', to which all young people should have access, which may need to be specialized, personalized and made 'accessible' to young people in particular circumstances. This approach should enable young people who 'need specialist support' to have a 'real voice' (DfES, 2005a, p. 56) and play a full part in 'planning for their gradual transition to adulthood'. One important vehicle for achieving this aim is seen to be the 'lead professional', mirroring the earlier *Every Child Matters* proposals for children (DfES, 2003), who would act as the coordinator, negotiator and advocate of young people with multiple support needs. The lead professional could come from a number of backgrounds, including social work, and would be expected to:

- act as a single point of contact who young people and families can trust, able to support them in making choices and in navigating their way through the system;
- ensure that children and families will get appropriate interventions when needed . . . ;
- reduce overlap and inconsistency among other practitioners; and
- ensure that where the young person requires more specialist services . . . the young person is involved in an effective hand-over.
(DfES, 2005a, p. 59)

The paper concludes that the commitment to integrated and participatory working will also be subject to inspection and review, and it will be an integral part of service evaluation to: 'assess how well the views of children and young people are captured [and] the extent to which young people are involved in designing services' (DfES, 2005a, p. 65).

The further government policy documents aimed specifically at 'children in care' have underscored this emerging commitment to consultation and promoting children's rights to participate (DfES, 2006b, 2007b). The Care Matters programme includes a significant strengthening of the care planning procedures to put young people's 'wishes and feelings' at the centre of the process (DfES, 2007b, p. 110), to be given legislative force from 2008.

Whilst the commitment to greater participation and control is set out clearly at the level of generalized policy and strategic aims, it is also important to consider some of the ways in which these are to be operationalized in service delivery. Thus, for example, guidance sets out the role of the 'lead professional' (who may or may not be a social worker) in coordinating intervention (DfES, 2006d). Whilst bringing together the range of agencies and providers who might be involved, the lead professional is expected to 'build a trusting relationship' with a young person and her or his family, to 'secure their engagement and involvement in the process', to act as a 'sounding board for them to ask questions and discuss concerns' and to 'continue to support' them through further assessments and 'key transition points' (DfES, 2006d, p. 3). Where children or young people are 'in need' or being assessed in that respect, where they are subject to 'child protection plans', where they are 'looked after' or (normally) where they are leaving care, the social worker will be expected to act as the lead professional, carrying out these diverse responsibilities (DfES, 2006d, p. 15). Amongst these duties, the lead professional is expected to facilitate young people in choosing who will take this role itself! Beyond this, she or he should be prepared to enable young people to express their own views and 'challenge when appropriate'.

As already observed, these principles are to be reflected at all stages of the process, through assessment, planning, intervention and

Box 3.1

- Participation is a right
- Children and young people are the best authorities on their own lives
- Participation depends on respect and honesty
- Participation must be accessible and inclusive
- Participation is a dialogue to influence change
- Participation is built in

- Participation is everyone's responsibility
- Participation benefits everybody
(Participation Works, 2007)

Do you think it is possible to enable full participation in every setting in which you might work with young people? What are some of the key obstacles? How easily can they be addressed?

evaluation of services provided. Government underlines this by stressing its commitment to the 'Participation Charter' developed by a consortium representing young people's interests. Box 3.1 lists the charter principles.

Participation policy and the social work context

As well as setting out these aspirations and standards in broad terms, it will also be useful to consider their application to specific social work tasks and settings. For example, the place of participation in the assessment process has increasingly been emphasized in practice guidance (for example, DH, 2000a, 2000b). Thus, the overarching framework for assessing the needs of children and young people under the Children Act 1989 stresses the importance of being and remaining 'child centred'. Attention should not be diverted towards other issues, or other individuals, especially in complex situations where the primary purpose of the task is to ascertain the child's or young person's best interests. It is important, too, not to rely on other people's definitions of 'the problem': 'The importance, therefore, of undertaking direct work with children during assessment is emphasised, including developing multiple, age, gender and culturally appropriate methods for ascertaining their wishes and feelings, and understanding the meaning of their experiences to them' (DH, 2000a, p. 10). Assessment is not simply something that is 'done to' children and young people, but should involve them as contributors to the process. They therefore need to understand the purposes and content of the assessment and to be given clear and regular accounts of what is happening and why. In this sort of context, it is incumbent on practitioners to avoid assumptions, for instance where young people may 'not communicate through speech and where professionals may be unclear how much of what is being said is understood' (DH, 2000a, p. 38). Communicating with and involving young people should not be given less emphasis simply because it is difficult or time-consuming, as the guidance recognizes.

Similarly, where there are concerns about possible harm to a child or young person, guidance makes it clear that her or his account should be considered: 'it is important to listen and develop an understanding of his or her wishes and feelings' (HM Government, 2006, p. 75). It is noted, too, that this is not just a matter of good technique or asking the right questions, because young people may require time and encouragement to develop 'sufficient trust to communicate any concerns they have' (p. 92). The practitioner's personal qualities may be as important as the skills required, and it is noted that children and young people identify certain attributes in professional workers which they value, such as:

- listening carefully;
- being available;
- being non-judgemental and non-directive;
- having a sense of humour;
- being open and honest;
- being trustworthy and maintaining confidentiality. (adapted from DH, 2000a, p. 44)

The inclusive approach to young people should be followed through, with a commitment to involve them in decision-making forms such as child protection conferences 'where appropriate' (HM Government, 2006, p. 96). This clearly has implications for the shape and conduct of this kind of formal procedure, where it is possible that young people (and other family members) may feel intimidated. Thus, for example, a child or young person should be enabled to 'bring an advocate, friend or supporter if s/he wishes' (p. 98). Subsequent actions, too, should be informed by a commitment to keep the young person 'up to date with . . . any developments or changes' in the planned intervention (p. 105), and planned interventions should be dependent on their agreement (p. 107). Once again, this underlines the important principle that 'participation' is a continuing process and not just a preliminary exercise.

Similarly, policy and guidance for 'looked after' young people also emphasize the value and centrality of choice and participation. Government has recently offered a 'pledge' to those in care, which should include:

- A choice, made with their social worker, of high quality placements;
- 24/7 support from their social worker or an out of hours contact; . . .
- An independent advocate;
- The choice of when to move on to enter adult life, up to the age of 18; and
- The right to have their voice heard.   (DfES, 2006a, p. 11)

These aims build on the existing standards for practice in children's homes, for example, which emphasize the importance of consultation which takes account of individual characteristics and differences. Thus, it is stipulated that the opinions of children and young people must be obtained in relation to 'key decisions which are likely to affect their daily life and their future', and systems should be put in place to ensure that this happens, such as 'written agreements, private interviews, key worker sessions, children's or house meetings'. These should be appropriate to 'differing communication needs' (DH, 2002, p. 13).

For all 'looked after' children, the recognition of their difficulties in accessing good-quality educational opportunities has led to a specific policy drive in this respect, and here, too, the emphasis is on 'taking account' of the individual child's or young person's views in 'identifying and meeting his/her educational needs' (DfES, 2005a, p. 12). And when young people cease to be looked after, here, too, there is a requirement to involve them in the planning and decision-making process. The relevant agencies and practitioners are expected to actively 'seek' the young person's views and 'take all reasonable steps' to involve her or him in meetings to prepare her or his 'pathway plan' (DH, 2001, p. 36). Importantly, here, there is an emphasis on taking proactive steps to identify young people's views and aspirations and then ensure their involvement in the process, because: 'Clearly, the further the young person can be involved in the process, the more successful it will be.' Once the plan is prepared and implemented, it should also be the subject of regular reviews, with the facility for the young person herself or himself to trigger a review if she or he wishes (DH, 2001, p. 46). In order to support the young person's involvement and promote her or his interests, provision has also been made for the appointment of a 'personal adviser' for young people 'living in and leaving care' (p. 47).

These examples are not exhaustive but they demonstrate the extent to which an explicit commitment to participation has been incorporated into all aspects of consultation and service delivery with young people, especially in those contexts where there is a direct role for social work intervention. This is a growing and increasingly sophisticated initiative in policy and practice, which recognizes the importance of tailoring approaches to specific circumstances, notably the diversity in young people's backgrounds and the need to adapt the means of communication in some instances. It is consistent with a broader recognition of young people's participation rights, such as those reflected in the United Nations Convention on the Rights of the Child (Box 3.2).

Notwithstanding the clear and growing recognition of the right of young people to 'have a say' both in general terms and in specific circumstances, this, of course, leaves open the key question as to whether, and to what extent, consultation and participation lead to substantive change, both in the way in which 'problems' and needs are defined, and in the way in which these are addressed.

Having their say?

It will be important now to consider some of the available evidence as to the ways in which consulting with and involving young people has

Box 3.2

UN Convention on the Rights of the Child
Article 12

1. States Parties shall assure to the child who is capable of forming his or her own views the right to express those views freely in all matters affecting the child, the views of the child being given due weight in accordance with the age and maturity of the child.

2. For this purpose, the child shall in particular be provided the opportunity to be heard in any judicial and administrative proceedings affecting the child, either directly, or through a representative or an appropriate body, in a manner consistent with the procedural rules of national law.

(United Nations, 1989)

What role does social work have in ensuring that young people have access to appropriate representation?
As a social worker should you take a lead role in enabling young people to speak out?
What if you disagree with their views?

led to a refocusing of concerns and a readiness to include their perspective in service planning and interventions.

Consulting with children and young people in both policy and practice arenas has certainly, and rightly, become something of a growth industry in recent years, and there are many examples of work undertaken to promote a range of approaches and to evaluate their effectiveness (see Franklin, A., and Sloper, 2004; Hine, 2004; Park et al., 2004; Durant et al., 2005; Harris and Broad, 2005, among others). The starting point for these may be somewhat different to that of the community in general, which may be concerned with young people primarily in developmental and (dys)functional terms, but that is one of the reasons why it is important to consider the similarities and differences emerging from young people's own perceptions. This should help us to understand and hopefully address any 'mismatch' between the way in which they and their problems are characterized by others and their own perspective(s).

Firstly, then, what can we glean from broad surveys of young people's views and experiences in general? Well, it seems that for the most part, the views, attitudes and moral judgements of the young are broadly similar to those expressed by 'reasonable adults', according to one extensive study of the views of 7–15 year olds. Their ideas about rules, citizenship and mutual responsibility do not appear to set them apart. Even if these are expressed somewhat simplistically, it is observed that this may not be much different from the ways in which adults would articulate them: 'What is noteworthy is that these children and young people demonstrated the same range of views and opinions as similar groups of adults might have done . . . The ideas put forward were clearly well understood by the young people and not simply repetition of adult or media views' (Hine, 2004, p. 39). Several 'key points' emerged from this study, indicating the ways in which young people see their world, and their place within it. Thus, for instance, these children and young people perceived their communities as dangerous places to grow up, perhaps partly because of the way in which the sample was recruited. In addition, respondents tended to hold inaccurate views of people from different backgrounds, which may mean that 'the seeds of racism can germinate easily here' (Hine, 2004, p. 39).

Interestingly, the young people surveyed for this study held a strong sense of social justice and fairness, but also a very strong sense of the ways in which they could be unfairly treated themselves. Indeed, this appeared to feed into a general scepticism about the integrity of the social institutions around them, and wider social systems such as the political process. Thus, for example, it is clearly anomalous for the notion of active 'citizenship' to be promoted in the school setting when so many aspects of the school experience are perceived to be unfair and disempowering. Children and young people are: 'sceptical of participative initiatives in schools because they detect tokenism within them. Children do not trust the teachers within schools because they often feel the teachers do not respect them' (Hine, 2004, p. 40).

This study concluded that young people feel that they have little control over key aspects of their lives and that the opportunities to exert an influence are limited They feel that their actions and the outcomes of their behaviour are predetermined, so that, for example, young offenders see their actions as largely shaped by the adverse circumstances in which they are living. It is of some interest in this context to draw parallels with psychological theories concerning the 'locus of control', which attribute individuals' attitudes and behaviour to beliefs about their potential to influence the world around them (see Peterson et al., 1993). These theories suggest that the efforts people make to control or change their lives depend substantially on their prior beliefs as to how much control they have to achieve their desired outcomes. The risk is that a pessimistic view of one's capacity to achieve change will lead to an unwillingness even to try.

To some extent, these findings are reflected in wider studies of young people's attitudes and perceptions (Park et al., 2004). Young people's interest in formal politics in the UK is low and falling, and there is a distinct class dimension to this, with young people in poorer households being less likely to see any value in political activity. Despite this finding, this particular study also found a high level of belief amongst young people that they *should* be given a say in important matters affecting them, such as the closure of a local sports centre (Park et al., 2004, p. 26). Likewise, there was support in this survey for the idea that young people should have some say over 'what is taught in schools', and what forms of punishment should be used in schools for unacceptable behaviour (Park et al,, 2004, p. 6).

Other studies, too, have indicated that, generally, young people 'take seriously the question of their relationship to the wider society' (Lister et al., 2005, p. 47), contrary to assumptions held elsewhere. Grounds for this argument are also provided by the widespread evidence that young people are willing and enthusiastic when it comes to 'constructive social participation in the local community'. However, differences were identified between those defined as 'insiders' (more highly qualified, 'successful') and 'outsiders' (few qualifications, unemployed), with the latter group seeing themselves as 'second class citizens' (Lister et al., 2005, p. 48). Concern is expressed about the impact of this kind of two-tier model of citizenship on those who are socially excluded:

> The more that exclusionary models of citizenship dominate, the less likely it is that disadvantaged young people will identify themselves as citizens. The same is true if politicians, educators and others who work with young people promote a deficit image . . . and impose a model that has no resonance with young people's own experience.
>
> (Lister et al., 2005, p. 48)

For those groups with whom social workers are more likely to be involved, the disparity between their perceptions of fairness and of legitimate participation and their lived experience may be of particular significance. In one sense, perhaps, it is encouraging that the rhetoric of participation and the changing policy agenda have ensured that there is now considerably greater emphasis placed on identifying the views and aspirations of young people who use services, both individually and collectively. However, the evidence produced suggests that often their 'voice' is not heard or acted on, and that services find it hard to adapt to a more inclusive way of working.

In the specific context of disabled children and young people, for example, it has been reported that their participation 'remains patchy' (Franklin, A., and Sloper, 2004, p. 9). In this case, it was concluded that 'little is known' about children's experience of participative processes, what they would see as 'good practice', or what sort of outcomes they would wish to result from their involvement. Despite much enthusiasm for the idea of participation, research demonstrated that 'not all [disabled] children and young people are being involved in decisions regarding their individual care and . . . only small numbers are being involved in service development' (Franklin, A., and Sloper, 2004, p. 38). The authors of this study note that participation is about creating a sense of 'continuing dialogue' rather than just a matter of formal involvement in specific events. Their review of existing practice was not all critical, however, and they conclude that positive lessons could be learned from imaginative initiatives already in place. The checklist in Box 3.3 helps to prepare practitioners (and their agencies) to engage with disabled children and involve them in assessment, planning and decision-making.

Other studies have highlighted the point that appropriate avenues to participation are important, but they must also be linked with substantive outcomes. Young parents, for example, identify a range of problems that they would like addressed, but they feel that these are not always taken seriously by professionals. What is needed is a willingness to see things from young parents' perspective and to work on their priorities. This group would like to see: 'a change in professionals' attitude

Box 3.3

- be clear about your aims and objectives;
- be realistic and not expect too much at first;
- consider practical arrangements such as wheelchair accessibility, transport;
- undertake involvement as early as possible;
- tailor methods to each individual child – there is not a single solution;
- not treat disabled children as a homogeneous group;
- be creative;
- use available resources such as I'll Go First, pictures, symbols, photos;
- allow sufficient time to prepare, and have protected time in order to undertake the work satisfactorily;
- allow time for young people to build up their own confidence and skills;
- build up relationships with young people in longer term service development initiatives;

- spend sufficient time with the child/young person in order to get to know them and understand their communication method;
- consider that children with complex communication methods might be best supported in their communication by someone who knows them well or that this person can offer advice;
- have sufficient funding and resources available;
- access training;
- keep information simple, jargon free
- [do] not make assumptions;
- be honest;
- have a positive approach;
- [do] not be afraid! (Franklin, A., and Sloper, 2004, p. 36)

Can you distinguish between general participatory principles and those which might apply specifically to disabled young people? If so, what is the basis for this distinction?

towards young parents. Professionals . . . providing services for young parents need to have more empathy with them and be proactive in helping them to find out about services available to them or claim benefits' (Durant et al., 2005, p. 20).

In the case of young people in and leaving care, the connection between improved participation and concrete outcomes is clear. Care leavers have said that improved support through personal advisers and pathway planning[2] enabled them to identify key tasks in 'moving on', which, in turn, helped to ensure that these issues were addressed effectively (Harris and Broad, 2005). For instance, the informality and accessibility offered by leaving care workers are contrasted to the restrictions and frustrations of more formalized processes, which constrain young people and practitioners alike. In another study: 'There were complaints that any plans made were not implemented, that their wishes were over-ruled with no explanation given, that their concerns were not addressed' or: "*They say they'll talk about it at the next review but they never do*" (Munro, 2001, p. 9). The point made by young people in this study is that they are regularly allowed to 'influence trivial decisions' but do not have a say in the big issues such as where they live, or how often they have contact with significant others.

This observation helps us to make a crucial link between applying participative principles and achieving substantive outcomes. It focuses attention on the central issues of power and control in the relationship between practitioners and young people who use services, and it helps us to recognize that achieving effective participation can only be demonstrated to the extent that it leads to better outcomes. Thus, for example, it has been noted that leaving care services are 'often called upon to play an advocating role' and that 'this could help develop young people's perception that the service was "on their side", helping to keep them engaged' (Harris and Broad, 2005, p. 50). This led the researchers in this instance to conclude that: 'Perhaps "engaging with other services" is at least as important as "engaging with young people" if better services and not disappointment brought about by raised expectations can be the result' (Harris and Broad, 2005, p. 59). A commitment to empathize with and advocate for young people is therefore integral to effective participative practice.

The challenge of achieving participative practice

This chapter has specifically sought to underline the importance of taking account of the perspectives of young people themselves. The emergence of a 'participation' agenda at the level of government and other key opinion-formers has been an important development in recent years. There is thus a much greater level of recognition and legitimacy accorded to the idea of involving young people in both service planning and individualized decision-making. Policy and practice guidance now requires agencies and practitioners to take seriously young people's views and to demonstrate that they are doing so. Thus, inspections of 'children's services' now incorporate 'universal inspection standards' which specify the degree of participation and choice which should be offered to 'looked after' children and young people, for example (Joint Chief Inspectors, 2005, p. 123).

In this climate, the way seems to have been opened for the development of specific forms of practice which take account of and act on the priorities for change set by young people themselves, and, indeed, the effectiveness of this kind of approach is demonstrated in a number of recent studies (e.g., Harris and Broad, 2005). The kinds of question that this gives rise to relate to the extent to which practitioners can be 'empowering' and enabling of young people with whom they work in a context of competing 'problem definitions'. It is quite likely that social workers will become involved not in response to an approach from a young person, but because the young person (or her or his behaviour) has been defined as problematic in some way for others, whether these are family members, other individuals or the 'community'. In addition, these problems are likely to be defined in terms of incomplete development or inappropriate transitions, based on conventional judgements as to what is 'normal' and acceptable. Young people, on the other hand, may well experience these processes of definition and categorization as marginalizing or socially exclusive, with negative consequences for their own sense of 'identity' and self-worth. If social work is to be positive, validating and able to engage constructively, then it must take an implicitly critical view of the problem definitions imposed on young people. In this way, participative approaches will start from a common recognition of what brings the young person and practitioner together, and at the same time, a mutual recognition that there are alternative 'starting points', notably the perceptions and priorities of the young person herself or himself. Thus, for example, young people view 'pathway planning' positively because:

> *The pathway plan is more what you want and what you think but the care plan is basically what social services decide for you.*

> *It feels better that I'm actually contributing to it and actually putting something down, instead of it being done for me and me looking at it thinking there's things that should've been done and hasn't. So I prefer if I've sat down and looked at it myself read it through and checked every possible bit of it.*   (quoted in Harris and Broad, 2005, pp. 29, 30)

Chapter summary

This chapter contrasts earlier external definitions of young people and their needs with an emphasis on their own perspective, and the importance of taking this seriously as a practitioner. Key points are:

- Young people's priorities very often differ from those of the wider community or those agencies working with them.
- There has been a growing recognition of the validity of young people's views and the importance of taking these seriously.
- Key policy documents and statements of rights (such as the UN Convention on the Rights of the Child) have given substance to this.
- Practice guidance is being developed to enable practitioners to put these principles into effect.

Further reading

The New Handbook of Children's Rights (Franklin, 2002b) offers a comprehensive collection which discusses the changing context of young people's rights in the UK and elsewhere, whilst also considering the issues from the perspective of specific groups, such as refugees, and developing a range of ideas for promoting rights and participation in practice setting.

Children Taken Seriously (Mason and Fattore, 2005) similarly offers a variety of perspectives on the social and practical implications of paying attention to the views of young people and moving beyond this to give them control over key decisions in practice.

Increasingly, too, young people's experiences of welfare interventions are being recounted in their own words. One such example is *The Looked After Kid* (Hewitt, 2002) Described as a 'mixture of fact and fiction', it none the less captures an important sense of the service user perspective from the viewpoint of a young person who is (or was) an essentially involuntary and powerless client of statutory care.

PART II

SOCIAL WORK AND YOUNG PEOPLE:
CONTEXTS AND PRACTICE

4 The relationship between ideas and practice

Changing models of practice

Having given space in the previous part of this book to some of the ways in which youth and its problems are conceptualized or 'constructed', we will now turn to the more concrete terrain of social work with young people as it is and has been practised. The development of distinctive models of assessment and intervention can be traced over time, and this will help to give substance to the recurrent themes and challenges likely to be encountered by practitioners in contemporary settings. Not only do the kind of influences set out previously shape our ideas about the causes of and solutions to young people's problems, but also they act directly to influence the frameworks within which interventions have been developed.

As we shall see, the consequence has been an emphasis on categorizing young people according to a relatively narrow range of stereotypical attributes, and intervening accordingly. Institutional forms of care, for example, have tended to apply a 'deficit' model, which locates identified problems with the young person, and seeks primarily to change her or him in order to ensure that she or he fits into the normal expectations and social roles prescribed. Middleton's (1999) account of the experiences of disabled young people, for example, refers to a persistent emphasis on the 'correction' of 'physical faults', as a preferred option, irrespective of whether 'the young people may have other concerns and priorities' (p. 20).

The aim here will be to explore some of the patterns and trends in social work with young people over time, not just to identify any apparent shortcomings, but also to explore the potential for change, and emergent examples of new thinking and good practice, for instance in promoting a 'children's rights' perspective and a greater emphasis on participation, which appears to have become evident in the present day. These will hopefully 'signpost' future possibilities for progressive development.

Styles of intervention reflecting competing perspectives

A number of previous studies have suggested that the nature of social work intervention with children and young people depends on the prevailing 'perspective' held by practitioners and their agencies (Fox Harding, 1997, for example). Accordingly, the particular approach

Box 4.1

Typically, when young people become 'looked after', there is available a substantial amount of prior information about them, their behaviour, family circumstances, characteristics and needs. Decisions about interventions inevitably depend to a large extent on this prior 'knowledge'. I once worked with colleagues at a children's home who believed that it was better to work with as little prior knowledge of their residents as possible. They felt that this would enable them to avoid making prejudicial assumptions about the young people living there, whilst also enabling them to start with a 'clean sheet'.

Might it be more helpful, in some cases, to attempt to work with a 'blank slate', in this way, in order to avoid prejudging the young person concerned?
What are the risks in this kind of approach and can they be managed effectively?
Would it be better, do you think, to 'open up' case files and share information with young people as fully as you can, as a specific exercise to enable them to question, challenge and renegotiate what is 'known' about them officially?

undertaken in any given case will depend on the relative influence of competing views as to the origins of the 'problem' and the most appropriate way of dealing with it.

As I have suggested elsewhere (Smith, R., 2005), these perspectives are not mutually exclusive, and indeed each can be seen to exercise an influence on distinct aspects of the service framework for young people. The different perspectives identified vary in the extent of their influence according to time and place. Some, notably Packman and her colleagues (Packman, 1981; Packman et al., 1986; Packman and Hall, 1998), have argued that the evidence shows that young people are, indeed, dealt with according to the way in which they are categorized, and that this process itself is variable (but see Box 4.1).

In her earlier work, Packman found evidence of a clear distinction between 'depraved' and 'deprived' children and young people, with the former group being dealt with on the basis of their unacceptable behaviour, and the latter group being addressed primarily in terms of their needs. This distinction was blurred, in her view, following the Children and Young Persons Act 1969, with the result that both groups came to be seen as 'children in trouble'. Problem behaviour was simply one manifestation of a broader range of needs linked with possible deprivation or harm. As a consequence, ideas of positive intervention to 'treat' (Packman, 1981, p. 148) the problems of young people became prevalent. The 1970s thus became a period when the 'child protectionist' ethos was highly influential in shaping the form and content of social work practice. Residential care became seen as a viable form of intervention which would provide not only the basis for meeting material needs but also a structured and supportive environment to enable underlying problems to be explored and addressed. Whilst the models of intervention varied, from organized programmes of learning and activities to more 'therapeutic' options incorporating counselling and groupwork (p. 146), they shared a belief in the positive value of focused regimes to tackle young people's underlying difficulties.

This belief in the positive potential of residential care was associated with a substantial rise in its use at this time, and a greater willingness to dispense with 'voluntary' admissions in favour of compulsion, such as the use of Place of Safety Orders (Packman and Hall, 1998, p. 6). This was indicative of a view that parents' position and partnerships with them were less important than the identified needs of children and young people themselves. Further study revealed that it was often 'parenting behaviour' that led to children being considered for reception into the care system (Packman et al., 1986, p. 45). Standards of physical and emotional care were questioned, and often it was 'irresponsible' behaviour by parents which was held to be the source of these 'perceived deficits' (p. 46).

Aside from concerns about parental performance, it was the behaviour of children and young people which was the next most significant perceived causal factor, although broadly defined 'health' issues were also felt to be associated with the emergence of problems for children and young people. More detailed investigation, however, appeared to identify distinct pathways for those children who eventually came to be 'looked after', depending on their attributes and the precipitating factors involved. A clear distinction emerged between different groups of children and young people, which were characterized by Packman and colleagues as 'victims', 'villains' and the 'volunteered' (Packman et al., 1986, p. 59). This distinction was manifested in a number of ways, such as the age profile of the different groups, with the 'villains' more likely to be teenagers, male, and viewed as responsible for a number of forms of unacceptable behaviour, such as criminal activity, truancy and running away. Their parents, too, were often felt by social workers to be lacking in the quality of emotional care and control provided. 'Victims', on the other hand, were found to be generally younger, more at risk of material deprivation and 'harm', with a background of family disruption and perceptions of limited parenting capacity, in the view of social work practitioners. The third group of those 'volunteered' for care were found to share some of the characteristics of both the others, differing largely because it was their parents who instigated intervention because of their own concerns about 'unmanageable', 'aggressive' or 'withdrawn' behaviour on the part of their children (p. 62).

The authors of this study were careful to note that these distinctions were not absolute and that young people coming into care should be viewed as occupying overlapping places on a spectrum. However, it also seems that these perceived differences could be traced through the patterns of decision-making and intervention subsequent to the initial referral. Thus, for those typically older members of the sample whose behaviour gave cause for concern, the use of compulsory measures was associated with a short-term aim of gaining 'control', and putting a stop to their disruptive activities.

Differences were also observable between the two local authority areas chosen for this study, with one relying more on 'voluntarism' and preventive measures to support the care of children by their families; whilst the other viewed the use of admission and compulsory measures as 'a legitimate form of help; where troublesome teenagers were willingly absorbed into the care system; and where indeterminate care was not necessarily seen as a bad thing' (Packman et al., 1986, p. 172). A number of factors were thus found to affect the orientation of practitioners towards intervention in specific cases, including the cultures and ideological climate evident in differing geographical areas, the 'positions' (Smith, R., 2005) adopted by specific teams, and the attributes ascribed to young people depending on the category to which they were notionally allocated at the initial point of referral. These apparent distinctions might tend to obscure similarities between young people falling into these different categories. For these authors, the key message was, indeed, to take a pragmatic rather than a prescriptive approach:

> We have seen . . . that social workers are frequently called in to 'do something' . . . at a time of crisis, when [a child or young person's] behaviour appears intolerable and when the reactions of others to [her or him] are at fever pitch. Yet, in a sizable proportion of such cases, both the behaviour and the reactions will subside . . . This tells us not that social workers should keep away or do nothing; but that their most useful role might be to keep this hope alive, and to try to help the children and all the involved adults (teachers and policemen, as well as parents) to *survive*, without taking drastic or irreversible action or applying immovable labels.   (Packman et al., 1986, p. 206)

A subsequent study returned to this subject to review changes in policy and practice following the implementation of the Children Act 1989 (Packman and Hall, 1998). This provided an indication of the continuities and changes in values and practice as they applied in child care over time.

By the mid-1990s the prevailing mood had altered, and the emphasis had clearly shifted from a 'child protectionist' perspective to one geared towards 'family support' and, to some extent, 'laissez-faire'. This could arguably be attributed to a fortuitous coincidence of a political drive to minimize state intervention, and an emerging professional consensus in favour of preventive work to support children and young people in their families, rather than removing them. The two authorities involved in the study approached this common objective of reducing admissions in contrasting ways, one by effectively cutting off the supply of residential places and promoting alternatives such as fostering and adoption, the other by putting additional measures in to 'support families' (Packman and Hall, 1998, p. 28). By this was meant measures such as short-term respite care, befriending services, counselling and material help. The implementation of the Children Act 1989 offered further impetus to the development of a partnership approach, and as the study notes, one obvious consequence was a shift in the profile of those 'accommodated' to reflect a much greater use of 'voluntary' admissions. These changes also led to a shift in the balance between the three groups identified previously ('villains', 'victims' and 'volunteered'). These groups could still be distinguished, albeit in a slightly different form (this time as 'difficult adolescents', 'children at risk' and the 'volunteered'). Thus, for example, 'difficult adolescents' were less likely than their predecessors to be 'persistent offenders' and much more likely to be characterized in the wider sense of being 'beyond control' (Packman and Hall, 1998, p. 73). Running away, persistent truancy and being 'aggressive' were more likely to be factors associated with the decision to accommodate this group of young people (all were over the age of 13). As the authors observe, there was also evident here a reframing of historic concerns about 'moral danger', often associated with the behaviour of adolescent girls and young women: 'For example, half the youngsters were believed to be putting themselves at sexual risk, and here the concerns were mostly confined to the girls whose recklessness and promiscuity were regarded as unacceptable and sometimes dangerous' (Packman and Hall, 1998, p. 73).

These authors go on to note that the broad range of concerns and behaviours giving rise to the admission of young people from this group also had implications for the nature of the interventions offered or attempted. Thus, 'partnership' could be difficult to achieve in a situation where young people were in conflict with their parents; but it also seemed that practitioners had a rather negative view of the services they were able to offer. There were concerns about the shortage of suitable placements; the risk of exposing teenagers to a 'rotten system' which might compound behavioural problems; or their own limited prospects of changing entrenched difficulties, whether in terms of fractured relationships or of challenging behaviour.

The new 'victims', or children at risk, were a different group, although many of them were still over the age of 13 (43 per cent). This group was much more likely to have featured on the Child Protection Register, and to have associated family problems such as parental mental health issues or financial difficulties: 'Where the circumstances of the families of children at risk *do* differ from others is in the degree of mental and emotional stress, in strained family relationships and in parental behaviour which is considered dangerous or undesirable, and here the heightened concerns of professionals clearly have a rational base' (Packman and Hall, 1998, p. 99). It seems, too, that for those older children and young people in this group, these problems might well be persistent, given that many had already featured on the register. Despite the fact that much had been done to anticipate the problems identified, the authors also note that many admissions were still 'emergencies', though: 'the hurried, unplanned and potentially traumatic nature of admission to accommodation in an emergency has continued unabated' (Packman and Hall, 1998, p. 99).

The third group, who continued to be known as the 'volunteered', were significantly different in character at the point of admission to accommodation. Virtually all of these children were aged 12 or under, and they 'had proportionately more health problems and more medical, educational and behavioural' needs (Packman and Hall, 1998, p. 100). Indeed, special educational needs were a common feature of this group, and the authors suggest that this may be indicative of the fact that the Children Act was now catering for children with disabilities as intended. Families' social circumstances and health problems often seemed to be an issue, and admissions were thus more likely to be associated with these problems combined with children's 'special needs'. Although these children were generally younger, the planned and recurrent nature of their admissions might indicate that they would continue to be involved with social services throughout their childhood, raising specific issues in relation to the provision of age-appropriate services and 'transitions' as they got older. This group was often provided with temporary or 'respite' care, and would be likely to require different types of placement over time.

In summary, the argument developed by Packman and her colleagues over a considerable period of time is that a broad typology can be developed to capture the distinctive characteristics of different groups of children and young people being accommodated by local authorities. This, in turn, has implications for the type of relationship between agencies and young people and their families, and for the type of service offered, and whether or not it is appropriate. For example, where children are 'volunteered' for accommodation, and continue to use it on this basis as they grow, a genuine spirit of partnership is most readily identifiable. However, in other cases, where social workers are seeking to 'protect' a child or young person who may be at risk, cooperation cannot be relied upon, and 'suspicion and resentment' are likely to be apparent. On the other hand, in some cases it is parents who expect social workers to assume responsibility for young people who are beyond 'control', leading to frustration and possible attempts to 'force professionals' hand', perhaps by precipitating a crisis.

The distinctive patterns of young people's backgrounds and characteristics, and the variations in response and trajectory through the care system, suggest that there may be some value in the idea of child care 'careers' that follow separate paths, with varying implications for practice.

Histories and careers: Routes through care

It may be difficult to distinguish the different types of influence (personal, contextual, social – see Thompson, 2001, for example) which shape the processes and patterns of intervention experienced by young people; however, in order to consider the implications for practice, it is important to try to identify how these might operate. Some sources, for example, have suggested that there is a degree of continuity in that 'early life experiences' can have a persistent influence on later behaviour and outcomes (Sampson and Laub, 1990). The problem, however, is that too strict a reading of this material might predispose us to believe that change is not possible, and that interventions may be no more than 'damage limitation' (Taylor, 2006, p. 64). A more positive reading of 'life course' theories is that in identifying persistent influences, they highlight those aspects of young people's lives which may be legitimate targets for change. This kind of approach should also help us to avoid making pejorative assumptions about young people based on their particular characteristics.

A number of comparative studies have considered the pathways followed by young people through care and other forms of intervention, and these have focused on a variety of factors, including family circumstances, individual characteristics and ethnicity. Barn's (1993) early work, for example, found that decisions about when and how to intervene with black children were often based on assumptions grounded in stereotypes, resulting in both excessive and insufficient action on the part of statutory services, dependent on the circumstances. Subsequent investigation (Barn et al., 2005) suggests that there are still variations in the form of service provided and the pathways followed by young people in care, but that these are quite complex. Thus, the nature and duration of placements, for example, differ quite widely depending on the 'racial and cultural background' of young people in care. Caribbean young people appear more likely to be placed in 'kinship' settings than other groups, and less likely to experience placement disruption, whilst white and mixed parentage young people were more likely than others to experience placement disruption. African and Asian young people were more likely to enter the care system at a later age; but for many of this group, this was to do with their status as unaccompanied asylum seekers, so their 'trajectory' through the system was quite distinctive.

In other respects, this study, which was based on the experiences of 261 young people who had been in care, found distinct variations between ethnic groups. Thus, overall educational attainment was low (only 47 per cent achieving one or more GCSE at grades A–G), although Asian, African and Caribbean young people were academically more successful than their white peers or young people of mixed parentage (Barn et al., 2005, p. 23). It was the latter groups, too who reported that they received least help from education professionals or social workers. Prior disruption notwithstanding, young people appeared to feel that their care status affected the quality of educational provision offered to them: 'They have no boundaries being in care, basically you could do what you wanted. Being a child I hadn't any sense of responsibility, I was pushing boundaries like teenagers do' (Care leaver, quoted in Barn et al., 2005, p. 25). The comments of these young people suggested that they felt that the workers involved with them took no real interest in their education except when they got into trouble: 'when I got suspended for fighting', as one young person put it.

The findings from this study seemed to confirm that young people from care are 'a heterogeneous group in terms of pre-care, in-care and post-care experiences' (Barn et al., 2005, p. 33). At the same time, some aspects of the experience seem to be shared across specific divisions, such as those of ethnicity and culture, like the educational difficulties facing 'white, mixed parentage and Caribbean young people'. These observations do seem to support the 'life course' thesis that common features of the experience of young people in care are also mediated by differences; in this case, these differences are framed in terms of ethnicity, but clearly other factors may also play a part.

Stein (2005), too, draws on the metaphor of a 'journey' through care to highlight similarities and differences for young people who come to be looked after by local authorities. For instance, he attributes the fact that they come to be accommodated to the inability of parents to care for them, albeit for a variety of prior reasons (p. 3). However, specific groups appear more likely than the population as a whole to become 'looked after' children or young people, notably disabled children (16.4 per cent), whilst around a quarter are of minority ethnic origin. In addition, an increasing number of young people are now looked after or 'supported by local authorities' as unaccompanied minors from abroad.

Although their points of origin may differ, it is recognized that aspects of their experience will reflect common themes for these young people, such as familial abuse, rejection, and disruption and loss in their lives (Stein, 2005, p. 4). This might suggest that stability and consistent relationships should be an aim of any form of intervention offered, irrespective of content or setting. But as Stein observes: 'one of the most consistent and depressing findings of research studies completed during the last twenty years is the amount of placement movement and disruption experienced by young people leaving care' (Stein, 2005, p. 5). He notes that studies in which he had been involved covering care experiences over a thirty-year period had consistently identified placement turnover as a significant problem. Thus, over time a figure of 30–40 per cent of young people in care has been found to be likely to experience four or more moves, with 6–10 per cent facing a very large number (10) of placement changes. This problem of instability confronts refugee children in a different way, in that over half of these are placed in temporary accommodation (such as bed and breakfast) with very limited attention to planning for their future care needs (p. 6). As Stein points out, the prevalence of placement moves in a young person's care career is not just disruptive in the material sense of changing living arrangements, schools and other services, but also has implications for young people's emotional security and sense of self-worth.

In this sense it is immaterial whether the placement change is initiated by social work agencies or by young people 'moving themselves' and going missing from care:

> For the young person, placement movement often means an abrupt end to a foster care or children's home placement accompanied by a sense of failure, guilt and blame – 'it's my fault, they don't want me' – and changing carers, friends, neighbourhoods, schools on several occasions with little security in their lives.   (Stein, 2005, p. 7)

For many young people, the impact of relatively abrupt change at the end of their time in care is also significant. They may feel that they are being 'forced out' or rejected once again, where purely operational criteria determine that their placement should come to an end on the attainment of a particular birthday.

Drawing on attachment theory (Howe, 1995), Stein suggests that there are significant consequences of instability for many 'looked after' young people. Given that they may well have experienced instability, mistreatment or rejection in prior family settings, the care system is potentially in a position to provide them with 'turning points', and a secure base from which to develop and progress. However, where this is not provided, or where there are further 'breakdowns', avoidant responses may become the norm. These young people appear to become 'emotionally polarized between dependence and independence' and unable to develop the emotional 'flexibility' to make sustainable and satisfying relationships (Stein, 2005, p. 9). Indeed, there is a significant risk that young people will become trapped in a kind of vicious circle, where their inability to engage effectively with others impacts across all aspects of their lives, inhibiting their chances of securing friendships, employment or other opportunities, which in turn results in a growing sense of isolation and lack of social competence.

These difficulties can also be linked to the challenge of establishing a positive sense of identity, particularly for those who may be isolated from their 'community', such as African-Caribbean and mixed parentage young people, and unaccompanied asylum seekers, whose attachments are likely to have been severed abruptly and traumatically. It should be recognized that time spent 'looked after' will contribute to the process of identity formation and reinforcement. Stein (2005, p. 10) suggests that there are a number of key elements to the task of helping young people develop a positive sense of identity on leaving care:

> 1 the quality of care and attachments experienced by looked after young people – a significant resilience-promoting factor . . . ;
> 2 their knowledge and understanding of their background and personal history;
> 3 their experience of how other people perceive and respond to them;
> 4 how they see themselves and the opportunities they have to influence and shape their own biography.

Education: A mediating influence?

More recently, the significance of education in the lives of young people involved with social work services has been recognized. Outcomes are variable depending on young people's ethnic origins, as we have already noted, but there are broader influences which appear to impact on this group of young people. Indeed, it seems that the interplay between the 'looked after experience' (Allen, 2003) and the education system provides one of the clearest illustrations available of the underlying challenges for young people entering the care system.

Studies report a persistently low level of educational attainment for young people in care, and a dramatic contrast with the population as a whole. One study, for example, found that almost half (47 per cent) of looked after young people were not entered for GSCE/GNVQ examinations in 2001, compared to just over 3 per cent of the general population of eligible young people. Unsurprisingly, this sort of disparity is subsequently reflected in outcomes, too. One survey of local authorities found that less than 10 per cent of young people in the sample achieved five or more GSCE grades A*–C (Fletcher-Campbell and Archer, 2003, p. 3), whilst another, more localized analysis suggested that 6 per cent of young people in care achieved this standard as compared to 59 per cent of school leavers in one county (Allen, 2003, p. 1).

Not only were the outcomes observed significantly different for young people who had experience of the care system, but their educational experiences were quite distinctive as well. One study (Fletcher-Campbell and Archer, 2003) found that, of 377 young people surveyed, only 101 (27 per cent) had experienced no change of education placement during their secondary school years. Indeed, a larger number had experienced at least three different educational settings, suggesting that interruption and delay are normal features of the school experience for many looked after young people. The reasons for these disrupted patterns may, of course, be varied, including: change of living arrangements; placement ending; exclusion from school; offending; or a planned move to an alternative educational setting. However, there may be similar consequences in terms of the quality of schooling overall. Attendance was found to be low for a relatively large proportion of this particular sample, and it is noted that accurate attendance data were not kept for a substantial number (41 per cent), suggesting that responsible authorities may not have been placing a high priority on their education. Indeed, it seems that managing their placement arrangements and the effective running of the care system may have assumed greater importance than individual needs and wishes in this context.

Further research in this area illustrates the complex interaction between young people's circumstances and the arrangements made to provide them an education (Allen, 2003). Interviews with young people who had recently been in care revealed that many of those questioned had 'few or no qualifications' and they recognized that this limited them to a narrow range of 'low-paid jobs' (p. 12). Indeed, they 'expressed regret that they had not made the most of their schooling, or been encouraged to do so by carers'. An interesting connection is made here with the 'timing' of young people's entry into the care system, recalling Packman's distinction between different pathways. Over half of the group studied in this case had become 'looked after' at the age of 13 or 14, as difficulties in their personal circumstances reached crisis point. Given that this is 'an important point' in young people's education as they prepare to start GSCE courses, it seems that accumulated problems are associated with disruption in this sphere of their lives as well.

In addition, placement moves were also likely to have a negative effect, not least because of the practical difficulties associated with changing schools. Friendships might be lost, and curricula could be different, so that young people were left with the task of 'catching up' in an unfamiliar environment. It should be noted, too, that young people are likely to feel particularly uncomfortable about being identified as 'behind' their peers, and this, in turn, may have a discouraging effect. One young person had to move from foster care to a residential placement a month before he completed his education, and blamed this for his failure to achieve a satisfactory end to his schooling. Allen (2003) notes, too, that social services agencies did not appear to keep much information on young people's education, confirming the findings from elsewhere that this was seen as relatively unimportant (Box 4.2).

The interplay between practical challenges to do with changes in setting on the one hand, and attitudes and expectations on the other, may result in cumulative damage to young people's prospects and performance in school. Thus, for example, a move into residential care might result in young people encountering 'negative' views about education from peers, or 'low expectations' and 'lax' attitudes amongst staff (Allen, 2003, p. 13); young people seemed to believe that 'there was too little support generally with education when in care'.

The effect of this combination of adverse factors could be identified in the damaging impact on young people's motivation: 'What was the point in trying to please people, because you would just get moved on again' (quoted in Allen, 2003, p. 13). Like care staff, teachers often seemed to compound young people's difficulties because of their own

Box 4.2

Although there has been much discussion recently of a more 'integrated' approach to meeting the needs of children and young people, it seems that this has not necessarily resulted in a holistic view of the circumstances of 'looked after' young people.

Does this suggest that the attitudes of practitioners need to change, both in social work and in other children's services? Or do you think the problems are structural, being rooted in the priorities imposed on practitioners by agency expectations and performance measures?

'preconceived ideas'. Of course, unlike many of their 'mainstream' colleagues, young people from care might still be grappling with the circumstances which had led to their placement initially, and this alone might have consequences for their ability to engage with educational regimes.

The general sense that is conveyed here is of the frequent incompatibility of a standardized school system with the specific difficulties faced by young people who become looked after. The challenges this presents may, in turn, be compounded by features of the care system itself, which also has its own dynamics and constraints. This illustrates the compound nature of the problems encountered by young people whose 'transitions' may already be difficult, when systems of help and support are not necessarily attuned to their specific needs.

Young people 'on the edge of care'

Of course, the provision of social work services for young people extends well beyond the population of those 'looked after' at any one time. Young people move in and out of statutory 'accommodation', for example, and there is now an increasing emphasis on preventing them entering the care system at all (DfES, 2006b). So, it may also be helpful to consider some of the pattern and dynamics of service provision which operates a 'family support' model intended to prevent breakdown (Biehal, 2005, for example).

Perhaps unsurprisingly, the characteristics of those approaching social services for 'support' are as problematic as in those cases where children are looked after. The difficulties they face are likely to be substantial and long-standing, and their backgrounds differ significantly from those of the wider population (Biehal, 2005, p. 71). In addition, research has found that there are a high number of specific problems identified for this group of young people by parents and practitioners, including a range of impairments, health problems and mental health issues. Again, these figures are much higher than for the community as a whole, and in this particular study 22 per cent of those referred had a statement of special educational needs (p. 74).

Like their counterparts amongst the 'looked after' population, this group of young people were also found to be affected by other difficulties, such as their parents' experience of adverse health conditions and mental health concerns. Most of their parents reported feeling depressed and over a third said that they had 'serious' problems with their physical or mental health (Biehal, 2005, p. 78). Levels of 'psychological distress' were three times those likely to be found in the general population, and the study found that these were massively underestimated by social workers. Of course, this has significant implications for those involved in direct practice, since failure to recognize these underlying problems might lead them to attribute young people's problems to parental irresponsibility rather than seeking other explanations.

Similarly, these young people and their families were often found to be experiencing significant 'material problems', including poor housing and low income; once again, however, consistently with earlier findings: 'Social workers and support staff appeared to be unaware of the stress caused by financial problems for many families. They may have viewed financial problems as the norm among the families they worked with, or families may not have shared these concerns with them' (Biehal, 2005, p. 81). Although the age range of the young people in this study was 11–16, it was found that the problems identified in most cases were long-standing, and for 17 per cent of the cohort had emerged before the age of five. Likewise, it was observed that previous patterns of social work involvement continued, in that more than half of the young people concerned had been involved with statutory agencies for over a year before the referral which was the focus of the research in question.

It is interesting, too, that this group, in common with young people going into the care system, were also differentiated, with those using 'mainstream' services demonstrating rather less deeply entrenched difficulties. Whilst the specific issue giving rise to the current referral tended to be similar across the sample as a whole, the research found that those subsequently referred to specialist teams for more intensive, focused intervention were experiencing more 'longstanding' and more 'severe' problems (Biehal, 2005, p. 111). In this sense, the process of assessment and classification could be said to be doing an effective job of identifying and assigning young people to targeted interventions. Nevertheless, this is also redolent of the kind of process identified by Packman and colleagues, whereby young people become effectively defined according to the nature of their 'problems' in a way which is one-dimensional and prescriptive. This is particularly likely to be the case where the process of classifying problems and risks involves the making of judgements which may subsequently be used as confirmation of that very classification.

Problematic interactions? Ideology, systems and transitions

The preceding discussion of the ways in which young people are referred, classified and then engaged with by caring agencies suggests that these processes are, paradoxically, both complex and predictable. That is to say, the paths which young people follow – their 'care careers' – tend to be determined according to a series of standardized assumptions, procedures and (often implicit) judgements about the young people. On the other hand, their individual characteristics, cultural differences and self-identities will ensure that their journeys through the system will be distinctively personal and often unpredictable. This, indeed, represents the dichotomy which they, and those who work with them, must negotiate. Stein (2005) has tried to capture some of the essential elements of this challenge in reflecting on the specific process of 'leaving care'.

As he points out, there has been a steady stream of research evidence over a lengthy period which has demonstrated the challenges facing young people who have been in care, and who often experience subsequent difficulties such as 'loneliness, isolation, poor mental health, drift and homelessness' (Stein, 2005, p. 16). Their experience is in sharp contrast to that of other groups of young people, and some of the difficulties they encounter can be linked with their experiences of 'transition'. For instance, young people who have been looked after, in foster care or children's homes, will have to take on major responsibilities, often with limited support, 'at a far younger' age than the population in general. Stein describes this process as one of 'compressed and accelerated transitions' to the state of adulthood. It should be noted that the challenges encountered by young people in this context are both practical, in the sense of having to manage their own finances and accommodation arrangements, for example, and psychological or emotional, in that they are less likely to be able to rely on a range of relationships and support networks than others. For young disabled people, transitions to adult services can be similarly abrupt; or they may experience an extended period of dependence, where they are denied the opportunity to make or participate in key decisions about where they live or what relationships they establish.

Stein suggests that there are two reasons that abrupt transitions for young people who have used the care system are particularly problematic, posing challenges in turn for those involved in providing services to support them. Firstly, he suggests that, if anything, changes in benefit provision, employment patterns and family structures have led to a prolonged period of semi-independence for most young people, which involves continuing material and emotional reliance on parents and other relatives. For care leavers, these resources may be much more limited, unpredictable, or simply unavailable. Secondly, and in similar vein, as we have seen in previous chapters, transitions are not uniform for most young people, and they tend to deal with significant changes steadily over a period of time, rather than having to deal with a series of major life events all at once. This, indeed, may help to illustrate why a change in one aspect of provision (say, a new residential placement) may need to be offset by additional input to ensure continuity in other aspects of the young person's life (such as parental contact, maintaining a school place, or supporting existing friendships).

In fact, as Stein (2005, p. 18) notes, it is probably unhelpful to conceptualize 'transition' as a unilinear, one-off process. It is more accurate to think of it as an extended and often iterative process, whereby young people may often return to a previous arrangement, such as living at the parental home, after a period of 'independence'. This flexibility in the move to autonomy is described as 'becoming more extended, connected and permeable', in ways which may not be readily available to young people who have been 'looked after'. Despite recent changes, such as the Children (Leaving Care) Act 2000, concern remains about the scale of the task for young people without strong networks of support or personal resources. Services and practitioners must be willing to recognize their continuing responsibilities in this respect:

> In promoting resilience, there will need to be more recognition of the nature and timing of young people's transitions from care. This will include giving them the emotional and practical support they will need into their early twenties, providing them with the psychological space to cope with changes over time, as well as recognising the different stages of transitions.   (Stein, 2005, p. 19)

It is encouraging to see this increasingly acknowledged in policy and regulations (DfES, 2006b, 2007b), with the need for continuing material and emotional support clearly acknowledged in the Care Matters programme. There are, too, some good examples of this principle being put into practice, such as extended foster care support provision in Hull (DfES, 2007b, p. 111). However, young people also make the point that continuing support should be provided in ways which suit their specific needs: 'What about residential care?' (young person quoted in DfES, 2007a, p. 25).

Conclusion: Working with complexity

For those engaged in practice with young people who draw on welfare services, there are clearly a number of important considerations relating to the nature and organization of statutory provision. These may be summarized in terms of three distinct elements which are fundamental, but which interact in ways which are not necessarily coherent and predictable: prevailing attitudes, service systems and individual biographies.

Thus, as we noted at the start of this chapter, the underlying assumptions which inform interventions are significant in determining what is seen as practicable and desirable. The shift from a historical preoccupation with institutional responses to a perspective which prioritizes 'preventive' measures may have obvious merits, but it may also be problematic in certain respects. Practitioners may, for instance, be inclined to think of residential provision as a 'last resort', to be avoided at all costs, whereas for some young people, it is clearly a welcome and necessary option (Ward, H., et al., 2005). It is important, too, that assumptions about the quality of care provided to 'looked after' children do not influence practitioners' views of the quality of service provided, or the likelihood of positive outcomes (Box 4.3).

There is no doubt that service systems do lend themselves to standardized and inflexible practices which do not mesh well with the

Box 4.3

Residential care has sometimes been viewed as an undesirable option for looking after children and young people. However, the problems of residential settings may arise from an assumption that they should be seen as a 'last resort' rather than as a positive option. As the Utting Report (Utting 1997, p. 22) notes: 'We lack neither the theoretical nor the practical knowledge to provide good residential child care.'

Under what circumstances, and with what safeguards, might a children's home be the right choice of placement to meet the needs and wishes of vulnerable young people?

variable nature of young people's experiences. Placement moves which may be necessitated for organizational reasons may have a profound effect on young people because of disrupted education or friendships (Allen, 2003). Not only do practitioners need to recognize this, but also they may have to be proactive in trying to influence placement decisions, or provide alternative arrangements to maintain continuity (of schooling, or peer relationships, perhaps).

Finally, of course, and following from the above, it is inevitable that young people will differ, and that it is crucial to take account of individual needs and characteristics in designing and providing suitable forms of intervention. This is clearly the case in terms of ethnic and cultural differences, for instance, but equally applies to the way in which developmental transitions necessarily vary from one person to another. Once again, Stein (2005, p. 10) helpfully summarizes this point by characterizing a young person's developing identity in the form of 'a personal narrative . . . , connecting the past, present and anticipated future'. This, in turn, has some important implications for practice and the use of standardized tools of assessment and planning, which may not always give appropriate weight to the factors or feelings which are most important to the young person concerned.

We will return to some of these key issues in subsequent chapters, but the most important observation at this point is that effective practice depends on utilizing an integrated approach to the different dimensions of young people's transitions. Standardized systems and prevailing beliefs may well be informed by sound principles, but they must also be seen as negotiable; services need to be responsive and accountable to young people first, and to prioritize their experiences and aspirations: 'She [social worker] was there for me when I needed her help. She also left me alone to be able to fend for myself and to get on with things. But the main thing was that the support was there when it was needed' (Looked after young person, quoted in Ward, H., et al., 2005, p. 14).

Chapter summary

This chapter has discussed a series of approaches to defining the needs of young people, especially those in the care system, and the impact of these approaches on young people's experiences of intervention. The idea of distinctive 'pathways' has been considered, with the associated implications for practice. Key points are:

- Approaches to intervention are shaped by the perspectives of practitioners and the prevailing assumptions about what constitutes 'good practice'.
- These perspectives may conflict..
- In parallel with this, the lived experiences of young people receiving services (variously thought of as 'care careers', 'pathways' or 'trajectories') will almost certainly follow distinct routes.
- Practice must be sensitive both to the differing needs arising from these variable experiences and to the contested nature of our prior assumptions about the most appropriate form of intervention.

Further reading

Values and Practice in Children's Services (Smith, R., 2005) and *Perspectives in Child Care Policy* (Fox Harding, 1997) are two parallel accounts of the way in which practice beliefs and underlying assumptions can create a predisposition towards particular forms of intervention. Practitioners need to be able to reflect both on their own value positions and on those which are likely to be held by others.

The work of Jean Packman (Packman,1981; Packman et al., 1986; Packman and Hall, 1998), carried out over many years, has been of great value in helping to identify and develop practice wisdom about the different ways in which young people in care are classified and the relationship between these and their care careers.

Resilience and Young People Leaving Care (Stein, 2005) takes a similar approach and helps to focus attention on the continuing needs of young people whose transitions from care vary significantly.

5 Care or control? Balancing responsibilities

A constant tension

One of the central dichotomies of social work practice is the requirement to promote the welfare of service users at the same time as
managing the risks associated with their behaviour. This is set out explicitly in the General Social Care Council's (2002) core statement of
practice principles:

> As a social worker you must protect the rights and promote the inter-
> ests of service users and carers.
> This includes:
> . . . Respecting and, where appropriate, promoting the individual
> views and wishes of both service users and carers;
> . . . Supporting service users' rights to control their lives . . .
>
> As a social worker you must respect the rights of service users while
> seeking to ensure that their behaviour does not harm themselves or
> other people.
> This includes:
> . . . Recognising that service users have the right to take risks . . .
> . . . Taking necessary steps to minimise the risks of service users from
> doing actual or potential harm to themselves or other people.
>
> (GSCC, 2002, p. 18).

Of course, stating these principles is important, but it is of limited value
in terms of providing operational guidance for resolving the inherent
contradictions in concrete practice settings.

In relation to work with young people, there are wider challenges,
too, in that they are subject to similarly ambiguous perceptions. As we
have already observed, they are often held to be collectively responsible
for a range of problematic or anti-social behaviour. At the same time,
certain sub-groups of the population are perceived as being particularly vulnerable to exploitation and abuse. Inevitably perhaps, much
social work practice revolves around the needs and actions of young
people who fall into these stereotypical categories.

In focusing on a number of the specific practice contexts in which
these dilemmas and conflicts are likely to emerge, this chapter will
elaborate the inherent challenges in more detail and begin to identify
some of the qualities and skills required by practitioners who are
continually expected to find an appropriate balance between 'care' and
'control'.

Young people and 'risk'

Contemporary discussions of social welfare have increasingly focused on the theme of 'risk', and the extent to which it is both a product of the behaviour of young people, and a representation of wide-ranging threats to their well-being. Much attention has been given recently to the ways in which the nature and level of risk associated with young people can be defined and quantified (Sharland, 2006). The coincidence of concerns about 'risk' with the continued problematization of youth should not be a surprise in the light of past experience (see Pearson, 1983, for example), but it is none the less important to consider how and why this takes the shape it does in the contemporary world.

According to some well-known theorists (Giddens, 1991; Beck, 1992), the recent past has seen the emergence of a 'risk society', as a product of wider-ranging social and economic transitions. In brief, this may be seen as a consequence of a series of interlocking factors, such as changing patterns of family life, shifting patterns of employment, transformations within communities and neighbourhoods, and (possibly) the emergence of new sources of potential threat and harm (such as the internet, for example). All of these, of course, may also be bound up with an increasing awareness of the 'risks' associated with young people, both in terms of the threat they are believed to present, and in terms of their own vulnerability to new forms of exploitation or abuse.

Giddens (1991), for example, has suggested that there is a relationship between changes in family structure and organization, on the one hand, and the nature of interpersonal relationships, on the other. As economic and social transitions seem to impose strains on 'pre-established forms of family life', he argues, so 'new forms of gender and kinship relation' emerge (p. 177). He is careful not to make moral judgements about these changing arrangements, but notes, nonetheless, that they will lead to the establishment of different networks, for instance incorporating new and former partners, 'biological children and stepchildren', with the resultant complexity and uncertainty this is likely to entail. The context for (late) modern life is thus often characterized by a sense of 'ontological insecurity', which acts as a kind of backdrop to more immediate social and personal problems. Thus: 'whenever fateful moments intervene or other kinds of personal crises occur, the sense of ontological security is likely to come under immediate strain' (Giddens, 1991, p. 185). As he points out, if this sense of rapid change and fragmentation is indeed a feature of the wider social world, then it has specific implications for the sense of individual identity: 'A self-identity has to be created and more or less continually reordered against the backdrop of shifting experiences of day-to-day life and the fragmenting tendencies of modern institutions' (Giddens, 1991, p. 186). For young people in general this poses some specific challenges in terms of the developmental transitions we have already considered;

and, clearly, where they are confronted with other crises, or abrupt changes in personal circumstances, the problem of sustaining a coherent sense of identity and self-worth becomes all the greater.

Beck (1992) has suggested that the uncertainties represented by changed social relationships are mirrored by a new generation of risks, which arise from the processes of technological modernization and social change. At the same time, failure to predict and control these changes has generated significant questions about the capability of 'scientific' procedures of investigation and knowledge generation. This, in turn, leads to the questioning of 'experts' and increasing doubts about their professional credibility. For social work, with its history of uncertain professional credentials, this erosion of belief is particularly problematic.

These developments have culminated in a number of radical shifts in the context for social work practice and the ways in which it is constituted. Recognition of the increasingly diverse and unpredictable nature of perceived risk has led to a desire to develop ever more sophisticated and failsafe means for assessing it, planning interventions and acting to prevent or reduce its impact. These pressures are observable at every level, from the political sphere, through organizational processes, to the practice setting itself (Sharland, 2006, p. 248). Thus, for example, government initiatives have generated action to tackle a range of categories of young people 'at risk', including care leavers, teenage parents, young homeless, those with mental health problems, or those who are 'not in education or training' (NEETS). These groups are complemented by another set of categories, of those young people who present a threat to the wider community, through offending, anti-social behaviour, substance misuse, or the refusal of opportunities in education.

At the same time, as Sharland notes, perhaps partly because of the decline of belief in the capabilities of welfare professionals, a whole range of new initiatives and agencies, from across various sectors, has been assigned responsibility and funding for tackling the problems of young people themselves. The role of statutory social work professionals appears to have been increasingly constrained and limited to formalized procedures of assessment and resource management. However, for the kind of reasons that Beck articulated, it is precisely these aspects of the professional task which have become the focus of attempts to develop more accurate and precise measures of risk, in order to enable targeted interventions to be provided. This, indeed, is the kind of language to be found in the emerging policy literature, such as *Every Child Matters* (DfES, 2003) and *Youth Matters* (DfES, 2005a). Services for children and young people are expected to provide, '**integrated targeted support** within the overall framework for young people's services so that young people at risk . . . are identified as early as possible' (DfES, 2006f, p. 36).

In support of this aspiration, a range of machinery has been developed, including the Common Assessment Framework and the

Information Sharing Index, both of which provide for the sharing of knowledge and concerns across services in order to provide the most comprehensive possible basis for intervention. Practitioners are advised that: 'As local areas move towards integrated children's services, *professional* [my italics] and confident sharing of information is becoming more important to realising the potential of these new arrangements to deliver benefits to children, young people and families' (DfES, 2006e, p. 7). It is therefore a collective responsibility to share information where there is cause for concern, and this should be carried out according to clear standards and principles, such as what is covered by the rules of confidentiality and when these can be overridden. This guidance has been drafted so as to apply to young people 'at risk', irrespective of the nature of the risk. Sharing information is described as 'vital' to ensure that services are provided for children and young people with 'additional needs'; at the same time, it is deemed 'essential' to protect them 'from suffering harm' or 'to prevent them from offending' (DfES, 2006f, p. 3).

The Common Assessment Framework (DfES, 2006g) purports to offer a systematic tool on which to base judgements about need, but the tools for assessing risk in detail are more comprehensive, and they are also distinguished according to the nature of risk identified. Thus, the ASSET tool (Youth Justice Board, n.d.) is for use with young people who offend, whilst a 'core assessment' utilizing the *Framework for the Assessment of Children in Need and their Families* (DH, 2000a) is the specified instrument for determining the appropriate response to the possibility of significant harm. At this point, it seems, it becomes impossible to apply a common framework for assessing risk and need, and a process of 'bifurcation' (Bottoms, 1977) is set in motion which may have significant consequences.

As is pointed out, these formalized instruments for identifying and measuring aspects of risk in young people's lives may not coincide readily with their own perceptions or experience. Sharland suggests that 'much of the psychological literature presents adolescence as a risky business, but one in which risk taking is not only normal but desired' (2006, p. 252). Indeed, too rapid or robust a response from others may 'prevent [adolescents] from achieving the maturity that risk taking and learning from mistakes might afford'. In order to illustrate this point, she introduces us to 'Jane', a 16 year old, whose 'risky' behaviours include truanting, smoking, clubbing and getting very drunk. These behaviours may or may not constitute a trigger for action from a range of external agencies, but they may not be far from the norm for Jane, and, importantly, for others in her peer group. As her repertoire of 'risk taking behaviours' widens, perhaps to include 'recreational drug use, unsafe sex or antisocial behaviour' (p. 254), agency and professional concerns may be heightened, but her perceptions of the nature and level of 'risk' remain highly significant, certainly in the context of any attempted intervention. In offering a critique of standardized risk assessment strategies, the disparity between subjective and external criteria is made clear: 'Risk, therefore, exists not as some external reality but as a "calculative rationality" of governance, through which particular groups or individuals may be identified as "at risk" or "high risk", and thereby observed, managed, disciplined' (Sharland, 2006, p. 255).

Taking this point somewhat further, other investigators have found an almost complete reversal in the way that certain groups of young people conceptualize 'risk' (Boeck et al., 2006). For them, too, the context and features of young people's lives are crucial in determining perceptions of what are and are not risky decisions and behaviours. Thus, young offenders have been found to have a 'fatalistic and often hopeless outlook in life' (p. 8). This is reflected in a sense of passivity and limited access to a range of possible 'futures'. Young people identified as offenders in this study either did not know what they wanted to do with their lives, or aspired to unlikely (if not impossible) outcomes, such as 'being a footballer' or a millionaire. These rather unspecific and ungrounded aspirations seemed to reflect a broader sense of indifference, and a distinctive view of risks to themselves and others.

This brings into focus some important considerations about the nature of risk itself. It seems that perceptions clearly vary according to experience and social position. Thus, for example, as the study above notes, the experience of risk may be contradictory, and may not operate in ways that are straightforwardly predictable. Young people involved in offending and anti-social behaviour may be in a state of what is termed 'risk stagnation', whereby they are unwilling to take the chance of leaving familiar surroundings and relationships. Where horizons are limited and there are clear risks involved in making changes, these factors might outweigh the alternative risk factors associated with maintaining a lifestyle which incorporates offending behaviour.

Similar influences may have a bearing on young people's capacity to make changes in other respects, too, such as moving away from situations where they appear to be exposed to exploitation and abuse. Where the alternatives are not clear and not discernibly better for the individual concerned, then the certainties and comfort of the status quo might have their own attractions. In practical as well as theoretical terms, this means that we must be very careful about basing our working assumptions on shared perspectives and common understandings of what characterizes risk, on one hand, and what strategies should be adopted to deal with it, on the other.

Emerging evidence seems to suggest that risks are indeed experienced variably, and lead to differing outcomes, depending on the individual concerned. Thus, in some cases, young people who are expected to be at high risk of offending do not go on to offend (Boeck et al., 2006, p. 3). This has been taken by some to mean that the crucial mediating factor is that of 'choice', and the judgements made by individual actors on the basis of their understanding of the costs and benefits of a particular course of action. The problem here is that whilst this may account for the variability of individual decisions and outcomes, it does not account for the patterns revealed, which demonstrate distinct variations between social groups. This means that perceptions of risk, cost–benefit calculations and the range of choices available to young people are dependent to a large extent on the social milieu and their own networks of relationships. Lupton (1999) suggests that the concept of risk itself acts to reinforce social divisions, and 'often serves to reinforce' certain groups' marginal status (p. 113). At the same time as these groups come under the scrutiny of more powerful representatives of the state, their own perceptions are accorded lesser value, and little account is taken of the restricted choices available to them. The capacity to analyse and act on one's knowledge of risk is more limited for those who are also disadvantaged in other ways. The sense of resignation, of 'hopelessness', which practitioners may encounter amongst certain groups of young people may therefore be understandable in terms of differential perceptions and access to the necessary resources to achieve change.

Nonetheless, practice is very often shaped for us by conventional categorizations of risk, as Lupton points out (1999, p. 114). The differentiation between those 'at risk' of harm and those who are 'dangerous to themselves or others' remains significant, and we will go on now to consider how this is reflected in the construction of social work with young people.

Young people 'at risk'?

Social work with children and families has historically been bound up with prevailing concerns about the mistreatment or abuse of children, and child protection work has often come to take centre stage in conventional understandings of its 'core business'. Thus, it is perhaps unsurprising that much social work with young people is driven by an emphasis on harm and the need to ensure that they do not put themselves at risk. In the case of 'young people' as distinct from younger children, the harms to which they are exposed tend to be fairly broadly defined, and these are often associated with underlying assumptions about personal responsibility and choice. Thus, for young children, it is likely that the risks they face will be identified as external and beyond their control; whilst young people may be assumed to take some share of the responsibility for putting themselves 'at risk'. For example, problem drug-taking, alcohol misuse, 'running away' and risky sexual activity may all be thought of as risks taken consciously by young people, for which they should accept a degree of personal responsibility. In this sense, our earlier discussion of transitions, and associated assumptions of increasing independence and autonomy, are reflected in the perception of young people as progressively more capable of exercising choice and control over their own actions. As we shall see, this kind of prior understanding may well affect professionals' ideas about the shape and scope of intervention. At the same time, it may also indicate a degree of commonality with the assumptions underpinning practice with young people who present an active threat, in the shape of anti-social or offending behaviour. In both cases, they are likely to be held largely responsible and therefore accountable for what they do.

Despite this observation, distinctions can be made between those 'at risk' and those who pose a risk to others. For example, the gender balance may be significantly different, with the former group more likely to include girls and young women, and the category of young offenders being largely male-dominated. This reflects both differences in perceived behaviour and long-standing beliefs about the differential risks faced by young men and young women. Young women are seen as being more vulnerable, and more at risk of sexual exploitation and abuse.

Grounds for these concerns have been provided by research evidence which associates harm to young women with experiences of earlier victimization, usually by adult males (Fergusson et al., 1997; Pearce, 2003). One study has thus found a close association between child sexual abuse and a range of both 'risky' behaviours and harmful outcomes in adolescence. Young women who had been abused as children were much more likely than the general population to become sexually active before the age of 16; to have more than five 'sexual partners'; to become pregnant; and to be subject to further sexual assaults or rape (Fergusson et al., 1997, p. 796).

Another study, focusing solely on young women 'at risk of, or experiencing sexual exploitation and/or prostitution', found similarly that their current experience could be associated with a range of prior problems (Pearce, 2003). These young women reported prior histories of: truanting; running away; and abusive relationships with older men.

In both studies, links were identified between wider influences and the immediate cause for concern. Thus, on the one hand 'elevated risks' are explained by 'social, family and contextual factors' (Fergusson et al., 1997, p. 801), and on the other young women who were sexually exploited were often 'separated from, or in conflict with, primary forms of support such as home, family, school and local authority care' (Pearce, 2003, p. 2). Indeed, in common with our earlier observations about perceptions of risk, the sense of futility felt by young women was reflected in their own behaviour. Over half of those involved in this particular study used heroin at least once a week and a similar number 'regularly self-harmed', whilst around a third had attempted suicide. This seems to provide further evidence of the implications of a fatalistic view of one's circumstances and capacity to change things. Tellingly, the author observes that: 'Many felt that they were not worth protecting from harm. One said: "*It's only possible to protect yourself if you think you're worth protecting*"' (Pearce, 2003, p. 2). This pessimistic accept-

Box 5.1

Young people and social workers alike often seem to share a sense of 'powerlessness'. However, it is important to recognize that everyone is able to make choices, even though in many circumstances these may be limited. The initial focus of intervention may be on identifying and expanding the range of feasible choices, rather than feeling constrained to accept 'the least worst' option available.

'The following are examples of questions and prompts that seem to work:
• Let's explore . . .
• How can we change . . . ?
• How can we look at this differently . . . ?
Let's take a step back . . .' (Merton et al., 2007, p. 282)

ance of their situation by young people may also have been linked to a lack of confidence that they would be believed if they reported their experiences of being abused (Box 5.1).

Of course, it is not just in the area of sexual abuse and exploitation that young people might be perceived as potential victims and therefore likely candidates for social work intervention; however, the categories of risk identified often seem to overlap. Thus, self-harm figures significantly amongst the group of young women just considered, but is also becoming recognized as a more widespread problem, as a recent national inquiry has demonstrated (Richardson, 2006). It is acknowledged that the subject has been largely 'taboo' in the past, and that self-harm may be difficult to understand. It is, however, something which is specifically associated with young people ('four times as many girls as boys'), and is much more common than might be assumed (one in fifteen young people are now believed to have harmed themselves at some time). Explanations are offered, sometimes by young people themselves, in terms of expressing 'hurt, anger and pain' associated with other pressures in their lives, and for some young people 'self-harm gives temporary relief and a sense of control over their lives' (Richardson, 2006, p. 7). It is, in turn, associated with other difficulties experienced by young people, including bullying, abuse, isolation, loss and other stressful situations.

Similarly, young people who 'run away' might be thought of as being at risk; and also similarly, their actions in running away might be seen as a form of attempt to exert 'control' over their situation in one of the few ways open to them. As discussed earlier, the relative judgement of 'risk' from their point of view might well be different from that of an external observer or professional practitioner. Young people may run away from their families, or from other settings, such as foster and residential care; and it is estimated that there are '129,000 overnight running away incidents per year in the UK' (Smeaton and Rees, 2004, p. 3). Young people run away for specific reasons, it seems, and these are often associated with problems of conflict and violence at home (p. 8). Running away is not a homogeneous category, and it seems that where young people do so persistently or for longer periods of time the kinds of problem they are escaping from may be 'deeper seated' (Biehal and Wade, 2002). These include domestic violence, (parental) drug and alcohol problems and sometimes sexual abuse:

> While conflicts may most often trigger running away, these may be symptomatic . . . Many young people using street work projects have been found to have experienced a high level of disruption in their lives due to relationship breakdown, conflict and violence and some have spent time in care earlier in their lives.   (Biehal and Wade, 2002, p. 14)

Studies of young people who run away suggest consistently that they may simply be exchanging one form of 'risk' for another, and that if they spend any length of time 'on the streets', this may be an inevitable consequence of their precarious situation. They may get involved in theft, begging or selling sex, for example, but they are also apparently vulnerable to other potentially damaging consequences, such as 'substance abuse . . . self harm and depression' (Biehal and Wade, 2002, p. 14) as well as sexual abuse and physical violence.

Whilst running away is quite a widespread phenomenon, it is none the less concentrated amongst the population of young people in residential or foster care. Given that they are likely to have been placed in care because of prior difficulties, it seems that for this group running away may be partly related to these unresolved issues, although it may also be related to negative aspects of the care setting. Young people who run away are not unaware of the dangers, it seems, so it must be assumed that they do not take the decision lightly. Young people expect to encounter threats from: ' "nasty people – men in particular"; "perverts and idiots"; "paedophiles and prostitutes". The dangers are obvious – "getting kidnapped, killed, raped, hurt" ' (Morgan, 2006, p. 14). Whilst some young people appear to have methods of anticipating and dealing with the threats they encounter, risk is still ever present because 'young people don't know how to protect themselves', and some make risky decisions to ensure their own survival: 'some girls become prostitutes to have somewhere to sleep'.

Another group of young people who may be seen predominantly in terms of their vulnerability are those with disabilities or learning difficulties. These young people are often provided with specialist services and education which take them out of the mainstream, focusing on their 'needs' primarily in terms of impairments. Although this focus may be supported by evidence which suggests that they are more likely to be at risk in certain respects (for example, Sherrard et al., 2002; Yeo and Sawyer, 2005; Emerson and Hatton, 2007), it may also result in a preoccupation with personal safety, care and protection, at the expense of other aspects of personal and social development.

Previous analyses have identified a preoccupation with what a disabled 'young person cannot do because of their impairment' (Morris, 2002, p. 4), and a tendency to think of transitions in terms of moving young people into specialist adult services (Stalker, 2002). These are considered more as 'care' placements than as 'a way of gaining qualifications or paid employment' (Morris, 2002, p. 3). A preoccupation with care and protection from risk may lead to a failure to recognize disabled young people's entitlements to 'take risks' in the same ways that others do: 'Friends and sexual relationships are important issues for young people but transition planning, assessments and services rarely address these concerns' (Morris, 2002, p. 4).

Thus, certain categories of young people with whom social workers are likely to practise may come to be defined essentially in terms of their vulnerability, particularly given the prevailing emphasis on risk assessment and risk management (Sharland, 2006). However, this perspective is likely to incorporate certain shortcomings, as we have seen. Although it seems clear that young people who use services may well be disadvantaged and potentially vulnerable for a number of reasons (for example, Emerson and Hatton, 2007), the way in which they perceive and experience 'risk' may not reflect the primary concerns of practitioners or agencies. Thus, for example, we have observed that young people who 'run away' may take risks in order to avoid alternative threats to themselves. Risk is rarely one-dimensional and may involve rational calculations, based on the knowledge available to them, as to the 'least worst' option. Interventions which fail to recognize this may therefore simply be irrelevant to the immediate issues facing young people (Box 5.2).

The choices young people make may be limited in a number of ways, and this is an important factor to acknowledge. They may, indeed, be limited by lack of knowledge, and because services either do not recognize a need or seek to make decisions on young people's behalf. However, choices are also limited because of the circumstances of disadvantage and poor provision which are the norm for many service users. The risks to which young people with learning difficulties and mental health problems are exposed are not simply to do with these two powerful labels, for example: 'Nearly two thirds of children with emotional disorders are living in poverty. Six out of ten have been

Box 5.2

Practitioners may frequently encounter the dilemma of whether or not to act on the disclosure by young people that they are engaged in risky behaviour. This may, of course, also be part of a 'testing out' process on their part.

What sort of criteria (e.g., likelihood of 'significant harm') might be applicable to

guide practitioners in deciding whether or not to take action to safeguard the young person concerned (or others)?
What undertakings can we realistically give about confidentiality in this kind of situation?

exposed to two or more different types of adverse life events. Over half are supported by a mother who is likely to have mental health needs herself' (Emerson and Hatton, 2007, p. 23).

The idea of being 'at risk' is complex and multi-faceted. Young people experiencing 'risk' from a particular source may also encounter a range of wider (and often unacknowledged) needs; they may sometimes also represent a risk to others; and they are almost certain to have distinctive views about the best way to manage the risks to which they are exposed. These observations have important implications for practitioners who must take account of a number of considerations: the young person's perspective and wishes are centrally important; risks may interact – removing one may heighten another; risks may need to be managed rather than eliminated; and risks may be less important to young people than other needs they identify.

Thus, for example, young people commenting on the appropriate response from care staff to running away suggest that 'there could be an agreement' to stay in contact by mobile phone, but that staff should not then use this link to insist that they return 'straight away' (Morgan, 2006, p. 16). For practitioners, the idea of allowing young people to take risks is sometimes uncomfortable, because it may conflict with other organizational requirements or professional values; but it may be the best option in complex and unpredictable circumstances, where relationships are more important than certainty.

Young people who pose a 'risk'

On the other side of the coin is the group of young people who are seen as offering a threat to stability and social order, whose behaviour is deemed unacceptable, and who are seen as the legitimate objects of social control. Social work has a particularly problematic relationship to this group because it is often seen as offering 'excuses' for behaviour which is unacceptable, and which should be deterred or punished. This tension between 'welfare' and 'justice' has long been recognized as lying at the heart of social work practice with young offenders, but it also reflects a continuing challenge to the legitimacy of a welfare presence in the criminal justice system. The question to be explored here is thus the extent to which social work is able to establish a credible and accepted basis for intervening in this particular context.

Sharland's (2006) view is that the present era is one in which 'the idea of youth at risk has become central to a range of discourses' (p. 247). However, the two aspects of risk appear to have become separated, so that it seems as if we are talking about a quite distinct group when we refer to those involved in anti-social or offending behaviour. As a result, the welfare needs of young people who offend appear to have become marginalized, and in the light of 'the risk rhetoric, there has effectively been an elision between the agendas of care and control' (p. 251). The concern to understand and explain young people's behaviour in the light of their background and circumstances has been replaced with practices focused on 'the management of criminogenic behaviour and situations through the use of actuarial styles of reasoning and technologies' (Gray, 2005, p. 938). The focus of intervention is the 'responsibilization' of young people, both in the sense of holding them accountable, and in 'actively involving' them in measures to reduce the risk of reoffending.

These developments in thinking and policy are reflected in specific measures such as the Crime and Disorder Act 1998, which established as the primary aim of the youth justice system 'the prevention of offending by young people' (Section 37). This approach was supported by assertions in policy documents that addressing the crimes of young people would reflect their welfare needs, by definition: 'The Government does not accept that there is any conflict between protecting the welfare of a young offender and preventing that individual from offending again. Preventing offending promotes the welfare of the individual young offender and protects the public' (Home Office, 1997, p. 7). This one statement seemed to provide justification for a sustained strategy of dealing with the problems of youth crime (and by extension young offenders) by identifying and controlling the risk factors linked to offending.

Reframing the problem of youth offending in this way led to a significant reorientation of thinking about intervention, which was now to be based on a calculative approach to assessing future risks and taking action best suited to minimizing these. Thus, what might previously have been prioritized as welfare needs were now of interest only to the extent that they represented possibilities of future delinquency: 'Deficiencies in family upbringing, peer contact and the school environment are framed as calculable risks which can be managed through preventative intervention' (Gray, 2005, p. 939).

The new machinery of youth justice established after 1998 incorporates an array of machinery designed to fulfil just this sort of function, including standardized and routinized assessment tools (ASSET, ONSET; see below), prescriptive forms of community-based intervention incorporating large doses of behaviour management, surveillance and control (for example, the Intensive Supervision and Surveillance Programme), and tightly enforced sanctions for non-compliance. Intervention programmes incorporate a variety of elements which are designed to ensure that young people address their offending behaviour and access formal education and employment opportunities. Success is measured in terms of further offending rates and satisfactory programme completion, and the 'welfare' benefits to young people are simply assumed to follow from these outcomes.

The place of social work in the 'new youth justice' has been assured through the establishment of multi-agency youth offending teams (YOTs), which represent a corporate commitment to the shared objective of preventing youth crime. This commitment thus appears to require a collective strategy based on combining perspectives and skills in order to maximize effectiveness. Different professional values and responsibilities are recognized, but they are to be subsumed under a common goal. Once again, the assumption is that differences are less significant than the mutual obligation to work together to prevent crime.

The Youth Offending Team has been described as a 'co-operative of practitioners[1] drawn from several public services whose mandate brings them into contact with young people at risk of (re)offending' (Burnett and Appleton, 2004, p. 26). The establishment of YOTs thus sought to put in place a joint mechanism on an equal footing to tackle the problem of youth crime. From a social work perspective, it could be seen as subsuming former 'welfarist' agendas under a 'justice model' focusing much more directly on problematic behaviour. This change can be seen not only as a substantive shift of emphasis, but also as one (among many) manifestation of a new belief in interprofessional collaboration, and the assumed efficacy of models of shared working towards commonly agreed goals. In the youth justice context, however, this did not necessarily mean that prior agency goals would retain their former significance, and this is certainly the case for social work practitioners.

Two contrasting views of these structural changes appear to have emerged. On the one hand, they are seen as effectively tying social work more closely into a system which is primarily concerned with managing risk by controlling the behaviour of young people who represent a threat to the wider community. On the other hand, becoming part of a wider collaborative network potentially opens up access to additional sources of help and support. In practice, however, the first of these two outcomes is more clearly observable, and it is noted that there has been a discernible 'shift in professional ethos away from welfare to the prevention of offending' (Burnett and Appleton, 2004, p. 27). The sense of a common objective, somewhat removed from the social work agenda, has led to other consequences, too, as the nature of the task has blurred professional divisions: 'Over the period of the YOT's development. . . team members' separate professional identities became less distinguishable and the unified identity of "YOT practitioner" emerged, graphically described by one practitioner as "this meltdown kind of thing where we are from other agencies but the edges are very fuzzy"' (Burnett and Appleton, 2004, p. 29). This development has been further underlined by the increasing reliance of youth offending teams on specialist practitioners (such as 'YOT Support Workers') who do not have any prior agency affiliations. In this context, the role and influence of social workers appear to be diminishing.

The new ethos of the YOTs has been reflected in working practices as well as structural arrangements, and, again, the emphasis appears to have shifted towards a technocratic approach to risk assessment and behaviour management. The ASSET tool, developed specifically for use with young offenders, is a central example of this trend. Its highly prescriptive, offence-focused format encourages a concentration on those aspects of a young person's behaviour, attitudes and circumstances which appear to be criminogenic, rather than considering need and well-being as parallel instruments for assessment in children's services would require (DH, 2000a, for example). Whilst some (usually less experienced) practitioners appear to find ASSET helpful as a kind of checklist, others see it as a hindrance. The routinized nature of the ASSET assessment appears to be complemented by an approach to planning and intervention which is also partial and minimizes the importance of good relationships in social work practice. The loss of previous working styles and their replacement with prescriptive programmes of intervention and 'case management' have been keenly felt by some practitioners: 'I never get a kid now dropping in to see me and saying "Is Miss [X] in?", "can I have a word?", you know, when they've got a problem or they want to tell me they've done well. That whole bit seems to have gone' (quoted in Burnett and Appleton, 2004, p. 33).

The preoccupation with behaviour and prevention of offending appears to mean that, for some young people, those aspects of their lives which may be more problematic to them are not seen as being important, or even relevant. Ironically, of course, failure to make the connection between offending behaviour and other aspects of young people's lives and experience may be counter-productive in relation to the narrowly defined objective of reducing criminality. Whilst workers in this particular study aspired to positive and caring relationships with young people who offend, their practices and procedures appeared to cut across this aspiration and undermine their welfarist principles.

Although the trends within the youth justice system appear as an extreme example, they are significant because they encapsulate an important feature of the current landscape, affecting both the way in which young people are viewed and the way in which interventions are shaped in line with these perceptions. Thus, youth offending is aligned in current discourse with a range of other 'risky' attributes, including problem drug use and school exclusion (McCrystal et al., 2007), as if these are all interchangeable features of a larger problem of 'social exclusion'. This assumption is partly a product of research findings which suggest that these behaviours and characteristics are concentrated amongst particular sectors of the population. Young people who are excluded from school are more likely to be involved in illicit drug use (McCrystal et al., 2007, p. 43), and in offending behaviour, according to their own accounts (McCrystal et al., 2007, p. 45; Smith, R., 2007). We also know from earlier studies (for example, Graham and Bowling, 1995) that there is a persistent gender difference in that boys or young men are consistently more likely to be involved in offending and other anti-social behaviour than girls or young women. On the basis of survey evidence, MORI claimed that the 'most common profile of a teenage offender was a white male aged 14–16, living in London or the north-east, who was excluded from school and had committed more than five crimes in the past year' (*Guardian*, 20 May 2002).

The programmes put in place for such apparently problematic young people focus on manifestations of risky behaviour which are seen as mutually reinforcing. In some ways, the antecedents or causes of these problem behaviours are not treated as particularly important, since the main focus is on developing the means to control and eradicate them. Because they represent a risk to society, these young people 'are increasingly designated worthy not of support but surveillance, control, punishment' (Sharland, 2006, p. 251). In this way, the notion of 'risk' constitutes the problem in a very specific way for practitioners. They are bound to see the priority as one of removing or reducing the threat, almost irrespective of its source, or other related circumstances. The extent to which the behaviour concerned represents a conscious choice, which may be culturally determined, and may be viewed as legitimate or 'normal' by young people, is not a relevant consideration. Thus, the part played by social work in engaging with, empathizing with and 'understanding' young people has no place in the repertoire of interventions, bringing to mind again, John Major's exhortation as Prime Minister that we should replace 'understanding' with 'condemnation' of young offenders (see Chapter 2).

However, in the same way as young people 'at risk' may be involved in making difficult decisions and choices about how to deal with alternative sources of potential harm, so those who represent a threat are also likely to be involved in complex patterns of relationships and to be subject to a variety of influences, such that their involvement in problem behaviour is not a simple matter of choice, or a result of endemic wickedness. The concept of risk is unhelpful in this respect, since it reduces complex interactions and outcomes to one dimension, and leads to a preoccupation with simplistic targets and outcome measures:

> In this scenario, it is often more expedient to engage in responsibilising interventions which challenge young offenders' attitudes and behaviour through structured, time-limited, restorative activities, such as community reparation, writing letters of apology and victim awareness training, rather than addressing the more nebulous and resistant social-exclusion factors. (Gray, 2005, p. 952)

The problem for social work is that different aspects of young people's lives appear to have been separated, leaving only manifest (and externally defined) 'risk factors' as the target for intervention. As a result, the range and diversity of approaches and techniques which might be relevant is significantly curtailed, leaving a limited range of behavioural and 'training' interventions on the table (Box 5.3).

The challenge for social work practitioners is to consider ways in which their principles of participation, empowerment and holistic practice can be reinserted into what has become an unpromising, even hostile, practice environment.

Box 5.3

Young people who are identified as perpetrators of sexual harm are often found to have been the victims of abuse themselves. In this context, the notion of risk is likely to have a powerful influence on assessment and decision-making processes.

How would you go about planning a process of assessment and intervention

which integrates current concerns about the risk posed by a young person who has offended in this way with a proper evaluation of their needs, which are likely to be grounded in their own prior experiences of being harmed?

Social work, young people and risk: Challenges and opportunities

Although some commentators have been tempted to draw pessimistic conclusions, it is important here to consider what the possibilities are for reframing practice positively in the context of a 'risk society' (Beck, 1992). One issue, for example, is the increasing extent to which young people have become 'not social work's problem' (Sharland, 2006, p. 259), either because they have been redefined as a client group of the criminal justice system, the youth services (Connexions, for example), or perhaps mental health provision or the voluntary sector. Nonetheless, it is suggested, this does not mean that social work is no longer relevant or important to some or all young people 'at risk'. Social work is particularly important precisely because it does link concepts of risk with other aspects of young people's lives, including the personal and structural factors that shape their choices and risk-taking behaviour. It is also a central feature of social work that it aspires towards holistic responses to these issues, supporting young people in their efforts to achieve positive outcomes.

In addition, as Sharland (2006, p. 259) observes, social work principles of self-determination and user control fit well with our understanding of young people as 'agents of their own lives'. Their choices might be constrained, but their perceptions of their own risks and needs are crucial elements in the processes of assessment and planning interventions. Whereas there has been a tendency in recent times to highlight particular aspects of 'risk' as if they are objective and operate independently of young people's own experience, this is not an accurate reflection of the variable influences which impact on them, and which will also necessarily lead to specific personal responses. Young people will necessarily follow 'their own trajectories' and make their own choices about risks and how to negotiate them. Risk taking and 'risk making' are perhaps inevitable features of the transitions that young people undergo, and social work needs to retain the capacity to 'question the distinction between what is normal and abnormal, acceptable and unacceptable risk – between youth in transition, youth in trouble and youth as trouble' (Sharland, 2006, p. 260).

Social work is also well placed to initiate a process of reframing 'risk', both in individual cases and in wider debates, precisely because it works with young people whose experience of 'risk' may well span experiences of disadvantage, mistreatment and oppression *and* involvement in behaviour which is itself unacceptable, anti-social or potentially oppressive. We know, for example, that many young people who enter the care system will also come to the attention of criminal justice agencies (Taylor, 2006). Although the relationship between these aspects of young people's lives may not be clear cut in terms of causation or consequences, the fact that it is acknowledged has certain implications for practice. At a minimum, these include not contributing to the 'labelling' of young people in care as failures or potential criminals, but it may also mean identifying and highlighting positive aspects of young people's lives, promoting their strengths and speaking out on their behalf.

In essence then, the task for practitioners is to resist defining young people solely in terms of apparently neutral and external 'risk' factors, but to find ways of exploring what these mean for those concerned and to work with them to develop effective responses. This is often recognized by practitioners who experience a considerable degree of frustration with narrowly prescriptive managerial approaches. Thus: 'traditional methods and values were regularly reasserted as necessary and important [by practitioners] . . . Faced with the chaotic lives and often desperate social circumstances of their young charges, the provision of a supportive relationship and attention to welfare needs were the assumed essentials of the job' (Burnett and Appleton, 2004, p. 132).

Chapter summary

In this chapter we have considered the influence of contemporary concerns about risk on the processes of assessing need and intervening with young people. The consequences of a risk-based approach may be a preoccupation with harmful behaviour, and this may in turn create problems for social work practice. Key points are:

- Risk has become a defining feature of contemporary society, exercising pervasive influence on organizational and individual behaviour.
- Practice has become constrained by a concern to minimize or avoid risk, at the expense of meeting need.
- Young people can be identified as posing a risk as well as being 'at risk', and the nature of service responses may be determined by which category is applied.
- For most young people, these categories create an arbitrary distinction which does not reflect the complexity of their lives.
- Social work must not become preoccupied with risk at the expense of a more complete understanding of the young person, his or her own perspective and a holistic approach to intervention.

Further reading

Risk Society (Beck, 1992) remains a compelling account of the processes by which the concept of risk has become pervasive in contemporary society. It offers a clear insight into the dynamics of 'defensive practice' and the way in which organizations become preoccupied with maintaining and improving systems of damage limitation and control.

Sharland's article 'Young People, Risk Taking and Risk Making: Some Thoughts for Social Work' (2006) is an insightful and authoritative account of the way in which the concept of risk and the associated attempts to control it have exercised a pervasive influence in social work with young people.

Youth Justice: Ideas, Policy, Practice (Smith, R., 2007) includes an account of the way in which youth justice systems and procedures have become preoccupied with managing behaviour at the expense of meeting need, creating significant problems for social work practitioners in this sphere.

6 Young people's experiences and expectations of social work

The rights of young people: Growing awareness

As the rights of children and young people have become more explicitly articulated and recognized, so there has been a process of rethinking their relationship to service providers. The UN Convention on the Rights of the Child, ratified in 1989, and adopted by the UK government in 1991, has been particularly important in setting out the basic entitlements of children and young people, as well as the responsibilities of others towards them. In the light of this, increasing attention has been paid to the way in which services have been provided for them, and questions have been asked about whether or not their best interests have always been served. The issues here arise on at least two levels: firstly, whether or not young people are routinely engaged in exercising choice and control over decisions affecting their lives; and secondly, whether or not their rights have been actively breached by the very systems put in place to help them. These two questions are clearly connected, although the implications of failure in each respect are rather different.

Thus, the growing concern with the rights of children and young people has had some important consequences for the way in which services are constructed and evaluated (see Chapter 3). It has brought into much sharper focus historical problems over the treatment and sometimes abuse of children and young people in the care system, for example, and we will go on to consider some illustrations of these problems. In addition, there have been signs of an increasing emphasis on participation, and an active commitment to take young people's views seriously. This, in turn, has led to a re-evaluation of the nature of the relationship between agencies and practitioners, on the one hand, and young people who use services, on the other. Should the role of the agency be seen as parental, administrative, customer-focused, befriending, participative or collaborative? Are these mutually exclusive? Can they be sustained consistently in the light of external expectations and demands?

In order to consider these and related questions in more detail, this chapter will focus on the documented experiences of young people who have received services from social work agencies, and consider these in the light of the legitimate expectations young people might have of those who are providing for their welfare and taking responsibility for their upbringing. This may help us to gain a clearer understanding of the challenges for practice in ensuring that young people's voices are heard and their wishes and feelings respected.

Uncomfortable lessons from the past

Despite the contemporary emphasis on rights and participation, it is important to recognize that the history of social work with young people, especially those in the care system, has often been characterized by failure and examples of mistreatment. Institutional care, in particular, appears to be prone to instances of abuse, not only of children and young people, it must be acknowledged (Butler and Drakeford, 2005). As Thomas (2005, p. 128) points out, 'abuse of children in residential care has been the subject of a series of major scandals'. Several major inquiries were held during the 1990s, which revealed systematic and highly damaging forms of abuse against young people (Levy and Kahan, 1991; Kirkwood, 1993; Waterhouse, 2000).

Certain common themes could be identified from these inquiries, such as the isolated nature of many residential care regimes, and the opportunities these afforded for systematic exercise of power over young people who were often vulnerable and unable to make their concerns known to anyone outside. In some cases, it appears that mistreatment was justified in terms of the need for specialized forms of 'treatment'. Thus, in Staffordshire, the 'Pindown' regime was deliberately built around processes of isolation and humiliation of young people, based on 'the principle that we were establishing control', in the words of the regime's architect (Levy and Kahan, 1991, p. 167). Similarly, the abuse of children in care in Leicestershire was initially legitimized by claims that it was based on a new 'therapeutic' approach, incorporating a form of 'regression therapy' (Kirkwood, 1993, p. 309).

An even more comprehensive inquiry into the abuse of children and young people in care in North Wales (Waterhouse, 2000) also found that mistreatment was systematic and resulted from failings at all levels of practice, management and strategic oversight. This inquiry found evidence of the abuse of children and young people in foster care as well as in residential settings. Again, there appeared to be consistent problems associated with a lack of concern for the interests and rights of young people when placed in care. It seems that there are particular risks associated with the way in which vulnerable individuals are treated in isolated or institutional settings, where they may be liable to exploitation by those in positions of power and authority.

It was in the light of these concerns that the then government initiated a substantial review of the 'safeguards' available to children in care settings, in 1996 (Utting, 1997). The starting point for this inquiry was the cautionary note (also voiced by Kirkwood, 1993) that it would be unwise to assume that any system put in place to safeguard children and young people living away from home could guarantee that 'nothing like it would ever happen again'. The investigation was targeted not simply at extreme examples of mistreatment, as the previously mentioned inquiries were, but also at 'institutional and other impersonal factors' which might impact adversely on the quality of young people's lives. The review accepted that safeguards for children and young people in care had been strengthened under the Children Act 1989, but it did not take this for granted, arguing that certain groups might be particularly vulnerable, such as those children and young people with learning or communication difficulties, those with emotional and behavioural difficulties, and those in public care generally (Utting, 1997, p. 18). At the same time, additional risks might be presented to children in these circumstances from predatory adults, who might seek positions of trust, and from institutional problems associated with staff stress. Beyond this, system failure could lead to damaging outcomes for children and young people, notably where organizational priorities were 'substituted' for what should be 'the primary objective of promoting the welfare of children'. Indeed, Utting suggests a straightforward rule to be applied, which is that 'everything that goes on' in child welfare agencies 'should be put to the test of whether it serves the interests of children. If it does not . . . , it is likely to harm their interests directly or indirectly' (Utting, 1997, p. 19).

The Utting Review quickly drew the conclusion that the safety and well-being of children looked after were dependent on the 'overall effectiveness' of the service provided. However, a number of aspects of provision at that time were not sufficiently attuned to the needs and aspirations of children and young people, including staffing arrangements, instability of placements, and health and education services for children in care. The report was forthright in asserting that the 'persistent deficiencies in children's homes are symptoms of a lack of commitment by political and service managers to unpopular, expensive but necessary provision' (Utting, 1997, p. 22). Problems such as financial constraints and a consequent unwillingness to invest in residential care were seen as endemic, and indeed its relative expensiveness is clearly a factor operating at all levels to discourage its use. Difficulties arise, however, where this understandable concern over cost impacts on professional judgements and attitudes towards an important element in the service portfolio.

Other recurrent problems identified by the review included the pattern experienced by some young people of repeated moves, and a failure to pay attention to basic education and health needs, which should be seen as universal entitlements. The review did not restrict its criticisms to residential care, but also expressed concerns about the quality of foster care provision. It noted, for example, that the 'isolated nature' of foster care placements meant that children and young people might be liable to abuse. Problems of inadequate training, for carers and staff, and insufficiently robust assessment processes were

Box 6.1

'A number of reports and inquiries have recently shown that young people in custody may be at risk of "significant harm" according to the Children Act definition. Indeed, in some cases, young people have died in penal institutions' ('29 since 1990' – Goldson, letter to the *Guardian*, 18 August 2007).

What are your obligations as a social work practitioner if you think a young person is 'at risk' in a secure establishment?
How can you exercise your responsibilities under the Children Act 1989 to safeguard him or her?

noted. Lying behind these shortcomings might have been implicit assumptions about foster care being inherently 'better' than residential care, and an unwillingness to probe too closely into family-like settings which appeared to be in the best interests of those in care. In addition, the review observed, some forms of care, such as private fostering, were subject to relatively little protective activity by statutory authorities. The review concluded that: 'It is not known how many children are privately fostered since statistics are not kept but it appears the number may be substantial. Children in private foster care are extremely vulnerable and at very considerable risk of abuse' (Utting, 1997, p. 29).

Other settings, too, were identified by the review as giving cause for concern. In the case of residential schools, the limited amount of interest in taking a proactive approach to safeguarding the well-being of young people came in for criticism. For young people in penal settings, the review took the line that custodial regimes would inevitably pose risks to their safety and well-being, and should be avoided wherever possible. In addition, a much more stringent approach should be taken to applying and enforcing safeguards to protect young people from harm (Box 6.1).

Changing attitudes: The impact of *People Like Us*

The Utting Review was significant not just because of its comprehensive approach to the welfare of children in care and other institutional settings, but also because it gave over space explicitly to the voices of young people, and this was an important step forward, in terms of public acknowledgement of the centrality of their perspective. It was thus extremely revealing to find, even at this point in time, that: 'Young people felt that they were not routinely listened to or involved in planning and decision making' (p. 76), and that 'participation' often meant just 'turning up' to find out what had already been decided for them. Young people in this consultation expressed concerns not just about their opportunities to have a say, but also about the unacknowledged risks they faced whilst in care.

Learning our lessons?

Following this highly critical account of practice in relation to a particularly vulnerable group of young people – those 'living away from home' – government did act, taking as guidance a key sentiment of the review: 'quality protects'. Extensive changes were initiated in the organization and content of services for children and young people coming into contact with the care system. The government-led Quality Protects[1] (QP) programme ran throughout England from 1998 to 2004, targeting a series of key objectives intended to improve services for children (the equivalent initiative in Wales was titled 'Children First').

Importantly, the QP programme acknowledged the scale of the problem, and its deep-rooted nature. The context of the initiative was one in which the wider problems of social exclusion and marginalization were being highlighted, and this is clearly of particular importance in relation to children's social services. Inclusive principles were emphasized, for example, in terms of creating better educational opportunities and promoting secure and lasting attachments. In practical terms, this led to targets to reduce the number of placement moves experienced by looked after children, and limit delays prior to placement (not necessarily compatible aims, it should be noted). Particular emphasis was placed on improving the life chances of looked after children with disabilities, or from ethnic minority backgrounds.

Following this massive programme of investment and improvement, it should be possible to identify clear evidence of better practice, and thus better outcomes for young people who have been involved as users of children's services. In particular, the consistent message that children and young people have not been 'listened to' seriously or effectively should have prompted a robust response, it would seem. As Thomas (2005, p. 178) notes, it is incumbent upon us to 'think about the results of all our work with children and young people'. He argues that there is some evidence that those areas on which attention has been focused, such as education and health improvements, indicate some positive gains, with nearly three-quarters of the 'looked after' population having regular health and dental checks by 2002. However, he also comments that other areas which have received less attention may offer a rather different picture. Thus, in contrast to improvements in physical health for young people in care, 'their mental health is still an area of high concern', with a 'high proportion' experiencing difficulties which might lead to mental health problems, for which suitable services are 'very limited indeed' (Thomas, 2005, p. 181). Indeed, the wisdom of adopting a target-driven strategy of this kind is questioned, partly because it leads to an over-concentration on some (usually the most amenable) areas of intervention at the expense of others. In addition, as Thomas notes, it is difficult to know how to interpret a particular outcome:

> For instance, when we read that 10 per cent of looked after children aged 10 or over were cautioned or convicted for an offence during a year, three times the rate for all children this age [DH, 2003b], are we to interpret this as an indication of how badly the care system is looking after young people, or as a reminder that the young people it is looking after are already at a high level of risk of poor outcomes when they come into care? (Thomas, 2005, p. 182)

Setting unrealistic targets or placing unattainable demands on those responsible for assessing and meeting young people's needs may be counter-productive. At the same time, however, we should at least make some attempt to discover 'how we are doing' in order to be able to identify practical and feasible ways in which we can maintain and improve standards of practice.

Continuing concerns: Young people still at risk?

Current evidence is mixed. There are clearly examples of service improvements and a greater attention to the expressed wishes and feelings of children and young people, but there are also persistent failings in the systems put in place to meet their needs and promote positive outcomes (Joint Chief Inspectors, 2005, for example). Thus, it has been concluded through service inspections that greater priority has been given to 'safeguarding' children and young people in recent years, and as a corollary to this, more attention is paid to 'listening to and consulting with children' (Joint Chief Inspectors, 2005, p. 5). However, the picture is not consistent, according to this source, with limited monitoring in some cases, some evidence of complacency amongst agencies, insufficient attention to the needs of specific groups, such as young people with mental health conditions, and concerns about what happens to children and young people in 'unregulated' settings. Out of this overview, other specific issues arise, such as the relatively low priority given to asylum seekers who are legally still children, and the challenge of 'reconciling immigration requirements and welfare considerations' (p. 9). The limited nature of support offered to this group is perhaps a reflection of wider difficulties some children's services departments have in responding to need, with the result that other agencies do not draw concerns to their attention. Similarly, this major inspection exercise found that whilst children's voices are heard in some settings, there remain widespread reservations about the 'lack of opportunities to express their views or concerns' (p. 6).

Whilst these issues can be attributed largely to systemic failings or inadequate resources, there are also significant practice implications, given that we have already observed that the mistreatment of young people, in and outside the care system, is often associated with a failure to seek out their views or to take account of what they say. Thomas (2005) again stresses that it is important not to place blame or responsibility on individual workers, who may be operating in the context of

structural or resource constraints, but that there are messages for practice from the evidence available about persistent shortcomings in
provision for young people. He makes the point that listening carefully
to young people's concerns is crucial, but that this depends on establishing an effective relationship with the young person concerned,
and sustaining that relationship. Young people will only share their
concerns, especially about sensitive personal matters or their treatment by carers, if they believe that what they say will be heard, acted
upon, and not misused or dismissed. They are unlikely to be able to take
this step unless they feel they can rely on a positive response from
someone they know and trust. The notion of making and sustaining this
kind of relationship may cut across the demands and constraints of
many social work settings, as Thomas (2005) acknowledges, but it
seems clearly to be a prerequisite of being able to engage effectively
with young people and respond to their concerns on their terms: 'children actually complained more about changes of social worker than
they did about changes of placement'. Whether or not it is possible to
generate performance indicators which measure the quality and
sustainability of relationships, the suggestion here is that lying at the
non-negotiable core of effective practice are 'the social worker's relationship with the child' and 'continuity in this relationship' (Thomas,
2005, p. 189).

Having their say: What young people tell us about children's services

As the Utting Review demonstrated, serious shortcomings appear to
have been endemic in children's services, especially in the residential
sector, over a long period of time. Many of these shortcomings, and
mistreatment of children and young people in particular, seem to be
associated with a lack of attention to their views and expressions of
concern: 'I don't like people making decisions about me and they think
they know what's best for me just by reading my file' (Young person
quoted in Utting, 1997, p. 77). It is consequently a positive sign that in
recent years much more emphasis has been placed on hearing young
people's perspective on the services provided and how they should be
improved.

Indeed, a wide range of strategies has been adopted in order to
ensure that young people are firstly consulted, and then able to participate in decision-making and service planning. There have been
small-scale research projects (Munro, 2001), wide-ranging surveys
(Viewpoint, 2006), focused consultations (Jigsaw, 2003; Knight et al.,
2006) and strategic-level policy initiatives (Gunn, 2005; DfES, 2007a,
2007b). This has been reflected even at government level with wide-
ranging consultations to enable young people to influence change in
service provision: 'Lots of you said that this was the first time you had
been asked what you thought about being in care' (DfES, 2007a, p. 1).

The common strand has been a strengthening commitment to engage with young people using services, to hear their experiences and their ideas for change, and to ensure that these are acted upon. In addition, there is a clear aim behind some of these initiatives to move from a position of seeing consultation and participation as something of a special event, to embedding this kind of approach in day-to-day practice, and in the ethos of service providers and practitioners. One study, for example, was prompted by a local authority's desire to initiate the improvement process by making 'some initial investigations of the views of children in their care' (Munro, 2001, p. 129). In this case, the researcher involved effectively acted as a mediator between the young people and the agency. This investigation was, on one level, quite reassuring for practitioners, in that it found that the young people taking part all recognized the importance of their social workers to them, and 'most' were able to identify 'at least one' who had got on well with them and provided positive support. As is often the case, apparently mundane activities such as phoning regularly and taking an interest in the young person were valued.

However, these young people also expressed a number of concerns about social worker involvement, such as high staff turnover and disruption (as many as six social workers in a two-year period in some cases), and unreliability was also a matter which came in for criticism.

It is undeniably the case that the demands of social work practice sometimes create difficulties in meeting commitments to service users, but social workers may also sometimes underestimate their own importance in young people's lives, and the impact of letting someone down who may have become used to being ignored or devalued[2]: 'Children interpreted this carelessness as a sign of their low priority in the social worker's life. One young person, reporting on the failure to hold her reviews regularly, was very angry but also felt helpless to alter matters' (Munro, 2001, p. 131). Whilst it may be difficult for practitioners to set reasonable boundaries between professional responsibilities and over-involvement, the point is made here that young people may well be seeking some form of human engagement which at the very least demonstrates that someone cares about them. Importantly, in this connection, this study likewise made the distinction between changes of placement and changes of social worker, the latter being seen as *more* disruptive by this group of young people.

In other respects, too, the quality of young people's participation in decision-making and planning appeared to relate to their wider experience of the care system. Thus, some felt that formal reviews were helpful and relatively unproblematic, whilst others 'felt powerless and frustrated'. It seemed that the ostensible purpose of the review, to consider young people's future needs, was not reflected in the kind of outcomes this group experienced. For them, it felt as if plans were not put into effect, their views were not taken into account, and they were fobbed off with promises of future actions which never materialized. It was noticeable that older children and young people, in particular, felt excluded from meaningful participation, and as a consequence they concluded that the purpose of review meetings was to 'talk about, rather than to, them' (Munro, 2001, p. 132).

There were other examples, too, in this study of the way in which the expectations and formal procedures of statutory agencies can cut across the expectations of young people. Thus, their reasonable assumption that information about them would not become common knowledge appears to have run counter to the implicit agency assumption that the 'corporate parent' role means that information can be shared widely and without seeking additional permission from the young person. This is a particular challenge for practitioners who may feel that it is professional good practice to keep a proper record of significant information concerning the young person and her or his safety and welfare. In the words of one young person: 'I felt really let down because I thought I had been talking to her [social worker] privately but I saw she had written it all down in the file for anyone to read. I wouldn't have said anything to her if I had known she was going to do that' (quoted in Munro, 2001, p. 133) (Box 6.2).

This study concluded that despite the widespread acceptance in principle of young people's rights to 'participation', in practice certain aspects of their experience of services appeared to run counter to this ideal. They would therefore find themselves unable to control the use of information about themselves, and, similarly they would find that they had little say in determining the nature of their working relationships with practitioners. Whilst it seems that children and young people increasingly have the capacity to make their views known and they want the right to be involved in decision-making processes, difficulties are likely to be encountered in practice. As Munro observes:

> The problem is: who has the power to listen to the child's voice? The social worker may be willing and anxious to empower the child yet themselves feel restricted in the autonomy they have. Management will be setting out objectives and priorities they are under pressure to meet. If a 16-year-old says he thinks the action and assessment record

Box 6.2

Practitioners are increasingly expected to demonstrate that they have consulted young people in order to find out their views about what should happen to them. However, as this example also shows, organizational agendas sometimes mean that the approach and style of consultation do not reflect young people's wishes. The process as well as the outcomes must be meaningful to them.

How can practitioners ensure that they engage young people effectively?
What mechanisms can be put in place to encourage a proper sense of dialogue, and 'checking out'?

> is intrusive and unhelpful and he would prefer to spend the time talk-
> ing to his social worker instead of completing it (as one young person
> in this study did), the social worker would face the dilemma of listen-
> ing to the child or to the manager.   (Munro, 2001, p. 136)

Some of the concerns identified in this small study about whether or not young people feel that they are listened to or their concerns are taken seriously are also to be found replicated in larger surveys (Viewpoint, 2006). Whilst 'the great majority' of young people looked after are generally positive about their experiences, 'there is a significant minority' who have a negative view of their treatment by the care system, and at the same time, those in this group are 'less content with' the quality of their relationships with social workers and the level of involvement in decision-making offered to them. Thus, there appears to be a clear connection between the quality of the care provided for young people and the ways in which they are involved in planning and decision-making. So, the group of young people identified as 'less settled and safe' were less likely to report that they were able to talk to their social worker, less likely to be praised for doing well, less likely to see the social worker as often as they wanted, and offered less information than they needed to help them make decisions (Viewpoint, 2006, pp. 15–16). It is not easy to demonstrate causal expla-nations or connections between these findings, or to suggest in which direction they might flow, but it is none the less important to acknowl-edge that where young people do not feel properly involved in decision-making processes they are also likely to have a more negative view of the care experience itself.

There are other published examples of exercises undertaken to engage specific groups of young people directly in evaluating the serv-ices they receive. For example, initiatives have been undertaken to engage and consult with disabled children (Jigsaw, 2003; Knight et al., 2006). Once again, it is clear that young people are positive about the principle of effective consultation: 'One young person said that he did not feel his mother or those at school really heard him, but felt that the consultation had given him a voice' (Jigsaw, 2003, p. 9). He made the point that he did not want 'people' to communicate with him via his 'mum', but to 'talk to me direct'. This potential difference of perspective between young people and their parents, and their understandable wish to be treated independently, appears to underline the importance of using appropriate tools to communicate effectively and directly with disabled young people.

For those young people taking part in this consultation, their experi-ences and aspirations mirrored those of other young people using welfare services. For example, most felt positive about their schooling, but for some, especially in residential settings, there were concerns about being away from home, feeling excluded and being isolated (Jigsaw, 2003, p. 9). Equally, respondents in general felt that they should be provided with 'more information, more options and more involve-ment in decision-making' (p. 7). And, like the broader population of 'looked after' young people, this group often saw formal reviews as being unhelpful processes, with little opportunity for them to partici-pate directly or to say what they wanted: 'Most found the experience boring and talked of wanting to talk or contribute in some way. Many felt that professionals directed their questions to parents rather than the young people themselves' (Jigsaw, 2003, p. 8). This observation tends to support concerns aired in earlier chapters about the way in which transitions for young disabled people may be different from those for other young people, with a tendency not only to underesti-mate the desire and capacity of young disabled people to act inde-pendently and express themselves autonomously, but also to overem-phasize their dependency and vulnerability.

Despite this, the exercise itself was important in that it did demon-strate young people's capacity to express themselves independently and positively. The broader message from specific consultation proj-ects is that young people have a right to be consulted and expect to be asked about the services they receive, whatever their circumstances and characteristics, and the onus lies on agencies, practitioners and others involved in consultative exercises to make these genuinely participative. This in turn means that there should be a conscious effort to engage young people, to take their messages seriously, and to ensure that they are acted upon. Therefore, 'the process of consulting young people should be positive and empowering not exploitative', and there should be clarity about the purpose of any consultation and whether it will 'benefit young people' (Knight et al., 2006, p. 12).

Two key elements of the process are emphasized here. Firstly, consulting young people 'about their views and experiences must be based on effective communication skills' and relationships based on trust; and, secondly, young people must be reassured that it is, indeed, worth the time and effort to take an active part. In the words of one disabled young person:

> We are used to people saying we cannot communicate, but of course, they are wrong. In fact we have powerful and effective ways of communicating and we usually have many ways to let you know what it is we have in mind . . . But by far the greater part of our difficulty is caused by 'speaking people' not having the experience, time or commitment to understand us or include us in everyday life.
>
> (quoted in Rabiee et al., 2005, p. 386)

Even when communication is effective and messages are clear, there remains the crucial issue of how agencies and practitioners respond. One unfortunate possible consequence of the increasing emphasis on the importance of young people's participation is that this might be seen as an end in itself, and the link between consultation and influencing outcomes might be lost. Indeed, young people have become somewhat cynical about attempts to include them in decision-making processes (Gunn, 2005), and have been heard to observe that there is often an ulterior motive underlying the effort to seek their views. In one case, previous 'experience of the social services department left . . . young people with a jaundiced view of the department's motives for participation' (Gunn, 2005, p. 134). Was it really being carried out just '[s]o it can make the department look good', as one young person put it? Undoubtedly, the mood of scepticism detected here may be related to wider processes of marginalization and neglect, and so the challenge for those engaged in direct practice is not just to do with establishing meaningful and effective consultative processes at a personal level, but is also about demonstrating in concrete terms that these are worth investing time and effort in, and can lead to concrete and positive change.

Effective participation and good practice

We began this chapter by considering some of the lessons from the past which indicate that the mistreatment of young people in service contexts has often been based on a process of isolating and disempowering them, individually or as a group. The denial of a 'voice' has left them in a position of weakness, where the absence of complaints has been taken as a sign that there is nothing wrong. More recent developments, associated for instance with the Utting Review (1997), have led to a recognition that participation is and should be a basic right for children and young people who receive services, which should be recognized as an essential precondition for effective service delivery. Whilst attempts have been made to put this principle into practice, serious concerns remain, in relation both to the extent to which it has been realized, and to the potential for consultation to lead to significant change. Young people themselves remain sceptical, and indeed, the potential value of consultation may be irreparably diminished for them if it consistently proves to be ineffective in achieving positive outcomes. These negative consequences will be all the more corrosive for those young people whose lives have already been shaped by processes of marginalization, discrimination and mistreatment. Nonetheless, participation is a fundamental principle and the work of practitioners and agencies should be geared towards ensuring that it is embedded at the core of their involvement with young people. It has been identified as being important for a number of reasons:

- To uphold children's rights
- To fulfil legal responsibilities
- To improve services
- To improve decision-making
- To enhance democratic processes
- To promote children's protection
- To enhance children's skills
- To empower and enhance self-esteem. (Sinclair, 2000, p. 1)

Importantly, this list connects the broad principles of rights and social justice with the specific benefits of enhanced services, protection from harm, and the inherent benefits to be gained from taking part in deciding what happens.

It is also clear that these and other benefits can only be achieved where practice is supported by an effective 'whole systems' approach (Wright et al., 2006), whereby the four components of 'culture', 'structure', 'practice' and 'review' are consistently oriented towards establishing and sustaining effective involvement. Thus, practitioners should expect to be acting as mediators between service users and their agencies; they 'need to be able to work in a way which enables participation and ultimately affects change or improvement within the organisation' (Wright et al., 2006, p. 7). If children and young people are to have confidence in participatory processes then they must be assured that practitioners will act on their behalf, and that advocacy will produce results. Clearly, if this is not the case, then confidence in the process will be undermined. Practitioners in turn need to feel that they have permission and will be supported in pursuing a participatory approach which may lead to awkward questions and necessitate change from within the agency. So, for example, it seems that a 'clear lead' from management is important, and that explicit support should be provided for those in practice, such as a stated 'commitment to participation' in written job descriptions.

What is needed is a change of mindset, so that both agencies and practitioners see participation as beneficial, in terms of both outcomes for children and the quality of service that is provided. Involving children and young people in decision-making processes should not be seen as threatening or as an abdication of responsibility, but as a means of achieving mutually beneficial ends.

In order to ensure effective involvement of young people in accessing and using services, it needs also to be recognized that this is not just a 'one-off' exercise, but should be embedded in all stages of design and delivery: 'Children and young people need to participate actively and meaningfully . . . from start to finish. They should be involved in defining the aims, objectives, processes, outcomes, and ways and means of measuring success' (Wright et al., 2006, p. 8) (Box 6.3).

Ceding control to the young person may be a more or less problematic aspiration, given that some aspects of these processes are not negotiable, such as conditions which are predetermined by a court order, in a youth justice setting. At the same time, practitioners will be aware that they have quasi-parental responsibilities where a young person is 'looked after' by the local authority, and that certain obligations follow from these.

Nevertheless, promoting participation remains important, as does openness and honesty about what is and is not negotiable in a specific context. The importance of 'scene-setting' should be stressed here. It is likely that young people will be engaging with social work services in a

Box 6.3

Social workers have to find a way of resolving the tensions between respecting young people's wishes and protecting their interests, which may not always coincide. Young people may, for example, be involved in relationships with others whose motives or behaviour are questionable.

As a practitioner, would you feel threatened by the idea of giving up control over key decisions about the care of young people with whom you work and allowing them to choose? What criteria should you apply? Can you think of situations where you would want to 'veto' their choices? What would you do if you knew that a young person who was being sexually abused was determined to continue to live with the suspected abuser?

context which is not of their making, either because they have specific needs, because they are at risk of harm in some way, or perhaps because they are subject to statutory requirements under a court order. In this context, their involvement with the service will not be seen as entirely voluntary or desirable, from their perspective. Thus, effective participation may well necessitate an initial process of information sharing (which needs to be accessible to the young person) and agreement of ground rules and mechanisms for ensuring that young people feel that they are able to contribute in ways that are acceptable to them. Implicit power relationships need to be recognized, and practitioners may have to vary their own work patterns to promote active engagement. It seems, for instance, that much modern-day practice is based on a standard working day, and relies on formal contact at agreed times in office settings. It may be necessary for us to reflect on the implicit barriers these very mundane forms of arrangement may put in place, which may actually create significant difficulties in creating the right conditions for participatory practice: 'Adults often fail to acknowledge the need to adapt their ways of working to accommodate children and young people' (Wright et al., 2006, p. 27). Thomas (2005, p. 77) makes an important point when he contrasts the formal settings and procedures within which practitioners often find themselves operating, and the ability he and co-researchers had to use 'games and activities' to explore young people's views and feelings about being looked after. Thus, ironically, the very processes set up to promote participation, such as statutory reviews, may themselves inhibit young people's involvement because they are experienced as alien and off-putting. It is not enough just to set up a formal activity such as a review meeting which offers a procedural mechanism for ensuring 'participation' by young people. Any such opportunity needs to be supported and incorporated into a process of engagement and dialogue:

> The benefits for children's involvement of seeing it as a process, where this happens now in practice, are numerous. It was clear to us . . . that building relationships of trust, giving clear information in terms

> that the child can understand, and encouraging children to speak up
> for themselves in 'little' matters as well as 'big' ones make a huge
> difference.   (Thomas and O'Kane, 1999, p. 228)

In order to support participatory work with children and young people, Sinclair (2000, p. 6) has offered a checklist to be followed by 'adults', who need to:

- *Inform.* Although it may seem self-evident, it is important that young people know what is going on, what is being decided, what format a meeting may take, when and how they can have a say, how to raise any concerns, and who is involved in making decisions which affect them.
- *Consult.* 'At its best, consultation is continuous dialogue.' It will be important to acknowledge both 'normal' feelings of apprehension about talking openly about personal issues, sometimes with people you don't know, and the additional problems that may be associated with past experiences which may be stressful and difficult to share. Clearly, practitioners must be prepared to offer additional support and to proceed at a pace which suits the young person.
- *Prepare.* Particularly for formal events, such as planning and review meetings, preparation may be necessary, either through careful explanation, or even through the use of the kind of training and resource packs made available by a number of organizations, such as the Children's Rights Alliance for England or Children in Wales.
- *Take account of the child's or young person's agenda.* This agenda may not be the same as that held implicitly by a statutory agency or laid down as part of a formal process. Involvement must be flexible, even if this means changing the central purpose of a meeting or rescheduling.
- *Consider the young person's needs.* The young person may want to meet on her or his own terms, and may wish to determine who attends. She or he may also have specific requirements in terms of preferred means of communication, or interpretation. The ease with which such arrangements are made also conveys important messages about how much priority is given to the young person's perspective and personal preferences.
- *Facilitate the use of independent support.* Similarly, young people may want to be supported by people with specific skills in assisting them to communicate, or by friends, relatives or other professionals of their own choice, who can help them articulate their needs and aspirations and assert themselves in what may be seen as an unfriendly setting.
- *Rethink the style and nature of meetings.* 'Given the strong evidence that children take their role in decision making seriously but find current practice unhelpful, promoting active participation means re-thinking the style and nature of meetings. Are they trying to serve

too many purposes? Can they be broken down into smaller, more focused occasions?' (Sinclair, 2000, p. 7).

• It is important to remember, too, that wishes and feelings expressed outside formal settings by young people should be given as much weight as those articulated in meetings or other official settings.

• *Treat children or young people with respect.* Clearly, this point is fundamental, and should not be subsumed under the requirement to meet procedural expectations.

• *Give feedback.* Young people often find it immensely frustrating to find that views which they have expressed clearly and strongly are not acted upon (Thomas, 2005), even when they feel there has been an explicit commitment to do so. In order to ensure that participation is, indeed, an ongoing process, young people should be provided with follow-up information and explanations as to why things are or are not happening once decisions have been made and actions promised.

Translating these principles into practice may present particular challenges, and may necessitate new ways of working which attempt to reframe existing power relationships. For instance, enabling young people to represent their needs and wishes as a group rather than isolated individuals may well be a more effective way of opening up discussion and initiating change, over problems which may well be experienced as oppressive at a personal level. Thus, in one local authority, 'Just Us' Groups were established to enable young people in care to play an active part in agenda-setting and expressing their views (Cambridgeshire County Council Children and Young People's Services, 2006, p. 9). The groups have been able to express concerns which might have been difficult for young people to articulate on their own, with significant results. For instance: 'social workers are more aware of the needs and views of young people and what they feel makes a good social worker'; 'possessions [are] not moved in bin bags' any longer; more support is available from the education service than previously; and young people have been directly involved in recruitment and training activities. Their work has also informed the code of practice which applies to the conduct of individual reviews. Thus, as indicated previously, cultural change is an important prerequisite for positive developments in practice.

It is also important to emphasize here that social work with young people should not be seen purely as a transaction between individuals, and it may well be seen as easier for young people, and more empowering of them, to find opportunities to ascertain their views and share ideas in group settings, notwithstanding issues of confidentiality and privacy. This approach is also helpful in enabling practitioners to distinguish effectively between what may be common concerns amongst young people, say about safety and personal security, and issues which are specific to a particular individual, where, for example, victimization would take on an entirely different meaning. Social work as an activity is very often structured in such a way that practitioners are required to focus on individuals, such as the review and planning process, but it is important not to overlook commonalities and shared aspects of young people's experience, needs and aspirations. Social workers and their agencies therefore need to think actively and creatively about utilizing the normal frameworks and settings for their interventions in order to promote opportunities for young people to get together, share problems, set their own agenda and identify ways forward. It should also be noted that this kind of collective forum also offers potential safeguards against the kind of systemic abuses of young people identified by the Safeguards Review (Utting, 1997) and other similar inquiries.

Protection, participation and progress

The purpose of this chapter has been to try to draw on some of the lessons of experience to demonstrate why and how a participative approach needs to be at the heart of social work practice with young people. It has been well documented that a disregard for the views and aspirations of young people has not just led to unproductive practice, but has also contributed to damaging and harmful treatment by those systems (and some individuals) meant to care for them. Partly, this perspective can be associated with a tradition of 'problematizing' young people themselves, and thus devaluing their perspective, but this should also be seen in terms of an inherent imbalance of power between those in positions of authority (including social work practitioners) and young people who, by definition, are likely to be in a vulnerable position themselves.

It is thus incumbent upon social work practitioners to take an active part in engaging with young people and supporting them in the expression of their wishes and feelings. This means both structuring and conducting formal processes, such as case reviews, in ways which are supportive and 'user-friendly', and seeking less formal and more open-ended opportunities to establish a proper dialogue with young people who are service users. This may mean taking risks as a practitioner, since effective dialogue depends on maintaining honest and meaningful relationships, and redefining the notion of 'professionalism' to incorporate principles of collaboration and commitment. Practitioners will therefore need to negotiate carefully the boundaries between involvement and 'over-involvement' as well as the challenge of representing young people's needs forcefully and effectively with (and sometimes against) their own and other agencies. Nevertheless, effective work with young people necessitates an approach which demonstrates that they are valued, and that their views will be listened to, heard, and acted upon.

Chapter summary

This chapter has focused on the origins and dynamics of the growing commitment to children's rights and its impact on social work with young people. In particular, it has been noted that past failings and mistreatment of young people in public care have led to a focus on involvement and participation. Key points are:

- Major reports have identified consistent mistreatment of young people in care settings.
- These failings have been attributed, in part, to a failure to 'listen to' children.
- Recent policy developments have emphasized the importance of participation and dialogue.
- Practitioners must distinguish between formal processes of consultation and substantive involvement of young people.
- Participation takes time and depends on effective engagement and sound relationships with young people.

Further reading

Thomas (2005) offers a detailed account of the requirements of delivering effective social work for young people who are 'looked after' (*Social Work with Young People in Care*). This book also incorporates a range of helpful practice illustrations and exercises.

Practical guidance about effective relationships and communication with children and young people is offered in the collection edited by Bannister and Huntington (2002), *Communicating with Children and Adolescents*, including those at risk or with specific communication needs.

Sinclair's (1998) article 'Involving Young People in Planning Their Care' was an important introduction to some of the key approaches and techniques involved in a young-person-centred intervention strategy.

PART III

MEETING THE CHALLENGE: WORKING
EFFECTIVELY WITH YOUNG PEOPLE

7 Starting from where young people are

Grounding practice in reality

So far, the specific challenges of understanding and engaging with young people and youth transitions have been explored. We have also considered some of the implications these have for social work practice, in terms of broad principles and intervention strategies. Thus, it has become clear that it is important to avoid compounding processes which problematize young people; by contrast, the task of professional practitioners is to validate their experiences, concerns and aspirations. This, in turn, provides the basis for effective dialogue, collaboration and empowerment, with the aim of ensuring that young people do, indeed, acquire responsibility for their actions and the capacity to make positive choices in their own right.

In the face of these aspirations, we have also identified a number of barriers, some structural, some organizational and procedural, and some at the level of practice. These cannot be wished away, especially not those which are rooted in long-standing attitudes and social structures which have tended to identify youth (and young people) as inherently problematic, and therefore as something to be managed and controlled, rather than explored and experienced. Social work stands somewhat ambiguously at the juncture between formal (and informal) systems representing authority and constraint and young people with their divergent and diverse lives and experiences. This ambiguity of position and role necessarily leads to a feeling of awkwardness and uncertainty – the recurrent question 'whose side are you on?' reverberates in professional consciousness, and practitioners continually find themselves having to negotiate the fine line between care and control. Nonetheless, as this and the subsequent chapters will seek to illustrate, it remains possible for social workers to practise with young people in ways which negotiate these dilemmas creatively and positively in the interests of service users. Achievements may sometimes be partial and limited, for the sorts of reasons already discussed, but the opportunity remains none the less to promote positive outcomes and to 'make a difference'. In order to achieve this kind of change on behalf of young people, it is important to get our interventions right from the start, so this chapter will focus on this aspect of the task, addressing the need to adapt our initial assessment and analytical processes to the perspective of young people living in difficult circumstances.

Social work must not start by seeing young people as 'the problem'

Young people who come into contact with social workers and social services agencies probably do so involuntarily, and often do so because they are defined as problematic in some way, whether because of their behaviour, their characteristics or their circumstances, or possibly because of a combination of all three. Social work practitioners have a crucial role in seeking first to understand, then interpret and provide legitimacy for the judgements made about young people, and their risks and needs. These initial decisions will probably have a significant effect on the nature and extent of any future services or resources provided, as well as shaping the young person's view of the nature of the service itself and her or his place in relation to it. Preparation, awareness and sensitivity are therefore essential components of the social work task. This is particularly well illustrated in the case of work with 'unaccompanied asylum seeking young people' (Kohli and Mather, 2003). For these young people, the transitions they would be expected to make are complicated by a range of other factors. Thus, the dynamics of biological, psychological and cultural change are overlaid for them by the major upheavals associated with moving away from their place of origin. Challenges may be encountered on at least three levels:

> Firstly, as 'strangers in a strange land', they may not know the habits, rules and customs of their new territories . . . Secondly, they may be carrying memories of disintegration following war and be traumatized or haunted by ghosts from the past. They have to depend on the comfort and skills of strangers . . . Thirdly, if they are looked after by social services . . . they have to find their way through a maze of systems of care and protection, having been through the immigration maze. (Kohli and Mather, 2003, p. 201)

Thus, as the issues of autonomy, choice and control over their lives become more pertinent to young people, so this particular group experiences a 'series of fractures' in their lives which undermines their ability to 'take charge' of what happens to them. Insecurity is generated not just by virtue of a change of location, but also because of the disruption of attachments and a lost sense of belonging. Given what we know about 'resilience', and the factors which provide positive supports to young people in difficulty, it becomes clear that young asylum seekers are likely to face serious consequences as a result of the disruption they have encountered. However, whilst it is realistic to anticipate a range of difficulties associated with these young people's particular circumstances, it still remains important not to pathologize them or accord them 'victim' status. Projects working with young asylum seekers have thus found it important to acknowledge the capacity they have to sustain a positive outlook and achieve change, with 'ruggedness, hope and creativity' being observed to coexist with 'pain' (Kohli and Mather, 2003, p. 202).

For practitioners, the process of assessment and identifying needs is necessarily complex in these circumstances, and involves consideration of relevant factors on a number of levels, as, indeed, the *Framework for the Assessment of Children in Need and their Families* (DH, 2000a) acknowledges; a 'holistic' approach is needed which integrates personal, family and wider factors into a coherent picture, and which focuses on 'strengths and hopes' as well as 'fears and worries' (Kohli and Mather, 2003, p. 203). The process of assessment is therefore unlikely to be straightforward, and requires careful application of professional skills, supported by the key social work values of respect and recognition of personal integrity.

It may be helpful in this context to consider the application of a number of 'tools' which potentially enable practitioners to make meaningful connections between different aspects of service users' lives and to avoid oversights. For example, Thompson's (2003) widely recognized 'PCS model' offers a basic framework for linking different 'levels' of experience which will be familiar to most social work students and practitioners. Thompson uses the model specifically as the basis for analysing oppression, but it also offers a broader framework for undertaking integrated assessments in social work. In distinguishing between the *personal, cultural* and *structural* aspects of people's lives, he offers a mechanism for distinguishing different types of influence and process, without suggesting that they are detached from one another, or that one necessarily takes primacy over the others. Thus, for example, at the personal level, one's 'thoughts, feelings and actions' will, in part, help to shape one's individual identity, as will immediate interpersonal transactions with others. So, in the specific context of inequality and oppression, prejudice is expressed directly and may involve the attribution of simplistic 'stereotypes' (Thompson, 2003, p. 13). However, it is insufficient to focus solely on the level of individual characteristics and interpersonal interactions. These, in turn, are 'circumscribed by the cultural context in which they occur' (p. 17). In the case of young asylum seekers, of course, more than one culture is clearly significant: 'They may grow up within a culture so different from their culture of origin that settlement results in a desiccation of roots and connections with their families left behind' (Kohli and Mather, 2003, p. 204). The social worker's task in this respect is therefore multi-faceted. She or he must firstly recognize the reality and importance of difference, and how this may create a sense of detachment or disorientation in itself. At the same time, it will also be necessary to consider the substantive implications of particular cultural expectations or obligations as they may impact on the service user.

Beyond this, too, Thompson highlights the relevance of 'structural' factors, such as 'the macro-level influences and constraints of the various social, political and economic aspects of the contemporary social order' (2003, p. 17), which, themselves act as contextual forces shaping cultural and personal experience. Clearly, for young people who are displaced from their place of origin, these factors are important in that their position within the economic and social order has been subject to massive upheaval and has become highly problematic, especially in the context of immigration policies which limit their ability to play an economically active role. Once again, the interplay between different levels and elements can be readily illustrated:

> The family funding the [young person's] flight may result in the children expecting to give the family a return on the investment. An economic subtext to exile is generated which they may try to live up to by carrying all the expectations of the economic migrant, on top of the particular pressures of being an asylum seeker.
> (Kohli and Mather, 2003, p. 204)

In similar vein, the present author (Smith, R., 2005, p. 96) has developed an ecological map which offers practitioners a more detailed framework for understanding and linking influences on young people's lives (Box 7.1).

This map distinguishes not just between 'levels' of experience, but also between 'types' of influencing factors, enabling judgements to be made with a greater degree of accuracy about the dynamic interplay between these. Thus, again, it becomes possible to make sense for and with young people of the complex currents which they are seeking to negotiate as asylum seekers. Leaving an uncertain and possibly dangerous political situation behind may have a direct influence on their feelings about their own personal relationships and family responsibilities:

> For unaccompanied minors – those who are sent to countries and authorities with whom parents have no direct contact – the effects of leaving are . . . complex . . . For example, in being sent away to safety because they are loved and treasured, they may feel discarded. Or being told that they must move away from a situation of danger, whilst the family remains exposed to it, can leave them pre-occupied with worry for the family's well-being.   (Kohli and Mather, 2003, p. 204)

These illustrations therefore seem to offer social workers a nuanced approach to understanding the varied and changing dynamics of young asylum seekers' lives, whilst ensuring that their own perspective remains central to the assessment process. This is crucial, not least because it helps to retain a balance between identified needs and 'resilience factors', as Kohli and Mather point out. They stress that the understandable focus on aspects of disruption and vulnerability may lead to a failure to identify strengths, personal resources and effective survival strategies. These young people, in particular, should not be further disadvantaged by being pathologized; they are not, for instance, as 'psychologically dishevelled' as many other children who may have been harmed by their families. Indeed, their own prior experiences in difficult and sometimes overwhelming situations may have been a source of valuable skills and personal attributes. According to these authors, this leads naturally to a 'focus on a practical and meaningful

Box 7.1

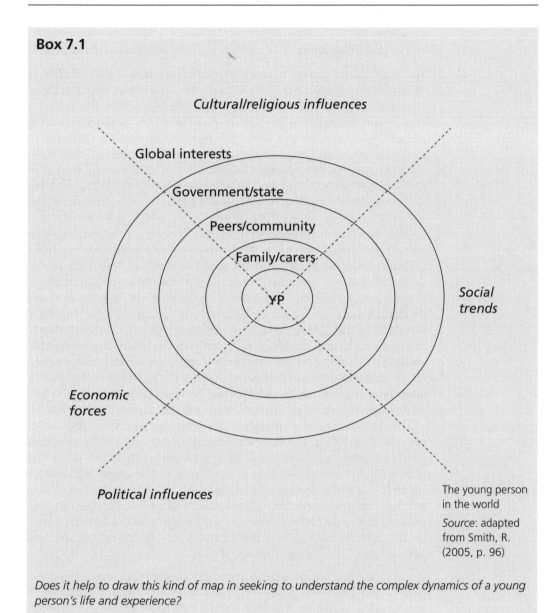

Cultural/religious influences

Global interests

Government/state

Peers/community

Family/carers

YP

Social trends

Economic forces

Political influences

The young person in the world

Source: adapted from Smith, R. (2005, p. 96)

Does it help to draw this kind of map in seeking to understand the complex dynamics of a young person's life and experience?

approach that welfare workers can take to capacity building in children in adverse circumstances' (Kohli and Mather, 2003, p. 204). Practice needs to link direct assistance and support with interventions which reaffirm the young person's sense of self-worth and identity and address those issues which are likely to be problematic as a result of their dislocation, such as:

- belonging;
- thinking;

- agency;
- cultural integration.   (Kohli and Mather, 2003, p. 205)

The practitioner cannot possibly expect to be familiar with all aspects of a young person's previous experience, and must avoid making simplistic assumptions about this, either negative or positive. Rather it is necessary to engage in an enabling process which supports the young person in making sense of new challenges and demands in the light of her or his past experience and prior attitudes and beliefs.

Clearly, too, in this specific context, the task of the social worker in providing validation and encouragement for young people who are asylum seekers is further complicated by her or his own procedural and organizational demands. The necessity of offering a reliable and consistent source of solidarity may run counter to the expectations placed on social workers by legislation and statutory agencies (Humphries, 2004, p. 104). Indeed, social workers have been accused of failing to demonstrate empathy or support for those subject to immigration policy, and of having actively cooperated with 'the removal and deportation of people even in the grimmest circumstances. They have not resisted the gate-keeping and inhumane role thrust upon them.' This raises a crucial challenge for practitioners, not just in the specific context of working with young people who are seeking asylum, but much more widely, and this is to consider the messages conveyed by aspects of their activities which may be experienced as hostile and oppressive, even if these are consistent with the terms of their jobs.

This, in turn, raises a number of important questions for practitioners who seek to 'start from where young people are'. Firstly, whatever one's individual qualities and skills, it is also likely that one's perceived 'role' will play a significant part in defining relationships with service users. It is impossible entirely to detach oneself as an individual worker from the attributes of the position one holds. As Humphries puts it, holding anti-oppressive values and aspiring to practise in ways which do not discriminate against service users may be unrealistic, or even self-deluding. She asserts that social work:

> Needs to stop pretending that what it calls 'anti-oppressive practice' is anything but a gloss to help it feel better about what it is required to do . . . It needs to inform itself of theories of power . . . It needs to begin to act collectively and in solidarity with those affected and impoverished by reactionary policies.   (Humphries, 2004, p. 105)

It may be because state social workers appear to be compromised by their position that some of the more positive examples of intervention with young asylum seekers are to be found outside the framework of statutory services. None the less, the centrality of these services to social work practice still demands that we try to maintain a positive and creative role for practitioners in formal settings. Some agencies clearly seek to maintain a positive approach, based on social work principles and a commitment to young people's rights (Cemlyn and Briskman,

2003, p. 174), and this enables social work practitioners to remain true to their core values. Social workers may need to prioritize 'rights-based practice' in contexts where the diminution of rights represents an over-arching threat to the profession's aspirations to provide help and support to vulnerable populations such as young asylum seekers. Returning to our assessment tools discussed earlier, social workers are able to draw on these to identify the contrary impact of policies and practices at national level on individual young people's well-being. However, responding to these negative impacts purely on an individual basis may not be sufficient. The situation of the individuals concerned may not be changed, and social workers themselves may find their own position becomes problematic. Indeed: 'Rights-based micro practice has an important role to play, but must be framed by a wider commit-ment by the profession to political advocacy and campaigning, if social work, particularly in the statutory sector, is not to perpetuate collusion' (Cemlyn and Briskman, 2003, p. 174).

Whilst the example of young people seeking asylum brings this chal-lenge into sharp focus, it must also be noted that other aspects of social work with young people are likely to generate similar imperatives, such as the treatment of vulnerable offenders in custodial settings. The process of engaging with young people and seeking to start from their experience and their own definitions of 'the problem' may lead the 'rights-based' practitioner to a position of actively confronting systemic denial of young people's best interests.

Disabled young people: 'What is normal?'

Whilst seeking to understand and engage with the needs of young asylum seekers may lead us inexorably in the direction of a rights-based approach, this is not the only social work context in which there are particular issues for 'person-centred practice'. For disabled young people, the issues of transitions, choice and control are problematic for a number of reasons, and these have a significant bearing on the approach taken by social workers to understanding and assessing their needs and aspirations. In short, the way in which processes and struc-tures tend to isolate disabled children and young people has contributed to a rather narrow and 'exclusive' approach to key deci-sions affecting their lives.

Whilst it is not the place here to go into the subject in great detail, much recent work has helped to demonstrate the impact of processes which have tended to segregate people on the grounds of perceived difference, specifically disability, and the consequences for the ways in which services are designed and delivered. Oliver's (1990) influential contribution drew attention to the way in which disability had become defined as a problem located within the individual rather than society. Associated with this was a range of assumptions and attitudes embed-ded in professional thinking and agencies' services, identified by

Thompson (2003, p. 89) with the terms 'welfarism' and 'medicalization'. Both of these terms represented an approach which tended to apply stereotypical categories, to underestimate people's capabilities, to create and sustain states of dependency, and to focus on care and maintenance tasks rather than rights and personal development. Whilst these assumptions were seen to be applied to disabled people in general, there were additional consequences for the way in which provision was organized for children and young people, some of which continue to impact on social work practices in this area, despite recent attempts to reframe assessment and planning processes.

The contribution of the Children Act 1989 is significant in this respect because it has sought to bring services for disabled children under the umbrella of children's and young people's services in general. Thus, Section 17 of the act specifically includes disabled children as one of the specified categories of 'children in need', and brings them within the assessment process which should apply equally to all children and young people who are thought to be 'in need':

> In the past, disabled children have often been excluded from or marginalised within mainstream services, and many standard assessment frameworks and approaches have been developed with only non-disabled children in mind. The Children Act 1989 emphasises disabled children are 'children first' and the Assessment Framework is based on this principle of inclusion. (Marchant and Jones, 2000, p. 73)

This practice guidance makes some important points about the ways in which assessment tasks should be approached on behalf of disabled young people. It makes the distinction between needs associated with 'impairments', and the needs which arise because of the 'disabling barriers' which originate in the wider society and stop young disabled people achieving their aims. Social workers are explicitly encouraged to adopt a 'social model', rather than an 'individual' or 'medical' model, in carrying out their work. Thus, assessment cannot be solely focused on the individual, but must also address the relationship between that individual and her or his wider networks and social systems. Three distinct elements to the assessment process are identified:

- The direct impact of an impairment;
- Disabling barriers that the individual encounters; and
- How to tackle the problems created by these barriers.

(Marchant and Jones, 2000, p. 75)

The task of engaging with young disabled people, and identifying their concerns and priorities, is thus established from the outset as a participative exercise, which necessarily involves working from their perspective. The aim, it is argued, should be to use the assessment process itself as a positive exercise in sharing knowledge and understanding in order to provide an agenda for change and development. Once again, a helpful template is provided for practitioners planning an assessment, including a prompt to reflect on one's own values and prior assumptions:

- Think about your own understanding of disability;
- Take into account the child's experience and understanding of assessment;
- Take into account the family's experience and understanding of assessment;
- Be clear about the focus of an assessment;
- Find out who else is currently involved . . . ;
- Gather information from existing assessments;
- Access helpful information on specific childhood impairments.

(Marchant and Jones, 2000, p.76)

Most of these suggestions probably apply in all cases where assessments of need are being carried out with young people, but there are some specific implications for those with disabilities.

For example, the starting point could be the practitioner's expectations and experience. We need to consider whether our own, and our agency's, approach is genuinely inclusive, and provides appropriate mechanisms to engage with young people. The issue of language and communication captures this kind of question quite well. In the process of moving away from practices based on notions of inadequacy and dependency, there has been considerable recent progress informed by a recognition of the importance of enabling and supporting disabled young people to make their views known (Whitehurst, 2006, for example). This has involved not just the development of a range of appropriate communication techniques, such as 'Talking Mats' (see below), but also and perhaps more importantly a shift in attitudes so that young people are engaged directly, rather than through a third party such as a carer, or ignored completely. This small study involving a group of young people with 'profound learning disabilities' drew attention to a number of key messages. Firstly, 'barriers' to communication can and should be addressed, and importantly, 'normal teenage' views and aspirations were identifiable. The young people involved were found to: 'have the same range of preferences and fears as mainstream children. They too are hesitant about making new friends and prefer their more familiar peers but are equally excited by new challenges and new horizons' (Whitehurst, 2006, p. 60).

As well as recognizing and addressing one's own prior assumptions and implicit barriers, the process of engaging with disabled young people must also take account of their own prior experience of assessment processes and interventions. It is perhaps an unfortunate and unacceptable consequence of existing patterns of assessment and provision that young people are likely to have experienced a number of prior investigations of their 'needs', perhaps extending throughout childhood, which may have been uncomfortable, intrusive and 'pathologizing'. They may have been both objectified and devalued in this process; in the words of one disabled girl: 'they're only interested in the bits of me that don't work . . . They want to see what I can't do' (Marchant and Jones, 2000, p. 76). The point is made here, too, that past experience may have encouraged a sense of passivity and apathy (Seligman, 1975), and it may be incumbent upon the practitioner to take proactive steps to avoid this, and to ensure that this is not misinterpreted as lack of interest or competence.

Importantly, too, the practice guidance points out that, in a rather different way to the general population of children, there is likely to be close and continuing involvement of other family members. Roles and relationships can be complex in these circumstances, with parents often being seen as (over)protective. These dynamics are further complicated by a tendency to see parents as co-providers, and therefore holding multiple roles in relation to young people: 'They are perceived, simultaneously, as resources for the statutory services, co-workers and service recipients in their own right, while their children may or may not be also perceived as service recipients. This can create an ambiguous and confused relationship' (Marchant and Jones, 2000, p. 77). Importantly, in the midst of all this, parents' needs, wishes and perceptions may be substituted for those of young people, whose aspirations for autonomy, independence and control over their own lives should be acknowledged.

This necessitates 'being clear about the focus of the assessment', which means being led by the needs and wishes of young people, rather than those of others, such as carers or service providers; it is crucial to avoid becoming 'service-led'.

The approach to understanding the needs of disabled young people may be further complicated by the sheer number of service providers involved, spanning education, health and specialist functions within these agencies. The experience of a series of assessments, all focusing on partial aspects of the young person's life and circumstances, may be another factor contributing to the depersonalizing and disempowering manner in which they have become involved with services previously. There are practical implications for service providers, here, in terms of better communication between them, and more consistent ways of working, but this also seems to offer strong support for the principle of putting the young person at the centre of the process and enabling her or him to exercise a degree of control over it.

Indeed, taking this kind of approach may be helpful in 'reframing' the initial question, and moving away from a problem-oriented approach. Use of tools such as 'Talking Mats' (Cameron and Murphy, 2002) to facilitate communication with young people with learning difficulties may help to achieve change in direct practical terms, but also offers a means of generating a more holistic understanding of their lives and their wishes and feelings. This kind of tool has been shown to be helpful in focusing on 'transitions', which are often seen as particularly problematic for this group of young people, directing attention towards their aims and expectations. Thus, in one evaluative study, clear benefits could be identified from the use of 'mats': 'For one young man with the most severe learning disability, two very positive likes emerged, horse riding and trains. Significantly, staff at the day centre he attends were unaware of these two interests, both of which motivated him to interact and engage in communication' (Cameron and Murphy, 2002, p. 107).

Significantly, too, this initiative had the effect of broadening practitioners' understanding of the individual and moving away from a preoccupation with case management. In this way, the emphasis is shifted towards questions about the service user's 'quality of life' and the kind of transitions which young people in the general population will be making. For young people with disabilities, or with learning difficulties, this is particularly helpful because the way in which services are structured, and some of the implicit assumptions about these young people's lives, may tend to deflect attention from the normal, everyday challenges and changes which typify youth transitions. The importance of using this kind of technique to put young people at the centre of the decision-making process is of particular relevance here, but has broader implications, too: 'Participants visibly relaxed as they realized that the "mats" were allowing them to express their views in meaningful and tangible ways in which they had ownership of the process, could change their minds and go at their own pace' (Cameron and Murphy, 2002, p. 111). Thus, for example, the process of engagement helped in this case to challenge the common perception that young people with learning difficulties 'are bored and unmotivated', and staff at the day centre concerned were able to adapt the 'mats' for use as a way of 'planning daily activities' *with* young people.

Questioning and 'reframing' what we already 'know'

Changing the way in which we frame the questions to be asked and the ways we communicate with young people when assessing their needs may be a powerful way of including them more directly and centrally in the process. It also helps to ensure that we take account of the things that matter most to them, as opposed to the formal requirements of carrying out a particular procedure. The Children Act 1989 was significant in that it brought disabled children into the broader category of 'children in need', in the attempt to identify them as 'children first'. However, this achievement stands to be compromised to the extent that 'needs' remain the principal determinant of assessment procedures and subsequent interventions. This may still lead to an emphasis on passivity and dependency, and a preoccupation with managing the 'presenting problem', that is, the child's or young person's disability, at the expense of her or his own priorities. Convenient assumptions and existing arrangements may need to be challenged, by finding space and methods which enable young people to make their views known clearly, and to influence decisions. Where this happens, new perspectives may emerge:

> Some participants expressed opinions that were not previously known to them and some raised sensitive topics, such as where they wanted to live and who they wished to spend time with. The 'mats' allowed differences of opinion to be explored and were used as a vehicle for further, deeper discussion.
>
> (Cameron and Murphy, 2002, p. 112)

As noted elsewhere, the ability to 'reframe' prior assumptions and thereby to open up discussion may be particularly important in the case of planning for transitions with young people, especially where assumptions may already have been made about their needs, wishes, characteristics and capabilities (Fook, 2002). This is especially the case in the present example, where young people's needs may in the past have been mediated and interpreted by those around them, perhaps in a parental or other caring role. It is not a typical expectation that young people should share all aspects of their lives with parents or carers, so clearly assessment and service planning needs to take account of this possible source of tension, and the increasing significance young people are likely to place on their independence and autonomy, irrespective of their formally identified 'needs'.

'Street work' and the challenge for social work of alternative problem definitions

In order to complete this discussion of the challenges for social work in assessing young people's needs, we will turn to consider some of the practice issues relating to young people who find themselves 'on the streets', whether by virtue of running away, or through other exclusionary processes. For this group, like others, there appear to be fundamental questions about how their 'problems' are defined and by whom, and how they can be included in the processes of assessment and decision-making.

For a number of reasons, the attempt to identify and assess the needs of this particular group of young people crystallizes certain key challenges for social work practitioners. These may be seen in terms of complexity, change and 'ownership', because, on top of the already multi-faceted and uneven transitions of youth, young people who are 'excluded' in the very physical sense of being out of or without a home are likely to be caught up amidst a variety of tensions and pressures. Thus, the UK Consortium for Street Children acknowledges that it is 'impossible to produce a single definition for "street children"' (Consortium for Street Children, 2003, p. 1), before going on to categorize them primarily in terms of their housing status, as:

- Children who run away, leave home or who are thrown out . . . 'Runaways'
- Homeless
- Street homeless.

It can be seen that these terms are likely to cover a very broad range of backgrounds, characteristics and circumstances. It is clear that the dynamics of young people's lives may vary considerably, even where they are viewed as falling into a common category, such as 'runaways'. For practitioners, the importance of clarifying what lies behind the definitional term is apparent. It should also be evident that the use of such broad terms by social workers themselves, and other colleagues, can have a significant impact in shaping how young people are seen and, quite possibly, how they are treated.

It is therefore necessary to take an informed approach, as it is in any area of practice. The Children's Society has been involved in working with 'runaways' since the mid-1980s, and during this time has developed a considerable body of knowledge on the subject. It defines a runaway as 'a young person under 16 who stays away from home for at least one night without the permission of a parent or carer or as a result of being forced to leave' (quoted in Consortium for Street Children, 2003, p. 1). This is not to distinguish in terms of needs and potential vulnerability between those under 16 and older young people, but merely reflects their legal status. Whilst as many as 100,000 children or young people under the age of 16 may run away every year in the UK, the patterns of behaviour this represents vary significantly: 'Many of these young people will not actually sleep on the street, going instead to the houses of friends or relatives or to hostels, refuges or night shelter provisions. However . . . a quarter of child runaways sleep rough in back alleys, fields or bus stations' (Consortium for Street Children, 2003, p. 1).

Not only are their destinations varied, but the 'running away' careers of young people also demonstrate different patterns. Most of those who run away will do so only once, and will stay away for between one and three nights, but certain groups appear more likely to stay away from their homes for longer, including young people from black and minority ethnic groups (SEU, 2002). It is also reported that for those who begin to run away at an earlier age, the pattern of behaviour is likely to become more entrenched, with more frequent and extended episodes amongst this sub-group. As with other aspects of social exclusion affecting young people, there appears to be a pattern of intensification of problems for some. Thus, young people who begin to run away before the age of 11 are more likely to become homeless at the age of 16 or 17; and those who run further away from home are also likely to experience other problems, which may be part of a repetitive pattern – returning home may not be the answer.

These observations draw attention to the significance of history in assessing current needs. Whilst it might be quite apparent in some cases, for example in relation to children with disabilities, that their past experience and involvement with services are relevant factors, this may not always be obvious where practitioners become involved with young people who have run away. However, there are a considerable

Box 7.2

The logical starting point for work with young people at risk on the streets may appear to be to try to re-establish contact with their family or carers. However, it is important to avoid idealizing this setting, given that the young person has already taken the drastic step of running away.

What kind of pressures would prompt you to run away from your home environment? How might you go about creating 'breathing space' so that young people can reflect on their circumstances and explore alternative options?

number of factors which prompt young people to this drastic action, and these are likely to be substantial and persistent; 'they are usually running *from* something, not *to* something' (The Children's Society, quoted in Consortium for Street Children, 2003, p. 4). The kind of factors which prompt young people to run include bullying and abuse, personal issues such as sexual orientation, family conflicts and relationship problems, and the breakdown of parents' relationships (Box 7.2).

Because young people might feel themselves under enormous and inescapable pressures, the decision to leave home often appears to be prompted by a belief that they have no choice; but in seeking to get away from an unbearable situation, it is also clear that they may be exposed to other risks, including physical or sexual harm, and potential involvement in crime or sexual exploitation (see SEU, 2002, for example). However, these risks may not always be obvious to young people themselves, or act as much of a deterrent given the severity of the situation from which they are seeking to escape (Turner and Jagusz, n.d.).

Good practice guidance underlines the importance of considering antecedents as well as the immediate problems faced by young people:

> In some instances it may already be clear that a child or young person is in need. But in many instances these problems may be hidden. **The fact that a child or young person has run away should alert agencies that there may be underlying problems and that the child or young person and his/her family may require support.**
>
> (Scottish Executive, 2003, p. 1)

The same guidance highlights the fact that in many cases young people feel that they have not had the opportunity to talk to anyone about these problems or to obtain information about where to get help. The response to a young person who has run away should not therefore be dominated by the concern to return her or him to the place of origin, and the opportunity should be made available 'to discuss with a professional' the reasons for running away, and whether or not the situation may arise again. In the light of this, it is important to offer the chance to discuss these reasons prior to returning the young person – it cannot be assumed that those with day-to-day responsibility for her or him, whether family or care settings, necessarily have her or his best interests at heart. The task to be undertaken in identifying and balancing risks needs to take account of the risk factors associated with returning the young person home as much as those arising as a result of running away.

It may be helpful, therefore, to think of assessment as at least a two-stage process in this context, with the concern to address immediate risks and needs being linked with a more detailed examination of underlying issues and the need to develop more systematic and longer-term intervention strategies. Whilst practitioners may feel that it is relatively easy to identify immediate risks associated with being on the streets, these should not be allowed to override other concerns. At the same time, the assessment process should seek to incorporate both dimensions of the young person's needs. This is clearly the view of young people who want services to be flexible and responsive: 'it's about giving that young person the chance to have that support if it's needed and not just at a certain time but when they decide that they need the support' (quoted in Turner and Jagusz, n.d., p. 5).

Indeed, one of the underlying problems for young people, and for practitioners, appears to be something of a mismatch between the circumstances and needs of those who run away, and the organization and response of services, which cannot always seem to adjust to immediate and unpredictable problems. It often seems to be the case that the immediate, practical problem of responding to a young person who is away from home is not prioritized by social work departments, or individual practitioners:

> Most social services departments use Emergency Duty Teams (EDTs) outside normal working hours, when runaways are most likely to need help. They are often very short-staffed, covering a large geographic area . . .
> Where they do make contact with EDTs, [other] organisations can find it difficult to elicit a helpful response. Nearly half of police forces surveyed said that their local social services department was generally unable to assist when they found a runaway out of hours.
>
> (SEU, 2002, p. 50)

> 'If you're having to deal with babies with broken legs and teenagers running away, then you do prioritise – that may not be right but it's a reality of the situation.'   (Social worker quoted in SEU, 2002, p. 50)

This report by the Social Exclusion Unit also found evidence that 'the initial response of social services departments when confronted with a runaway is often to send them home without an assessment.' This appears to be linked with a concern on the part of agencies that to acknowledge a responsibility at the outset might lead to further calls on limited resources, so practitioners, at least in statutory agencies, may well find that they are receiving mixed messages about the nature and extent of their professional responsibilities.

The way in which services are constructed may run counter to the expressed needs of young people, as well as underlying principles of good practice. Young people appear to find the arbitrary allocation of workers and resources frustrating and unhelpful, and they value some-one who will keep in contact and coordinate assessment and service provision. Good workers will:

> 'come to you, you don't have to go to them, they're excellent, they just seem to know you.'

> 'I had a key worker who I would see on a one to one basis so I could tell him anything about all that stuff in my life . . . so he could get a broader picture of what was going on.'   (quoted in SEU, 2002, p. 31)

By contrast, substantial frustrations were expressed where young people were passed 'from post to post', or where poor communication meant having to repeat yourself over and over again.

The apparent mismatch between the organization of services and the needs and expectations of young people 'on the streets' creates significant obstacles to good practice, it seems. Interventions need to take particular account of the issues which arise when young people become 'detached' from their normal living environment, focusing on specific needs which may be linked to both the causes and consequences of running away. It is not simply a matter of providing immediate protection and planning a return to an unproblematic envi-ronment, and because of this practitioners must be prepared to take an approach based on principles of engagement, making connections, continuing support and advocacy, even where they may have no prior relationship with or knowledge of the young person.

At the point of contact, the focus of intervention may well be the immediate risks to which young people are exposed, and which they may not have anticipated, but this should not lead workers to overlook or diminish the importance of underlying concerns which may have prompted the young person to run away in the first place – assessment needs to be holistic, and plans developed accordingly. It is also impor-tant at this point to provide some sort of continuity, partly because service and organizational boundaries tend to inhibit this, and partly because young people in extreme situations often have difficulty in accessing services (SEU, 2005, p. 69). It is therefore important that practitioners are willing to take continuing responsibility, even when formal lines of accountability may be unclear – being 'passed on' to someone else at this crucial point is likely just to compound the young person's feelings of alienation and worthlessness. As we have observed previously, this may involve the social worker in taking on an active role as advocate for the service user, in relation to her or his own agency and other organizations. In many ways, this is an easier role to adopt for those employed by specialist projects, or within the voluntary sector, but it is important for those in statutory services also to adhere to the same principles. It is at this point, indeed, that we have to think of assessment as being something more than a static, one-off exercise, and as integral to a continuing process of engagement, relationship building, and problem-solving. For young people in extreme circumstances, such as those living on the streets, it is unlikely that this can be achieved quickly or simply, especially where this can be identified as part of a continuing pattern. It is worth reminding ourselves here of the relatively straightforward message expressed repeatedly by young people themselves that their 'ideal service' would be one that is 'joined up', and provided by workers who understand and respect them and are 'prepared to listen' (SEU, 2005, p. 70); and that they need consistent support from someone they can trust, and relate to, and who is both available and able to 'give good advice' (Turner and Jagusz, n.d., p. 13).

Getting it right from the start

In addressing the issues which arise at the initial point of contact between service users and social work practitioners, this chapter has tried to draw attention to the kind of values and practices which are significant in shaping the young person's experience of intervention at this point and as it progresses. First impressions are important, and the circumstances of young people experiencing problematic changes in their lives make this all the more certain (Box 7.3).

The issues affecting young people and those around them are probably complicated, and problems long-standing; whilst their previous experience of services will have influenced their views of what these are like and what they can offer. It is unlikely that the intervention process will start with a 'clean sheet', and it is clear that ground work may be necessary to establish an effective working relationship. For some, such as disabled young people, this may mean recognizing them in their own right, and acknowledging their aspirations for independence and control; for them, the focus may need to be shifted from managing disability to negotiating transitions, in the same way as other young people do.

For others, who are marginalized or excluded, their limited expectations of what services can offer and feelings of being let down previously may make the process of engaging them and creating a basis of trust particularly difficult. The need for workers to take a particular orientation to their practice is clear. It is unlikely that effective interventions can be achieved without undertaking a process of relationship building and seeking a detailed understanding of the young person

Box 7.3

Services often appear daunting and unwelcoming to young people who are not sure what to expect and may be influenced by negative stories they have heard about social workers.

What steps can you take to make yourself available and accessible to young people who might seek your help?
What sort of things might put them off?

concerned, even in the face of her or his apparent suspicion or indifference. Creating space and time for this process to unfold therefore seems to be a central requirement, notwithstanding the organizational and procedural expectations which inevitably intrude. This, though, is what young people want from practitioners, and it clearly underlines the point that effective relationships lie at the heart of good practice.

Chapter summary

This chapter has sought to identify some of the challenges to social work practice in offering a service to young people which they can recognize as relevant to their needs and as accessible. Key points are:

• Young people will come to the attention of the service because of an identified need, but their life experience and their perception of their own problems are likely to be multi-faceted and interrelated.
• Services need to acknowledge that young people's lives and circumstances vary, and that interventions cannot be based on uniform assumptions about what is 'normal' or desirable.
• The shape and dynamics of young people's lives may not coincide readily with the way in which services are organized and interventions structured. Practitioners may thus find themselves having to negotiate the boundary between service expectations and the aspirations of young people in order to create space and time for effective practice.

Further reading

Kohli's and Mather's (2003) article 'Promoting Psychosocial Well-Being in Unaccompanied Asylum Seeking Young People in the United Kingdom' is an extremely helpful account of the way in which social work methods and understandings can be applied to the complex and often traumatic experiences of unaccompanied young people from abroad.

Fook's (2002) *Critical Social Work* provides an effective account of the technique of 'reframing' existing assumptions or categorizations which might be inhibiting the provision of relevant or effective services, especially where the perspectives of young people and agency agendas differ significantly.

The chapter by Marchant and Jones (2000) in the Department of Health guidance on *Assessing Children in Need and Their Families* is a very helpful resource in the context of engaging with and assessing the needs and wishes of children and young people with disabilities.

8 Dealing with risk

Preparing to intervene

Although it is slightly artificial to distinguish phases of intervention, for present purposes the focus now shifts from the initial stages of engagement and assessment of young people's risks and needs to those of preparation and delivery of services. We have already noted how important it is to undertake a process of building trust and a relationship from the start, and the aim here is to consider how these foundations can be built upon to enable practitioners to support young people in a context of diverse pressures and conflicting demands.

Once again, specific sites of intervention will be used in order both to illustrate aspects of the broader task of doing social work with young people and to highlight further some of the common themes which have emerged so far, such as the question of how to deal with 'risk'. The transitions of youth are by definition likely to involve uncertainty, and indeed decisions and actions which incur a degree of risk, both to young people themselves and possibly to others around them. For those with whom social work engages, these uncertainties are heightened by the sort of events and circumstances which trigger the involvement of welfare services. The task of distinguishing between what are normal, acceptable and manageable risks and those which need to be controlled in some way or removed is thus bound to be problematic. For practitioners, there is an associated question as to the use of authority and the impact this will have on working relationships, where, as we have seen, trust and a sense of mutuality may be hard to achieve, and even harder to sustain. The arbitrary use of power, even where it is deemed to be in the young person's interests, will almost certainly have consequences, and other aspects of the intervention strategy may be compromised as a result. For those wishing to establish a spirit of solidarity with young people, to enhance their rights and promote their interests, the judgement as to when and how to use statutory powers may be especially problematic, and will merit careful reflection. On the other hand, practitioners' ambivalence about this sort of issue is equally likely to be shared by young people, for whom the exercise of external authority may be seen as protective and enabling in some instances. In fact, the only thing we can be sure of is that it is essential to avoid being too prescriptive, and that judgements should be based on detailed understanding and dialogue, wherever possible.

Protecting young people from themselves:
Is it the task of social work?

Whereas it may seem uncontentious to accord social workers, and other adults, responsibility for ensuring that young children are protected from the adverse consequences of risky decisions and actions, this is less clearly the case as children get older. It becomes more acceptable to take the view that young people should learn from their mistakes, and even suffer for them, within reason. Thus, the appropriate point at which others should intervene, whether parents, carers or professionals, is not clear, and may be contentious. Judgements need to be made about the level of risk which can be tolerated before intervention is triggered, whilst it is also important to consider the extent to which self-determination can or should be compromised in order to ensure young people's safety, especially where no one else is at risk.

Indeed, it may be the case that it is only where this kind of problematic behaviour reaches extreme levels, or threatens to impact on others directly, that there is any real impetus towards intervention. Thus, for example, 'routine' drug and alcohol use, or sexual activity involving young people, may give rise to little professional concern, at least in the present era, even in the face of dramatic media campaigns. However, there is a point at which these behaviours, and others where thresholds may be clearer, such as self-harm and suicidal actions, trigger expectations of intervention of one kind or another.

Particularly in the case of young people, developmental assumptions may legitimize interventions where behaviour appears to fall short of what might be expected from mature adults. Where the tendency to take risks with health or well-being can be linked with developmental needs, it thus becomes easier to justify taking action to ensure that young people do not come to harm. For social workers and other practitioners, however, there remain a number of problems, partly arising from the way in which risks and needs are identified initially. Thus, for example, the principle of progressive empowerment does not sit well with processes by which concerns about 'problem behaviour' are based on external judgements, and then services are imposed on those who are the subject of these assessments. Nonetheless, this is often the path which services follow.

In fact, it may seem as if young people whose behaviour gives cause for concern over their own safety or well-being may find themselves in a sort of 'double-bind', whereby they are deemed to be both blameworthy for putting themselves at risk, and simultaneously less than fully competent and thus not responsible for their actions. Certainly this appears to be the case in the context of sexual activity, sexual health and teenage pregnancy. For example, young people who are 'looked after' are identified as being 'at a significantly greater risk of becoming parents in their teens' (Teenage Pregnancy Unit, 2004, p. 8). Whilst their backgrounds and experiences may impact on their capacity to exercise self-determination, the focus of interventions seems to be predominantly on changing their behaviour, implicitly (and sometimes explicitly) locating responsibility entirely with them.

One project in this area of work for example, states that it is 'reshaping who they are and their ability to communicate, to initiate and to have the confidence to put something forward' (Learning Mentor, quoted in Plant and McFeely, 2004, p. 157). This observation raises wider issues, especially in the context of practice to change unacceptable behaviour. The emphasis is clearly placed upon the young people themselves in this instance, and the project has sought actively to engage them in taking responsibility for monitoring and controlling each other's actions. The use of a set 'curriculum', with workshops focusing on a range of health issues, has offered an opportunity for young people to learn about this subject matter, and at the same time to participate in discussion and reflection on their own attitudes and behaviour: 'The young people talked at length about their behaviour. Mostly they referred to the improvements in their own behaviour since participating in the project' (Plant and McFeely, 2004, p. 156). Young people were said to be empowered through their involvement in these workshops, and to have gained in relevant knowledge and self-esteem. Significantly, the young people in this project were involved in its 'development and delivery', and they felt that their contribution to the learning was valued.

However, practitioners working in this way will need to consider a number of issues when establishing groups to address behaviours defined as problematic. For example, success criteria need to be drawn more widely than simply reducing the incidence of problem behaviour, since this may lead to an excessive focus on personal responsibility, at the expense of other contributing factors. Interventions which are skewed in this way may achieve short-term gains, especially those observable in the group setting, but offer little by way of sustainability, if young people do not gain in terms of the personal resources needed to resist exploitation, to improve their knowledge of the subject and the services available, or to establish networks of mutual support. Thus, the 125 Health Project described here tried to avoid blaming young people for their circumstances. It 'did not develop from a basis of telling young people what "they should" or "should not" do' (Plant and McFeely, 2004, p. 154), but tried instead to provide them with resources, information and support systems which would enable them to make informed choices about their sexual behaviour with confidence.

Importantly, too, this kind of strategy highlights the value of empowering practice in tackling gender inequalities and oppression. Young women working in groups were enabled 'to role play situations where they were placed under pressure to have sex' (Plant and McFeely, 2004, p. 161), and had a chance to discuss issues of choice, control and self-image openly in a way which had not been available previously. Such initiatives are not dramatic or highly original, but they illustrate some important principles for practice, and they are valued by participants. Firstly, it is clearly unrealistic and unhelpful to hold young people entirely responsible for their circumstances or the choices they make. Focused groupwork, however, provides an opportunity to reflect on these issues and to identify ways in which they may be able to influence outcomes and change what happens to them: 'the model of positive praise, reward and the ignoring of inappropriate behaviour is particularly effective when working with vulnerable young people' (Plant and McFeely, 2004, p. 166).

Similar issues of blame and control are apparent in relation to 'self-harm', where again young people appear to be putting themselves at risk, for reasons which are 'hard to understand' (Bywaters and Rolfe, 2002, p. iii). As with other forms of behaviour which appear irrational and clearly damaging to the individual concerned, the starting point for practitioners must be to 'see beyond' the behaviour itself, and address the multi-faceted and complex issues lying behind it. At the same time, it is pointed out, whilst there may be factors contributing to the practice of 'self-harm', the activity itself must be recognized as an attempt to stay in control, and as an act of 'self-protection not self-destruction'. The specific response to problematic and distressing circumstances in the form of self-harm may appear to be damaging, but it is also a form of self-expression, albeit one which is chosen from an apparently very limited range of options.

Indeed, the problem for practitioners in responding to self-harm may well lie in a preoccupation with the behaviour, rather than its meaning – thus, those who have self-harmed appear to do so for a variety of reasons, and their views about its purposes are also diverse (Bywaters and Rolfe, 2002). Young people are reported as seeing it as a positive form of self-expression, for example, in which context addressing it purely as a 'problem' would seem to be missing the point. Referring to suicidal actions, Souter and Kraemer (2004) also refer to 'self-harm as an *attempted solution* to [a] crisis. The young person feels that all avenues of help have been exhausted or closed off' (p. 262).

Those working with young people who self-harm must be aware of the need to distinguish between the behaviour itself and what it represents. Self-injury may be a way of trying to cope with or minimize other problems, and it may, indeed, be seen as 'beneficial' (Bywaters and Rolfe, 2002, p. 3). Simply tackling the behaviour may neither be very effective nor focus on the predominant areas of concern from the young person's point of view (Box 8.1).

Intervention is likely to be triggered by the incidence or recurrence of self-harm, especially where it is associated with a medical or psychiatric emergency (Royal College of Psychiatrists, 1998). However, an undue concentration on the immediate and sometimes shocking circumstances may draw attention away from more fundamental underlying issues. Young people, when asked about their experiences: 'stressed the need to listen and try and understand the meanings of

Box 8.1

'Anna described herself as severely depressed and found that cutting was a way of coping with this . . . she did not see the self-injury as a problem, but did see depression as a problem for her' (Bywaters and Rolfe, 2002, p. 2).

How easy is it to avoid over-concentration on the direct evidence of 'harm'?
What approach would you take to ensure that self-injury is viewed as part of a 'bigger picture'?

self-harm for them, rather than making assumptions about them based on their self-harming behaviour' (Bywaters and Rolfe, 2002, p. 9). The process is therefore necessarily an exploratory one, where the emphasis will be on 'unravelling' the complex and individual factors which underlie the behaviour itself. Traumatic past events, such as sexual, physical or emotional abuse, can often be found in the young person's past, but self-harm may also be a way of coping 'with current difficulties'. It seems to work as a sort of 'release' for pent-up feelings, and converting emotional pain into its physical equivalent (p. 13). However, the sense of relief achieved seems to be short-lived, and this contributes to the 'addictive' or habitual characteristics of self-harm: 'it's just something you've got to keep doing' (young person, quoted in Bywaters and Rolfe, 2002, p. 15). There is thus a certain ambiguity about the activity of harming oneself, which is about asserting control, on the one hand, but also becomes progressively more compulsive, on the other.

Self-harm is thus both complex and variable, and intervention is unlikely to be straightforward. Self-harm is an expression of personal control, and effective interventions will have to develop an understanding of the reasons for this and enable young people to achieve an equivalent feeling of control over other aspects of their lives. It seems then that short-term responses will not be sufficient, despite claims from some sources that: 'A crisis intervention is often most appropriate' (Hawton and James, 2005, p. 893). Indeed, it is recognized that 'compliance' is often problematic, purely because self-harm is often seen by the young person involved as a positive option. Instead, it may be better to think in terms of broader 'problem-solving' strategies, using techniques which enable the young person to reflect on her or his circumstances and identify opportunities for exercising greater control. Given the possibility of traumatic events in the past, it is suggested that it may sometimes be helpful to extend 'problem-solving' approaches to include the wider family. It is useful to work towards 'improvement of specific cognitive and social skills to promote the sharing of feelings, emotional control and negotiation between family members' (Hawton and James, 2005, p. 893). Importantly, too, this promotes acknowledgement from others of the validity of the young person's experience and feelings; she or he is put at the heart of the intervention, and thus is offered further recognition in her or his own right. Young people appreciate being afforded time and being taken seriously, and it is often quite mundane signs of 'caring' which help them to regain a sense of self-worth (Bywaters and Rolfe, 2002, p. 27).

Being available, offering the right kind of setting, and focusing on wider issues and interests than just self-harm all appear to be valued by young people. They recognize that this kind of support is likely to lead to longer-term benefits. They are uncomfortable with being judged or blamed for their actions, and it is crucial that respect for the individual is demonstrated even when her or his behaviour is apparently bizarre and problematic. From what we know of youth development and transitions, the issues of identity and control are highly significant to young people, and their attempts to negotiate this terrain, however counterproductive, need to be recognized and understood. As much as anything else, the task for practitioners in the context of self-harm is to offer validation, and the opportunity to reflect, in order to create the basis for change.

Young people and protection from others

The place of social work in child protection services is well established. However, the question of how to respond to young people at risk of harm from others poses rather different problems from those where the well-being of younger children is at stake. Once again, issues of history, identity and control are significant, given that the 'risks' from others to which young people are vulnerable may be seen as the result of their own choices and behaviour, in the same way as drug and alcohol problems might be viewed. Thus, in some circumstances, young people have been held responsible for their own victimization, for example where they have been the subject of sexual exploitation. This is clearly a position of some ambiguity, whereby the promotion of self-determination is a central social work principle, and consistent with the aspirations towards independence of young people; and yet, in order to safeguard them, it may be necessary to think in term of setting limits to their choice of actions. For those who become the subject of mistreatment, too, there is potential for 'victim blaming', and a failure to recognize the consequences for young people of being harmed or exploited.

There is considerable sensitivity about the subject of sexual activity in particular amongst young people, with a clear gender dimension, too, and this is something for which practitioners need to be prepared. They will need to be able to reflect on their own assumptions and beliefs, whilst also acknowledging the likely influence of others in this context, including young people themselves, family members, carers, other professionals and public opinion. 'Deep down', as Folgheraiter (2004, p. 31) demonstrates, the social work practitioner is 'unconsciously propelled to define problems according to moral sentiments'.

It is significant that this area of practice has been seen as sufficiently sensitive to merit specific guidance from government (DH, 2000c) and detailed protocols issued by local partnerships safeguarding children (for example, Lancashire Area Child Protection Committee, n.d.). The underlying assumption in these documents is that young people's involvement in sexual activity is often not entirely voluntary and should be seen in such cases through the lens of child protection, rather than as irresponsible behaviour. Thus, one local protocol makes its starting point clear:

> It is designed to assist those working with children and young people to identify where [sexual] relationships may be abusive, and the children and young people may need the provision of protection or additional services.
>
> It is based on the core principle that the welfare of the child or young person is paramount, and emphasises the need for professionals to work together.
>
> (Lancashire Area Child Protection Committee, n.d., p. 2)

This protocol goes on to make some important points about the impact of power and inequality on the quality and substance of relationships – emphasizing age differences as a key factor, but also drawing attention to different levels of 'knowledge' and the impact of gender, sexuality and race as possible variables. Additional consideration needs to be given in those circumstances where young people may have 'a learning disability, mental disorder or other communication difficulty', but this should not lead to denial of their rights to 'a full life, including a sexual life' (p. 3).

In prioritizing the needs and wishes of the young person, this protocol also reminds practitioners that the consent of parents or carers can be overridden in the discussion of 'personal or sexual matters' with a young person who is less than 16 years old where the young person is able to understand any information that is provided, and where it is clearly in her or his interests to take this step. Whilst provision is made for working directly with the young person without parental involvement or consent under these conditions, guidance also suggests that efforts should be made to encourage young people to 'share information' with parents or carers 'wherever safe to do so'. In common with most such policy documents, this protocol also stresses that confidentiality cannot be guaranteed in all circumstances, and that this should be made clear to young people from the outset. Of course, this is a crucial dilemma for practitioners who are committed both to empowering and to safeguarding young people at risk of harm. To stress the conditional nature of confidentiality may, of itself, result in young people becoming more unwilling to share crucial information or discuss their concerns. The 'distance' between the practitioner and service user is clearly emphasized through this kind of exchange, so it must be handled carefully, and the underlying rationale should be

Box 8.2

I can remember a case, which came to the attention of local agencies when I was in practice, of a 14 year old girl who was the subject of a care order and who consistently ran away from the children's home where she was placed to return to her father, who was believed to be sexually abusing her.

To what extent do you think practitioners should seek to 'understand' her feelings and explore the nature of their relationship?
Or is it better to establish clear and explicit boundaries at the outset? Do you believe that it is more important to bring their relationship to an end? Will this approach necessarily undermine your ability to build an effective relationship with the young person? What are the consequences of adopting either of these approaches?

explored with the young person. The use of specific illustrations, such as potential risks to peers or siblings, may help to clarify the issue.

Assuming that practitioners are able to establish a basis of trust and understanding with young people who might be subject to exploitation and abuse, the process of engagement, protecting, supporting and empowering them is none the less likely to remain complex and riven with ambiguities. Thus, for example, it will be important to enable young people to reframe their own thoughts and feelings towards those who may be exploiting them. In the context of young people involved in prostitution, for example, it is noted that: 'young people, particularly girls, may be physically and emotionally dependent on the coercer despite . . . violence endured, for the sake of "love". The fact that outsiders would consider this a delusion does not make it any less real for the individual concerned' (DH, 2000c, p. 16) (Box 8.2).

Social workers must be prepared in such circumstances to start from a different position to that of the young person concerned, similarly perhaps to cases involving domestic violence, but this does not mean simply imposing a 'professional' analysis, since the young person's feelings towards the abuser must also be recognized as genuine. The process of engagement and building trust is not simply a matter of inherent good practice, but is also a necessary part of the project of providing the young person with alternative perspectives, and the practical and emotional resources to make changes. The task of protecting the young person is largely achieved by building strength and resilience and enabling her or him to safeguard herself or himself: 'When working with young people . . . agencies must recognise the strength of this attachment [to the abuser or exploiter] and the time and difficulty there may be in breaking it and helping the young person to attach to appropriate adults' (DH, 2000c, p. 16).

Thinking in developmental terms, as we have previously, using the concept of 'attachment' (Howe, 2001) is helpful here, too, because it enables practitioners to consider the personal and emotional dimensions of abuse, alongside those which are related to structural factors and inequalities. Problematic experiences of attachment in earlier childhood are predictive of later patterns of relationship formation (Bailham and Harper, 2004). Young people with a history of unstable or problematic attachments may therefore adopt strategies to help counter this, which may themselves lead to further difficulties. As Howe (2001, p. 202) observes, the 'quality of the relationship' may be less fundamentally important than the fact that a relationship exists at all. This may be one of the reasons that exploiters of young people are able to maintain them in a state of dependency and abuse:

> the attachment system is designed to bring children into proximity with their attachment figure. Even when care-givers are rejecting, neglectful or abusive, children have to develop behavioural and psychological strategies that attempt to ward off anxiety or in which they try to seek alternative ways of psychologically securing the attachment figure.   (Howe, 2001, p. 202)

Translated into the context of young people subject to sexual exploitation, this helps us to make sense of the 'grooming process' and the way in which young people are befriended and drawn into abusive relationships. It may be their very isolation, stemming from problematic attachments, which places them at particular risk, to the extent that they 'are likely to be recognised as vulnerable by abusers or coercers' (DH, 2000c, p. 17). Young people in these circumstances may well be 'unpopular with their peers' and experience feelings of 'low self-esteem'. Their own social competence and understandings, for instance of what constitutes a healthy relationship, may also be skewed (Bailham and Harper, 2004, p. 63). They are also susceptible to 'messages' from those to whom they may become attached which confirm their perceptions of themselves as relatively worthless or socially incompetent.

Applying attachment principles

For practitioners, the form of intervention must therefore be based on modelling appropriate 'attachment principles', it is argued (Bailham and Harper, 2004, p. 64). Some of these principles, it must be acknowledged, may cut across the normal demands of a routinized professional role and job specification, such as availability and continuity. Despite this, it is felt to be: 'crucial for staff working with vulnerable adolescents to apply attachment principles in their work by encouraging openness (open communication unless the information is detrimental to the young person's well-being), the provision of choices, sensitivity and responsiveness' (Bailham and Harper, 2004, p. 64).

Honesty and consistency are required in pursuing agreed plans of action, and these must be demonstrated 'over time', too. The fact that young people may have become sensitized to the messages conveyed to and about them makes it particularly important for interventions to counter these, and to provide reassurance and continuity. Where young people have a history of insecurity, and where they 'have suffered neglect and maltreatment', they are particularly likely to 'avoid, resist or feel anxious about new opportunities' (Howe et al., 1999, p. 260). Clearly, adolescence is a time when many such opportunities are likely to present themselves, and these represent distinctive 'turning points'. Practitioners may need to provide support and encouragement at these crucial times, and it will also be important for them to assist others 'in appropriate positions (a youth worker, a school teacher, a volunteer) to encourage children to respond to social opportunities which they might normally refuse' (Howe et al., 1999, p. 260). The example is given of the role of foster care, and the importance of the approach taken by carers where placements are offered to young people in need of protection. It is not enough simply to arrange a placement, because the 'simple provision of foster carers holds no guarantee in itself of a positive impact'. Social workers are likely to have to provide active support to carers and to help them to engage effectively with the needs of young people seeking 'to accomplish some of the normal psychosocial tasks associated with adolescence' (Downes, 1988, p. 485).

The importance of 'being available'

Schofield and Brown (1999) argue that intervention with 'troubled adolescents' who have experienced harm depends on the social worker (and others involved) being able to establish some sort of guarantee of availability and certainty of response. In the first instance, this means simply 'being available'. Thus, for example, in one practice initiative studied, the idea of planned interventions quickly fell by the wayside:

> contrary to expectations, the worker had no difficulty in engaging the girls. The timing of the work, though, had to be flexible and, to a large extent, on their terms. Although the worker had an idea that offering a consistent and reliable time for meeting would be an important factor, it became rapidly apparent that these young women led highly chaotic lives and were quite unable to control their lives or contain their anxieties between appointments.   (Schofield and Brown, 1999, p. 27)

The ability of the young person concerned to set the agenda and the reciprocal response of the worker in 'being available' in themselves contribute to the development of certain key elements of an effective relationship, such as trust and consistency, it is suggested. They also offer a positive experience of being able to control the timing and nature of the interaction between worker and service user, which also contributes towards a sense of 'self-efficacy'. At the same time, it is made clear, the worker involved with young people in this kind of setting is also likely to have to deal with and 'contain' powerful and negative expressions of anxiety and anger: 'It was the worker's task to communicate the feeling that it was possible to survive and not disintegrate, by containing their powerful feelings' (Schofield and Brown,

1999, p. 28). Knowledge of attachment theory helped the social worker in this instance to appreciate the likelihood of inconsistent and angry messages, some of which may have been directed at her:

> The message for the young women was, 'I'm not afraid to hear about your anger, sadness, depression. I can cope'. This message can be turned around by the girls: 'If these feelings are bearable, perhaps I can bear them.'
>
> It is at this point that they could start to feel more in charge of their lives.   (Schofield and Brown, 1999, p. 29)

Importantly, the personal availability of the practitioner was complemented by the provision of a 'safe place', the family centre at which she was based, and which offered some physical certainties and safeguards to mirror the emotional support on offer. It is also suggested that it was this basis of trust and understanding which enabled the worker to be 'honest and open about risky behaviour and damaging choices' without being rejected.

Significantly, this practice model makes connections between the inner resources available to young people at risk, and the external environment (and the people within it) which is more or less threatening to them. It is seen as a way of 'revising the internal working model and enabling young people to enter new situations and new relationships with some capacity to trust' (Schofield and Brown, 1999, p. 30), as well as the ability to make informed choices and exercise a greater degree of control over their lives. That it was not glamorous or 'magical' should not detract from the recognition that the quality of intervention is often revealed through mundane but none the less significant actions, such as taking the trouble to visit a 'girl in difficulty in a residential unit'.

Working with young people who pose a risk to others

In balancing risks and needs, social workers often encounter significant dilemmas and competing priorities, and this is particularly so in the context of work with young people whose behaviour is problematic and appears to present an external risk, to other people or the wider community. It is worth perhaps reminding ourselves (see Chapter 5) that the formal statement of professional responsibilities, the General Social Care Council Codes of Practice, makes clear that practitioners have an obligation to take such risks into account in their work:

> As a social care worker, you must respect the rights of service users while seeking to ensure that their behaviour does not harm themselves or other people.
>
> This includes . . .
>
> Following risk assessment policies and procedures to assess whether the behaviour of service users presents a risk of harm to themselves or others;
>
> Taking necessary steps to minimise the risks.   (GSCC, 2002, p. 18)

In one sense, this requirement might be seen as entirely consistent with the statutory aim of the youth justice system as set out in the Crime and Disorder Act 1998, which is the prevention of crime by young people (Section 37). However, the problem for social workers is that this is only one aspect of a broad and eclectic range of responsibilities, which involve an active and ongoing process of making choices and prioritizing courses of action. This would be problematic enough in itself, but we should also take note of the observation that purely in respect of preventing crime and reoffending there is very little clarity about 'what works', and what forms of intervention are most likely to prevent the commission of harmful acts by young people in the future.

A further degree of complexity to the social work task is introduced by the acknowledgement that there is a very substantial overlap between those populations of young people 'at risk', and those who present a risk to others. Problematic transitions of one kind or another may well be interwoven with problematic behaviours, despite the tendency for 'official discourse' to suggest 'a sharp distinction between "troubled" and "troublesome" children' (Taylor, 2006, p. 14). Social workers, however, in line with their codes of practice, are expected to take account of and respond to both aspects of young people's experience.

Taylor's study is important in this respect, because her investigation specifically addressed the overlap between the 'care' and 'criminal' careers of young people, and the issue of what kinds of intervention might be effective in this context. Similarly to our previous observations, she also noted the importance of 'attachments', and how these impact on young people's experiences and outcomes. From young people's own accounts, she is able to draw out the value of relationships provided by carers and social workers even where young people's lives are disrupted and they become involved in offending. Perhaps contrary to expectations, it seems that it is possible to promote and develop meaningful relationships 'at a relatively late age' (Taylor, 2006, p. 122), especially with supportive foster carers. The significance of these 'attachments' to young people provides a positive endorsement of the 'care experience', whilst also contributing to additional benefit: 'several young people commented that they felt they were better people for being in care. It has been argued that secure attachments can enable resilience to previous psychosocial adversity by promoting an individual's self-esteem. Such attachments may also be strongly protective against offending behaviour' (Taylor, 2006, p. 122). Young people were able to identify a number of factors which helped them stay out of trouble, including: 'respect for a carer', recognizing rules and 'boundaries as fair and reasonable', being trusted by carers and feeling responsible to their carers for their own behaviour.

Whilst it is often foster carers who are identified as providing this kind of support, there is no doubt that social work practitioners also have a part to play, especially in helping young people to negotiate crucial 'turning points', at which they may be particularly vulnerable, or where significant new opportunities become apparent. It is particularly unfortunate when expectations are not met:

> I just found that as soon as I hit my eighteenth birthday just no one's wanted to know . . .. I switched social workers just as I moved out of care, and to a lady 'cos the man I had before just didn't understand about counselling and emotional problems . . . So . . . I said to her 'That's what I'm gonna need, a bit more emotional support . . . She said, 'I can't give that to you. I haven't got time for that sort of thing', and that was a real knock-back'
>
> (Young woman quoted in Taylor, 2006, p. 159)

On the other side of the coin, some young people were able to identify important positive attributes demonstrated by social workers, such as availability, 'listening', acceptance and good advice.

The distinction between behaviour and needs

It is important to make the distinction between young people's behaviour (which may be problematic or challenging) and their needs for and, indeed, expectations of support (Box 8.3). As Taylor points out, young people want (and need) a source of support which is constant and reliable, especially in the context of other changes and encounters with the justice system: 'Particularly important is the need to keep in regular contact and not to make promises or appointments that cannot be kept' (2006, p. 161). As others have noted (e.g., Robinson, 2005), the increasing fragmentation of roles and responsibilities within the justice system has militated against this kind of continuous engagement. The separation of assessment functions from case management and service delivery activities may make sense in terms of resource management or administrative simplicity, but it may be unhelpful for young people, for whom reliable relationships may be important (and unavailable elsewhere in their lives). This point is developed further in the arguments of those who promote 'pro-social modelling' (e.g., Cherry, 2005; Trotter, 2006), a somewhat jargonistic term to refer to processes by which 'workers should model the behaviour they wish to foster in their client' (Taylor, 2006, p. 161).

Box 8.3

On reflection, I feel that I failed to recognize the importance of one young person's background, whilst focusing on his vehicle-related offending. His mother believed that his behaviour could largely be explained by the fact that he was adopted, and although this was probably not a sufficient explanation on its own, I now feel that I should have explored this issue further.

Should social workers in youth justice settings concentrate on responding to offending behaviour, or should they be more concerned with child welfare issues? Or should they try to find ways of bridging the two?

Unpacked, the principles and methods of 'pro-social practice' (Cherry, 2005, p. 3) may appear to recall some of the historic values so central to social work practice traditions (Biestek, 1961). These include:

> Demonstrating 'genuine concern' for the person;
> Encouraging pro-social behaviour;
> Challenging anti-social values and behaviour;
> Transparent use of authority and enforcement powers;
> Clarity about roles and purposes;
> Actively working in partnership with service users;
> Treating the service user as an individual and valuing diversity.
>
> (Cherry, 2005, p. 3).

This list may appear relatively anodyne and uncontroversial, but it does provide a useful checklist for practitioners against which to evaluate their interventions with young people in trouble. It is interesting to note, for example, that young people respond to discipline and authority according to the legitimacy with which they invest those who seek to exercise power over them. Taylor (2006, p. 114) highlights the difference between 'pointless discipline' exercised by staff for whom there was no respect, and the response of the young person to a carer's use of authority in the context of a positive relationship.

Interestingly, Taylor links this observation to the practice of 'reintegrative shaming', whereby it is intended that disapproval of a young person's unacceptable behaviour can be expressed in ways which have an impact but do not alienate the individual concerned. This is a central element in some forms of restorative justice, a relatively recent but increasingly widespread development (Crawford and Newburn, 2003) in the search for approaches which effectively reconcile punishment and welfare. Certainly, restorative interventions may offer a vehicle by which social workers can retain a focus on the well-being of the young person whilst also engaging in the process of resolving the difficulties which arise from her or his offending behaviour. Whilst acknowledging that the social work task may well extend beyond the immediate concerns associated with an offence, this process may provide a helpful means by which specific problem behaviour is linked with wider issues and other needs.

Restorative justice services essentially offer a vehicle for all those affected by an offence (victims, offenders, families and others) to express their views about what has happened and what should be done about it, in a way which seeks to achieve mutually acceptable solutions. Importantly, these offence resolution processes should be 'voluntary' and should respect 'the dignity and equality of each person', whilst building understanding and 'promoting social harmony' through a mutual 'healing' process (Scottish Executive, 2005, p. 2).

'Conferencing' (Crawford and Newburn, 2003) has become a widely recognized mechanism through which restorative principles can be put into practice. Closely related to the New Zealand/Aotearoa model of family group conferences, which have become an accepted form of practice in child and family social work, restorative conferences adopt the same kind of inclusive, informal and flexible approach to dealing with the problems associated with the offence. However, different models have emerged, with consequences for both the process and outcomes for young people. Practitioners should avoid falling prey to an undue emphasis on 'happy endings' which ostensibly meet victims' needs at the expense of other considerations and wider issues affecting the young person at centre stage.

Importantly for social work practitioners, restorative interventions such as conferences should be seen as a way of approaching 'turning points' in a positive fashion: 'The restorative approach is focused on building and repairing relationships rather than managing and controlling behaviour' (Netcare, 2007). It acknowledges that the behaviour of the young person concerned may be harmful to others, or to the community in general, but the purpose of the intervention is to provide a constructive forum in which these issues can be examined and addressed. Significantly, the views of the young person are taken into account, and she or he is invited to be 'part of the solution making process'. The process of accepting responsibility in this way is an active one which enables the individual to learn from the experience, and to recognize her or his ability to contribute positively. At the same time, the involvement of other parties, including 'victims', also provides an opportunity to acknowledge the young person's wishes and feelings about the offence, and to endorse her or his efforts to put things right. In this way, the focus is shifted from the offence in isolation to the capacity of the young person to see herself or himself as part of a network of relationships and to take responsibility. Its empowering potential is significant: 'Before the restorative conference I felt that I was not listened to properly by the school. They blamed me for bigger things that had nothing to do with me. I was able to put things right and accept the things I had done wrong' (young person, quoted in Netcare, 2007). This example, taken from a school-based restorative scheme, illustrates some of the potential for this form of practice to shift attention away from the young person purely as a threat, and towards her or his capacity to solve problems and take control. For practitioners this is highly encouraging, but it also underlines the importance of applying certain key principles carefully.

Young people must be properly involved and consulted throughout the process, since their commitment can only be secured if they feel that they have a part to play in deciding what happens. The focus should be on wider issues of 'reconciliation', rather than relatively narrow concerns about 'making amends' for an offence, although this may well form part of the bigger picture. The restorative process must not be seen as an end in itself, but, as with other 'turning points', as an opportunity to engage with young people, to empower them, and to create opportunities to achieve change. And it must also be accepted that there may well be 'loose ends' requiring continuing involvement with the young person. For this reason, the social work practitioner may well have to consider how to remain supportive of the young person in the face of significant pressure from the justice system to 'cooperate'. There may be a temptation for social workers involved in youth justice to adopt the view that achieving compliance is a necessary part of the task, but this may at times be incompatible with the underlying challenge of establishing a sound and supportive relationship with socially excluded young people. Sometimes longer-term objectives to do with achieving better life chances for the young person may not be compatible with the aims and purposes of other interests in the justice system. Siding with young people whose attitudes and behaviour may be unpleasant or unacceptable to others may be difficult, but it may also be necessary in order to sustain the relationship which will form the basis for effective future practice. The social work values of 'non-judgementalism' and 'acceptance' (Banks, 2001) can sometimes be challenged by young people's actions, it is clear, but these remain key attributes to underpin practice rooted in ideas of social learning, growth, development and positive change. It is important to maintain the distinction between the individual and her or his behaviour. Addressing risky or threatening behaviour should thus be seen as a means to an end in social work rather than as an end in itself.

Social work, young people and risk: Towards effective practice

As risk has become a dominant theme in social work thinking and practice (Webb, 2006), it has become increasingly important to understand the implications of this for work with young people. It has been suggested, for example, that there is a generalized tendency to move away from face-to-face work, and rather to concentrate on the processes of 'calculation and regulation in the face of risk'. As a consequence: 'the move away from intensive direct work undermines personal needs for trust, recognition and intimacy [and] relations between people increasingly take on the appearance of relations between things' (Webb, 2006, p. 77). In the light of these concerns, this chapter has sought to focus on three distinctive aspects of 'risk' in relation to young people: risk from themselves, risk from others and risk to others. These categories are complicated by the fact that they represent an amalgam of concrete threats and dangers on the one hand, and the processes whereby certain young people come to be problematized selectively on the other. Thus, there are no readily applicable calculative approaches which can effectively identify and provide solutions to clear and specific objective risk factors. By contrast, the social work task must begin from a position of engagement and dialogue, whereby the young person's perception of risk, and its causes, takes centre stage.

This is not to suggest that young people are not exposed to potential harm, nor is it the case that their behaviour is never problematic and threatening. However, the social work task needs to move beyond the application of standardized assessments and routine measures to manage risk, and interventions must be based on a more nuanced understanding of the complex circumstances and influences affecting young people. As we have seen, given these factors, it is unlikely that social workers will achieve this aim without developing relationships of trust and mutuality with young people in difficult circumstances. Sometimes, as Webb (2006) acknowledges, the systems, procedures and underlying assumptions on which social work is based (especially in statutory settings) do not support this kind of approach. However, the discipline's 'ethics of care' requires a commitment to mutuality, dialogue and a critical perspective, which enables young people's wishes, feelings and aspirations to emerge and to influence decisions and outcomes.

The concept of risk may be helpful in drawing attention to immediate contexts of harm or potential harm, but practice must not be preoccupied with this or constrained by the terminology, which suggests a crisis response. This can only be partial, and may miss the point completely, as in the case of some young runaways. Crisis intervention and risk management can only have meaning and value if they are linked to more deep-rooted and longer-term strategies of relationship building, problem-solving and continuing support.

Chapter summary

This chapter has tried to draw out some of the key elements involved in effective interventions with young people, especially in a context where an element of 'risk' has been identified. Key points are:

- The authority of social workers creates a degree of tension and ambiguity around their relationships with young people, especially where young people's behaviour or circumstances place them at risk.
- Practitioners have to make difficult choices when trying to establish effective mutual relationships whilst managing risk.
- Despite this, young people clearly value positive relationships with social work practitioners.
- Relationships need to be developed over time, and sustained through transition processes.
- Principles based on our knowledge of attachment and simply 'being available' are important components underpinning effective interventions.

Further reading

Howe's *Attachment Theory for Social Work Practice* (1995) remains of significant value in reminding us of the way in which the nature of interpersonal relationships impacts on our ability to work effectively with young people, in terms of both their own past experiences and our professional capacity and commitment to engage with them.

Taylor's (2006) important study of *Young People in Care and Criminal Behaviour* reminds us of the importance of maintaining a social work focus on young people's well-being even where attention shifts to their offending behaviour and its consequences. They are still 'children first'.

Folgheraiter's (2004) *Relational Social Work* is a detailed exploration of the central place of relationship building in social work practice. It offers some valuable insights into the construction and use of relationships in supporting the empowerment of service users.

9 Social inclusion, young people and the role of social work

Taking a wider view of the social work task

Previous chapters have largely focused on the problems of young people as defined *for* them by social work, families, communities and other social institutions. In this sense, perhaps predictably, practice is sometimes constrained or compromised to the extent that it is concerned primarily with these externally defined concerns. Where formally defined problems, assessment and solutions coincide with the needs and wishes of young people, help offered may be beneficial, but, of course, this may not be the case. Selective definitions of risk may be unhelpful, as we have seen, and this can be graphically illustrated:

> I wrote to the directors of social services about children who were prostituting or who were violent. I begged for their protection, and then social services would write back denying the events as I described them. Imagine being told a teenager with a drug habit of £150 to £170 a day didn't have enough pocket money from social services to buy drugs and therefore she couldn't be addicted.
>
> (Batmanghelidjh, 2006, p. 11)

Importantly, the factors which generate problems for children and young people do not often fit into the relatively neat, atomized categories according to which welfare and other services try to capture and make sense of them. Some of this, at least, can be attributed to the limited capacity of agencies, and their inability to cater for every identifiable need. However, it is also the case that the formal agencies and systems of welfare have their own agendas and rationales which do not straightforwardly coincide with those of vulnerable and socially excluded young people. It is perhaps because of this that the practice of social work may feel somewhat incomplete, or even characterized by a sense of 'denial' as it grapples with just one aspect of the complex and damaging situations in which some young people have to live. Assessment processes might feel as if they are being utilized at least partly to justify screening out some needs, and redefining them as someone else's problem, or as insufficiently serious to warrant intervention, or sometimes just as intractable and beyond help.

Young people, on the other hand, will have their own definitions of need and aspirations for change, and when they encounter problems, they may well want and seek help on their own terms, rather than as set down by formal rules and procedures. Given the responsibility of social work to respect individual differences, and to promote the rights and wishes of those receiving services, this presents a significant challenge to practice. It may help, here, to consider some examples of the kind of settings within which young people's needs set the terms for intervention. How can and should social work respond when young people set the agenda?

Leaving care, social work and transitions

One area of intervention which appears to be based on the specific aspirations of young people concerns the transition from care to self-sufficiency. As has often been noted, leaving care is different in a number of key respects from the transitions to independence made by young people in the general population.

It has long been recognized that the pattern of experience, transitions and outcomes for 'looked after' young people is highly distinctive, and often disadvantageous in a number of key respects (Stein and Carey, 1986; DfES, 2006b). Thus, government acknowledges that 'children in care are being left behind' (DfES, 2006b, p.10), and that is reflected in substantially poorer than average educational qualifications, and unresolved problems which persist into adult life. The services that make up the care system thus seem to be falling short in addressing young people's needs whilst looked after, and their experience of transitions seems to compound these difficulties. Notably, the age at which young people leave care, and the manner in which this is accomplished, both give rise to continuing concern. Government concludes that the way in which this process has been conceptualized is a source of difficulty:

> For older young people in care . . . the care system must provide not only a positive living environment but a bridge into adult life. It is time to leave behind the unhelpful idea of 'leaving care' and recognise that every young person needs continuing help to make a smooth transition to adulthood. Any good parent continues to offer love and support to their children well beyond 18, giving them the greatest head start in life that they can. We should demand no less for young people in care.   (DfES, 2006b, p. 84)

The formal nature of statutory services and their inbuilt constraints of facilities and funds often appear to create contextual difficulties in enabling a flexible and supportive experience of moving on. As Thomas (2005) points out, both timing and structure can lead to problems. Young people from care are likely to have some continuing contact with friends and family, but they are less likely than others to be able to rely on these sources for 'financial support, . . . practical help, advice and emotional support' (p. 155). Young people from 'unsettled' backgrounds and with often limited educational attainments are expected to move to live independently at a younger age than their peers, and the break may well be much more final than it is for those in the general population, who are able to try things out, make mistakes and still rely on continuing family support.

Changes in legislation, such as the Children Act 1989 and the Children (Leaving Care) Act 2000, have sought to put in place mechanisms and services which offer continuing support and more closely mimic the 'normal' transition processes for young people. Subsequent recognition of the limited achievements of these measures has led to an increased emphasis on the views expressed by young people themselves. Young people say they want 'more support' and 'more choice' when leaving care, and their 'key messages' are that:

- they are not supported well enough and can't cope with work and education at the same time as learning how to manage money and fend for themselves.
- [they] should leave care when they are ready, not at a particular age, and . . . the right support should be there when they do.
- [they] should be able to stay with their foster carers after leaving care and be able to return to them after they have left, just like other young people do with their . . . families.   (DfES, 2006b, p. 106)

These priorities find endorsement in earlier research studies, which demonstrate the importance of a gradual, collaborative and planned approach to transitions (Thomas, 2005).

Research has identified different types of 'care career' and trajectories for young people on leaving, and this suggests that practice needs to be adaptable, whilst based on the fundamental principles outlined. Young people who have been 'looked after' tend to fall into one of three categories, according to Stein (2005): the *moving on* group, the *survivors*, and the *victims* group. Those in the first group have a number of positive factors in their favour, 'including a secure attachment relationship' and 'some educational success', as well as the capacity to 'make sense' of their own family relationships. Notably, for example, some young mothers from care backgrounds are able to draw on their experiences to renew family links and rebuild relationships with their relatives (Stein, 2005, p. 20). The kind of help and support this group tends to benefit from is continuing contact and positive reinforcement, which may be provided by former carers.

Survivors appear to be in a somewhat ambiguous position, seeing themselves as having gained in 'toughness' and maturity through previous adverse experiences (Stein, 2005, p. 21). However, at the same time, they appeared to be significantly reliant on other means of support:

> They believed that the many problems they had faced, and often were still coping with, had made them more grown up and self-reliant – although their view of themselves as independent was often contradicted by the reality of high degrees of agency dependency for help with accommodation, money and personal assistance.
>
> (Stein, 2005, p. 21)

Past experiences, such as sudden endings to placements, homelessness or relationship problems, are identified as contributing to their survival skills, but also leaving them in a position of continuing vulnerability and impermanence. For this group, the evidence seems to suggest that continuing support from key practitioners as well as their own networks can make a significant difference, and 'help them overcome their very poor starting points'.

For *victims*, the picture was bleaker. Being 'looked after', it seems, cannot 'compensate' for previous adverse experiences. In addition, their lives in care may be characterized by significant disruptions, such as repeated moves, constantly changing peer groups, educational problems, and loss or lack of supportive family ties. As well as this, they appear to be more likely to leave care younger than their peers, and to face a future of isolation, unmet accommodation needs and mental health problems (Stein, 2005, p. 22). For those seeking to provide continuing support and assistance to this group, the challenges are substantial, not least because their lifestyles and attitudes may tend to 'alienate' those offering help. None the less, as Stein has observed, 'it was very important to these young people that somebody was there for them, that they were not abandoned' (p. 22).

The constant theme for the three groups is the value of commitment, consistency and reliable sources of support. It is noted by Stein that one response to earlier research findings has been to develop more specialist services, providing a clearer focus on the needs of young people from care, and offering better-informed and more reliable points of contact. However, he also notes that these services have not always provided a comprehensive answer to the range of issues facing young people undergoing complex and challenging transitions. The advent of the Children (Leaving Care) Act 2000 appears to have given a sharper focus to the task of practitioners in helping young people to negotiate changes in their lives, with developments such as 'pathway planning' (Harris and Broad, 2005) providing a vehicle for this. The idea of pathway planning is helpful because it offers a clear and intelligible route by which formal expectations and procedures can be translated into a useful tool 'to focus direct work with young people' (Harris and Broad, 2005, p. 3). It provides shape and coherence to the process of moving on from care whilst also offering reliable support from practitioners (social workers and 'personal advisers') through this process. The plan uses the structure offered by regular reviews of young people's needs and services to maintain continuity whilst also enabling progress to be monitored and aims and objectives to be amended where necessary. The framework for the plan is designed to cover all the major aspects of a young person's life and aspirations, and to enable the identified needs to be addressed accordingly (DH, 2003a). In parallel with the agency version of the planning document, it is expected that young people are provided with the opportunity to prepare their own version of the pathway plan, and that this is used to shape discussions and influence decisions. Key areas should be covered including health, education, emotional and behavioural development, identity, family and social relationships, practical skills, financial arrangements and accommodation (DH, 2003a, p. 12). Thus, both practical living arrangements and personal and emotional issues should be covered systematically. Importantly, though, this should not be just a 'bureaucratic' exercise, and it must be revisited regularly, in order both to monitor progress and to sustain effective enabling relationships:

> When used well, pathway plans can be used to systematically assess and address risk, cover key aspects of everyday life, keep the young person's aspirational agenda in focus, share information, measure progress, introduce boundaries and help the young person to develop a sense of responsibility and adult autonomy. We found that for both personal advisers and young people, pathway planning is much more effective when viewed as a process rather than a form to be filled in.
> (Harris and Broad, 2005, p. 3)

Likewise, young people said in this case that they were enabled by this means to exercise choices and to 'hold others to account'. The plan and the support it guaranteed gave them a sense of purpose and direction (p. 4).

Built into this process should also be a commitment to regular monitoring, using the review process. Planned tasks should be allocated agreed timetables, and reviews undertaken at set intervals, in order to minimize the risk of 'drift' or losing sight of the young person's needs. Practitioners are able to identify key elements of pathway planning which enhance its effectiveness:

- There is systematic consideration of risk – problems are anticipated and crisis work reduced.
- Aspects of young people's lives are considered which might otherwise be overlooked.
- Young people's aspirations take precedence over professional priorities.
- Information sharing and agreed responsibilities are achieved more consistently.
- Work is focused on agreed areas of intervention.
- Progress and achievements can be regularly monitored.
- Structure can be provided, but in a 'subtle' rather than confrontational way. (adapted from Harris and Broad, 2005, p. 29)

As a consequence, where the pathway plan is used creatively and supportively, young people feel as if they have had the opportunity to express their views, exercise choice and take charge of decision-making and the arrangement of services.

Taking this kind of approach has certain other consequences for practice, not least because the mutual identification of young people's goals and aspirations creates an expectation that they will be supported in pursuing these. Thus, collaborative working with other agencies, effective networking and advocacy become essential elements of practice. Professionals need a sound understanding of what other services can offer, and a degree of specialist knowledge may also be helpful, such as how to 'steer a clear path through benefit entitlements'. Practitioners may find themselves: 'called upon to play an advocating role in terms of accessing other services and this could help develop young people's perception that the service was "on their side", helping to keep them engaged' (Harris and Broad, 2005, p. 50).

Of course, advocacy can take different forms, and it is important to distinguish between the individualized model suggested in the context of 'pathway plans' and the collectivized model associated with a 'social justice' orientation to welfare interventions (Broad, 1998, p. 258). A strong version of advocacy of this kind would require practitioners to take an active role in building and supporting networks of young people in and leaving care. This may be the only appropriate model of intervention in some cases, for example where young people leaving care should be supported in challenging 'individual and institutional racism' (Thomas, 2005, p. 166). It would be insufficient in the case of young people who have experienced oppression and disadvantage just to consider individual needs and 'welfare' interventions, because this would overlook a fundamental influence on their experiences and life chances. Practitioners cannot hope to provide a comprehensive response by dealing with young people in these circumstances in isolation. Effective intervention requires both individual work on issues such as 'identity' and educational opportunity, and network building, advocacy and challenging discriminatory practices (Thomas, 2005, p. 166).

As Broad observes, it is important not to adopt too single-minded an approach, for example pursuing social justice at the expense of individual need. An integrated practice strategy is likely to be more productive, linking approaches such as 'pathway planning', based on individual needs and circumstances, with a readiness to encourage and support young people in challenging the wider injustices and disadvantage they encounter. A multi-dimensional perspective is necessary, and social work should be ready both to act on immediate issues affecting young people leaving care and to take an active part in supporting movements for wider social change, especially those which are led by young people themselves.

Young people at (or beyond) the margins: The role of social work

The marginalized status of some young people, including a number of groups we have already considered, presents difficulties for social work practitioners in terms of engaging with them on their own terms. The circumstances and events associated with the process of social exclusion may lead to their being categorized in ways which deny social workers a role, whilst at the same time their own perspectives and experience of social work may engender a substantial degree of suspicion and mistrust on their part. In other words, there may exist a considerable gulf between practitioners and young people, with prior constraints and attitudes creating real difficulties.

How, then, can social work reconstitute itself to provide an effective service for young people who may not see its value or relevance to themselves? Batmanghelidjh's (2006) graphic description of the establishment of a community project helps to capture some of the challenges involved in making these connections. This initiative was inspired partly at least by a recognition that existing services did not (could not) address the needs of a large community of socially excluded children and young people effectively. Batmanghelidjh found herself, in fact, offering a drop-in service to a considerable number of young people who 'referred' themselves, often on grounds of 'neglect', but were not accorded sufficient priority to receive a statutory service of any kind. Her practice and that of her colleagues falls close to the boundary that distinguishes youth work from social work, but there are clearly elements which fall within the broad terms of what social work is and should do. Thus, for instance, the initial approach was based very much on principles of 'unconditional regard' (Batmanghelidjh, 2006, p. 18), with no conditions or constraints placed on the young people's attendance or behaviour. On this basis, it became possible to undertake practice consistent with 'life story work', equivalent to that undertaken in family placement services:

> as I got to know them they began telling me their life stories, and I began writing them down. They were horrific stories of young children battered, shot at, beaten, hurled to the wall as parents struggled with drug withdrawal. These were children who, in order to survive, had become drug couriers or drug-dealers. Some were doing bank robberies, some were making £4000 a week and sharing it among the whole group. And these were children who could not be returned to school, who'd been out of education for a number of years. Seventeen-year-olds who were capable of killing but could not write their names or addresses.   (Batmanghelidjh, 2006, p. 19)

In a sense, their lives ran parallel to mainstream society, with their own rules, structures and hierarchies. As is observed, the mainstream is often 'glad to lose them', conveying the ambiguous message that they should live by the accepted social norms and conventions, but that they are not welcome participants in its structures or activities. How then can social work practice ensure that it acts in a way which does not compound this confusion, but does offer useful and supportive interventions?

The project in question again offers some clues about possible strategies. It was found to be important to recruit individuals who both understood the young people's 'world', and could thereby demonstrate the capacity for empathy and collaboration. Alongside this, the project began to offer practical help to the young people who attended, in the form of food, bus passes and living allowances. As Batmanghelidjh (2006, p. 20) observes: 'In this way, we were addressing the core problems of poverty which were driving the children into criminal activity.'

As these basic methods of engagement were applied, an atmosphere of trust began to develop, so that young people would feel able to turn to workers for help irrespective of past behaviour or reputation. They also began to understand that support would be backed up by action, as when assertive methods were used to secure young people's rights.

Achievements were judged according to specific, personal and incremental measures. The point is made that conventional benchmarks of success, such as educational attainment or finding work, are simply not meaningful at the outset of such a project. We should start by judging our practice according to short-term and immediate indicators of trust and security: 'We have many, many successful outcomes which stem from vulnerable children's valiant struggle to survive abuse. They may not be visible in the league tables, and people may not value them, but the truth is that before an educational outcome there needs to be an emotional one' (Batmanghelidjh, 2006, p. 23). Importantly, we should acknowledge the value of positive recognition and reinforcement of achievements even if they are small and intangible. The tendency to focus on negatives, whether of behaviour or incapacity, should not lead practitioners to overlook positive gains, especially where these are self-defined.

Ironically, it seems, the task of responding to the consequences of structural disadvantage begins for the practitioner with a very individual approach to understanding, empathy and building trust. It is important, for example, not to be critical or rejecting when young people's progress is halted, or when they test the strength of the relationship, perhaps by behaving aggressively, offending, returning to a violent partner or reverting to drug use. The danger of being over-optimistic is that the worker may feel let down and express these feelings unhelpfully. Other risks are evident, too, for practitioners working consistently with damage and pain. Continuous exposure to young people's harmful experience may have a 'numbing' effect (Batmanghelidjh, 2006, p. 116), or the worker may simply feel 'overwhelmed'. In either case, the capacity to take action and promote the service user's interests may become compromised. Other emotional hazards also confront practitioners in these circumstances, such as the guilt of being unable to achieve or sustain better outcomes for young people, or anger directed at 'uncaring' agencies.

For professionals involved in caring for young people, there are clearly a number of key tensions here which need to be managed in order to sustain the capability to work effectively. These include the necessity of engaging with young people on a personal level, whilst retaining the capacity to stand back, reflect on interactions and avoid over-identifying with individual circumstances. In addition, practitioners need to be able to accept and move on from 'failure', without seeing it as confirmation of their own shortcomings or the service user's inadequacies. Equally, the achievement and celebration of positive change should also be set against a realistic understanding of the forces and constraints which may set limits to the gains that are made, or undermine them. It is crucial that the practitioner avoids internalizing 'blame' or allowing the mutual sense of failure to become reinforcing. Rather, it is important to think in terms of challenge and transformation.

A helpful framework for this kind of approach to practice is offered by Parton and O'Byrne (2000, p. 80), who describe it as 'the art of resistance'. The initial phase of intervention may be characterized by a process of 'validation', whereby service users' stories may be acknowledged and recognized as truthful, but should not be seen as confirming the 'impossibility' of change. This is important because it neither closes off the route towards taking action nor underestimates the difficulty of achieving change. The kinds of question asked seek to identify 'the tiniest possibility' of things being different, whilst demonstrating that as practitioners we understand just how substantial and apparently intractable are the problems faced by the service user. Talk tries to draw attention to alternative scenarios, when the young person may have seen things differently, or felt in control, or where a more optimistic view of the future can be envisaged *realistically*. Building resistance to the problem identified depends on a mutual process of recognizing and agreeing its size and severity, and once this is achieved, beginning to promote the belief that change is possible.

The next stage in the process, following the principles of 'constructive social work', is 'externalising the problem' (Parton and O'Byrne, 2000, p. 82). By this is meant drawing on accounts of the difficulties experienced to distinguish the individual from the issues and circumstances which are problematic. This helps to define what needs to be done as something concrete and understandable in its own right, whilst also enabling those affected to see it as something which they can manage and control. Thus: 'The externalisation of problems helps people to separate from their own subjugation' (Parton and O'Byrne, 2000, p. 83). This also helps them to question those factors which generate and 'maintain' the problem, whether these are their own or others' attitudes and beliefs, or other external factors which oppress and devalue them. This process also enables service users and practitioners to identify common ground, whereby the 'problem' can be tackled jointly and in its own right; it is no longer located with or owned solely by the young person concerned.

It is further suggested that this process of 'externalization' not only creates a sense of the manageability of difficulties, but also 're-politicises experience' (Parton and O'Byrne, 2000, p. 84), because it calls into question the assumptions and practices which define the individual as

Box 9.1

You stole money from [your] foster carer, and you aroused her rage. She should have forgiven you. She should have stayed and stuck it out. She should have shown comprehension . . . She should have understood your jealousy and your regret and your deeply, deeply painful yearning for your own mother. Instead, she slammed her doors in your face, and I watched you as you cried . . .

You took my cashpoint card and you took money, and with this you devastated yourself. But I wasn't going to give up . . . I knew how desperate you were. (Batmanghelidjh, 2006, pp. 126, 127)

How would you respond in a situation where you felt that a young person with whom you were working had let you down, or breached your trust?

the sole source of her or his 'problems'. The process of achieving this objective is described as having three stages: the person is encouraged to 'tell the story of the problem'; it is then recast in language which 'implies that the problem is external'; and then this is contrasted with the individual's 'preferred way of being', which enables change options to be identified (Parton and O'Byrne, 2000, p. 85), and the problem is reframed as something which is manageable and capable of resolution.

Of course, in practice the identification of a problem and routes towards a solution may be achievable as an important first step, but for young people in extreme circumstances, the difficulties they face are likely to be complex, and progress uncertain. Interim setbacks and new challenges are almost inevitable for those who are undergoing transitions in adversity. Knowing that there is a possible 'solution' may become even more dispiriting at times when progress is thwarted. At this point the role of the worker in 'holding on' (Rutherford, 1995) and reaffirming the distinction between the individual and the problem is vital (Box 9.1).

Challenging the inevitability of 'failure'

Responding to 'stories' which appear to demonstrate regression and repeated failure is a necessary part of the intervention process. 'Problematic stories' which suggest that change is impossible or that individual weaknesses will always block progress need to be challenged (Parton and O'Byrne, 2000, p. 87). This may be achieved, for instance, by distinguishing 'blame' from 'accountability'. The former simply alienates and stereotypes young people; the latter affords them the responsibility for taking the initiative and achieving positive objectives. Strengths and capabilities are thereby identified and underpinned. In a 'letter' to a young person, the practitioner states: 'We worked together as you determinedly battled against your addiction' (Batmanghelidjh, 2006, p. 127) – note here that the language reflects the principles of externalizing the problem and emphasizing accountability – even where this may be a battle which is fought time and again with uncertain outcomes.

These messages are particularly important in the context of practice with young people whose experiences are oppressive and who feel rejected, devalued and unwanted. Whilst the forces and attitudes which underlie their problems originate elsewhere, the consequences for them may be devastating not just in material terms, but also in the way that they see themselves, and in the limited opportunities they feel they have to change or influence anything. Thus, empowering and enabling practice begins (but does not end) with the individual, who may need to undergo a process of questioning, reimagining and constructing alternative futures which are realistic and achievable.

It has been suggested that the approach here is one which is best characterized in terms of the possibility of 'multiple explanations', because: 'along with uncertainty comes hope for change. This is postmodernism at its most positive, embracing pluralism and possibilities' (White, 1997, p. 750). Practitioners may find it more helpful to accept that 'deterministic explanations . . . have consequences' which may be counterproductive if they do not allow for the potential for young people to take responsibility and achieve change even in the most difficult circumstances. Often the task for the social worker may be about challenging the 'certainties' of personal shortcomings and failure, and replacing these with other alternatives, informed by 'creativity, imagination and hope' (White, 1997, p. 751). This may also involve challenging previous formal assessments and classifications which make incapacitating and oppressive assumptions about the young person concerned, and creating space for recognition of her or his positive qualities and potential in the face of institutionalized doubt and negativity.

Taking charge: Young people and user-led practice

The final part of this discussion will reflect on the potential for young people to take the lead in specifying and determining the nature of social work interventions with and for them. In this context, it is not simply a matter of redefining the ways in which they are problematized, but also one of rethinking how services are organized and who exercises control. There have been a considerable number of developments in the direction of user-led services in the recent past, notably in the context of disability and adult services, which suggests that there may be similar scope for progress in social work with young people.

Organizations such as Shaping Our Lives have taken a consistent lead in promoting service user interests and campaigning for greater control over services. Whilst they have had a degree of success in some areas, it is acknowledged that 'certain groups', including younger people, face additional barriers to involvement, and this is compounded where these young people are also from black and minority ethnic communities, or communicate differently. Similarly the organization Voice for the Child in Care has sought to promote a more central role for 'looked after' young people in shaping and influencing interventions. As we have been told previously though: 'Participation is a dynamic process, and real participation by children requires investment in time, energy and commitment. Children are much more able to contribute when they have been prepared' (Thomas and O'Kane, 1999, p. 228).

Despite this, opportunities to put young people at the centre of service delivery have not been consistently taken. It seems relatively straightforward, for example, that the principle of enabling 'looked after' young people to chair their own 'reviews' could be adopted by agencies and practitioners. However, this has been a relatively recent development in a limited number of areas, it seems (e.g., Bracknell Forest Borough Council, 2006), and implementation difficulties are noted. Where this has been facilitated, it is noted as a 'very positive' experience for the young people concerned (p. 5), although the point is made that it requires time and commitment on the part of practitioners, in terms of support and preparation. Thus, in this relatively small area of social work practice with children, progress towards properly 'user-led' services has been gradual at best. This is partly perhaps because of the limited time and capacity available to agencies and practitioners, but the question must be raised as to whether cultural and attitudinal changes might also be needed. Is there, for example, a tendency to make the assumption that because young people who are looked after have 'problems', they may not be capable of exercising choice and control appropriately? Might this be an argument for adopting a different perspective on intervention, perhaps following the 'social justice' model identified by Broad (1998, p. 258)? The emphasis here is on promoting legal and substantive rights, and pursuing an approach to problem-solving which gives priority to 'collective effort' expressed through 'campaigning and lobbying'. Practitioners would be encouraged to see this as part of their role, not just in individual cases, but in order to support collective activities and organizations of young people (Box 9.2).

For social work practitioners, this probably means taking risks, both in terms of exposing one's own practice to criticism and challenge, and in posing difficult questions for the agency, with potential consequences in terms of popularity and career progression! In practical terms, this kind of approach also points towards a change in emphasis. For example, the idea of 'collectivizing' problems suggests that it will be important to work with young people in groups, rather than as individuals.

Bringing service users together into groups is likely to be empowering, in itself, but it also provides an effective basis for them to generate different ways of conceptualizing and addressing 'problems'. Thus, for example, where children and young people are adversely affected by domestic violence, sharing may be beneficial: 'Groups are an ideal way

Box 9.2

Certain principles underpin this approach to intervention, identified as:

- encouragement of the collectivisation of problems, and attempts to tackle them
- a partnership approach to working with young people
- putting emphasis on the structural, not the personal aspects of the problems
- putting expressed or felt needs above professional or bureaucratic definitions of need
- an equal emphasis on the pursuit of process goals (promoting political organisation . . .) as on task goals (resource redistribution). (Broad, 1998, p. 260)

How would this approach change the way you would plan and carry out an assessment of need?

of bringing children together so that they know they are not alone in what they have experienced, as the atmosphere of secrecy at home has previously led them to believe' (Mullender, 2002, p. 68). Groups formed around a common theme offer access to a recognized source of expertise (peers with the same adverse experiences), and a mutually supportive context for problem-solving and challenging oppression.

Young people who are Lesbian, Gay or Bisexual often experience feelings of isolation and vulnerability in the face of prevailing negative or indifferent attitudes (Fish, 2006), so the creation of opportunities to meet together and provide mutual affirmation is often important for them (Hind, 2004). A 'safe space' is recognized as valuable, where young people can develop beneficial networks and relationships, underpinning positive identity development, where the role of workers is to enable and facilitate, rather than necessarily to lead interventions:

> Seeing a young person who's come to the group anxious, depressed, hopeless and despondent, unable to mention the word gay, after a few months seeing a very different person in front of you; comfortable, making friends, relationships, exploring their sexuality, has told family or parents and is in a very different place than they were before.
> (PACE[1] youth worker, quoted in Hind, 2004, p. 38)

A 'partnership' approach to work with young people indicates that practitioners must be willing to negotiate every aspect of their interventions. Thus, for example, it may be as simple a matter as rewording service objectives so that they are expressed in terms of the young person's goals and aspirations rather than those of the agency (Edebalk, 2005, p. 12). Equally, it may be important to rethink some of the formal settings within which decisions are made: 'It is, so to say, easier for adults because they know each other, they gang together. I don't think they are aware of what they are doing . . . They sit there as the worst crowd against you' (young person, quoted in Edebalk, 2005, p. 14). The implicit limiting effects of formal settings and routinized events have been documented elsewhere, too (Sinclair, 1998). The introduction of

Box 9.3

The conduct of an independent chairperson in review meetings might be very significant, because of the capacity to create space for the young person to determine what is discussed: 'It is important to give the child possibilities to control their future just a little bit. What is actually going to happen? Do I have a chance to say what I want? . . . it could be developed much more, but it is worth its weight in gold' (independent chairperson, quoted in Edebalk, 2005, p. 18).

How else can a young person be empowered to take control when their 'case' is being reviewed?

independent and peer elements into formal processes is one way in which these constraints can be addressed (Box 9.3).

Moving from the personal to the structural: Challenges for practice

More challenging for social work practitioners is the task of shifting the focus from personal to structural issues, given the way in which interventions and assessments are typically structured. This involves a principled approach to practice which means focusing on the structural aspects of problems which might be expressed initially in narrowly individualistic terms, and following this understanding through into the provision of specific forms of help and support. Hogeveen (2006) offers an important example of the way in which youth justice practitioners have been able to work alongside young people's groups to 'reframe' quite serious offences and generate positive responses which have had community support. In one case, a 'racially provoked knife attack' became the inspiration for a form of 'justice' determined by young people themselves, which addressed the underlying context of racism which led to the offence whilst also ensuring that the young person concerned recognized that violence was unacceptable (Hogeveen, 2006, p. 61). Thus, the immediate issues were connected to relevant structural factors in such a way that the agreed intervention could respond constructively on both levels.

The principle of putting 'expressed or felt need' before institutional or expert definitions might seem to have gained fairly wide acceptance in terms of guiding social work principles, but it is also the case that procedures and documentation threaten to compromise these. The constraining influence of standardized forms is widely recognized, and it seems that effective practice requires an active process of interpreting and supplementing this kind of document in order to ensure that it reflects the young person's perspective fairly and accurately. Some operational guidance documents, among them the ASSET form used in youth justice assessments, include sections explicitly framed in terms such as 'What do I think?' in order to draw attention to this.

Despite this, it appears that many formal approaches to assessing young people's needs are shaped and steered by the way in which they are constructed. Thus, for example, standardized procedures for assessing the 'needs' of young runaways have been found to overemphasize the family setting at the expense of young people's own concerns (Macaskill, 2006). The immediate problem of the young person running away seems to preclude an approach which prioritizes their perceptions and concerns. The conclusion drawn is that existing approaches to child welfare and child protection do not take account of the particular dynamics of adolescence, and that therefore alternative approaches are required. It may be necessary in such circumstances to change the focus of intervention, even from the point of initial contact; young people's definitions of 'risk' and 'need' must be accorded priority (Macaskill, 2006). As a result, it may also be necessary to think in terms of changing needs rather than a static picture, so that it is legitimate to record assessments in terms of uncertainties and provisional goals, rather than as predetermined whatever subsequent changes might occur. This fits more neatly both with the idea of adolescent transitions and with the specific challenges arising from disrupted circumstances or problematic relationships:

> Barif says that he most of all wants to take care himself. He thinks it is difficult to ask for help. He doesn't trust adults. He can handle physical contact, but is easily disturbed. It is better than before but he wants it to succeed more rapidly.
> (Record of consultation with young person at a review meeting, quoted in Edebalk, 2005, p. 12)

The approach to assessment and planning needs to be 'dynamic and active' rather than driven by administrative necessities. This will ensure that intervention more closely mirrors the indeterminate and 'unfinished' nature of young people's lives and changing circumstances.

The final element of Broad's 'social justice' model stipulates an 'equal emphasis' on process and on the achievement of agreed 'task goals'. This appears to be consistent with the points above which highlight the changing nature of aspirations and outcomes for young people, not only because of the inherently transitory nature of adolescence, but also because of the specific issues which young people may encounter as individuals who may be marginalized, mistreated or oppressed in one way or another. The challenge this raises for practice is therefore one of aligning the style of working with the currents and contradictions to be found in young people's lives. Often this means satisfying: 'both legal and administrative requirements, while at the same time involving both children and parents in close co-operation. This presupposes a combination of formal and informal attitudes and strategies' (Edebalk, 2005, p. 19).

As is observed, this means that giving substance to formal entitlements, such as participation in reviews or having the right to express a view, 'is complicated'. Factors such as age, understanding and past experience are clearly significant, as are the context and organization of the consultative process. Young people will understandably express themselves differently and perhaps more freely in places and under conditions in which they are more comfortable. We only need to think of the constraints that apply in highly formalized settings such as youth courts to recognize that these play a powerful part in determining how openly and fully young people will make their views known in these situations (Phoenix, 2007). As social work itself has become more institutionalized and office-bound, it may be that opportunities to engage effectively with young service users are becoming more limited. This is particularly problematic if it is assumed that guaranteed consultation rights in formal settings have somehow negated the need for informal and ad hoc contact, where the agenda is unplanned and different dynamics apply. Social workers themselves can take some steps to open up these opportunities for less highly structured interactions. For example, young people should be allowed, as far as possible, to determine the time, place and content of meetings. They should be able to feel comfortable about just 'dropping in' to see their worker, and that the practitioner is available and willing to act on matters which they deem important, as and when these arise. Trust building and empowerment depend on the detail of our interactions, as well as those more formal expressions of policy and intent: 'Despite the adults' good intentions, small details can appear that have been missed or omitted regarding the preparations and during the actual meeting, which can affect the child's attitude towards and willingness to participate' (Edebalk, 2005, p. 19). It has been pointed out consistently that there is a clear tension between the trust- and relationship-building elements of practice which are necessary to establish the basis for effective communication and meaningful interventions, on the one hand, and the 'instrumentalist and procedural agendas' (Roy et al., 2002, p. 117) which sometimes appear to dominate social work thinking, on the other.

This does not mean, of course, that young people should 'have everything their own way', as these authors confirm, but it does prioritize the task of 'engaging' with them as 'subjects' in their own right, and providing opportunities to make decisions and exercise control, for instance over how and in what format information is recorded and held, and for what purposes it is used. It has been suggested that use of Hart's (1992) 'ladder' of children's participation (see also Arnstein, 1967) may help as a checklist for practitioners (and their agencies) to determine the extent and manner in which young people are being involved in and exercising control over what happens to them:

- Manipulation (use of the child to get what the adult wants)
- Decoration (meaningless use of the child for appearances only)
- Tokenism (when children are apparently given a voice but have limited or no choice about the subject)

- Assigned but informed (given roles which are symbolic and functional)
- Consulted and informed (work as consultants for adults and are involved in all the stages)
- Adult-initiated, shared decisions with children
- Child-initiated and directed
- Child-initiated, shared decisions with adults. (as reproduced in Roy et al., 2002, p. 120)

It is suggested that effective 'critical practice' should prioritize the last four approaches. Practitioners may wish to consider (and seek young people's views on) which of these is appropriate in particular contexts, and, perhaps more importantly, which is actually being applied.

Young people taking the lead? Final thoughts

As we shall see in the next and concluding chapter, the social work task is continually compromised by the structural relationships which shape the dynamics of practice with young people. As a result, it is a continual challenge to find ways of effectively enabling young people to 'take the lead' in determining their own needs and goals, and then intervening in ways which support them in achieving these. As we have seen here, however, there are certain principles and strategies which practitioners can adopt in pursuit of this aim.

The ability to form and sustain collaborative relationships lies at the heart of practice which involves young people and enables them to express their wishes and needs openly and without fear of the consequences. This, in turn, requires practitioners to be open from the start, and to be clear about what they can (and cannot) guarantee in terms of ceding power and control to young people. It is equally important, given past experiences and perceptions of service providers, that this kind of approach informs everyday practices and processes as well as the 'big' decisions in young people's lives. Thus, for example, 'meetings', which constitute such a central part of the machinery of social work assessment and decision-making, must be prepared for and conducted in a way which caters for young people, rather than simply complying with agency rules and procedures (Sinclair, 1998). In an ideal world, perhaps it would be open to young people themselves to convene, plan and chair meetings in which, after all, they are the main agenda item.

Chapter summary

This chapter has tried to set out a series of possibilities for social workers to empower young people through their practice, in terms of both enhancing control at the individual level and challenging structural obstacles to effective transitions. Key points are:
- Young people's 'problems' may coincide with social work tasks and definitions, but they are likely to be seen and experienced very differently.
- Social work has the capacity to work with young people to enable them to take the lead in setting the agenda.
- This may mean questioning and challenging conventional definitions and agency priorities.
- Relatively small changes in the way in which work is organized, for example around reviews, can none the less have significant consequences in terms of young people's control over what happens to them.

Further reading

Batmanghelidjh's (2006) graphic account of the extent of need and deprivation for socially excluded young people, *Shattered Lives*, throws into sharp relief the challenge for social work in engaging effectively with young people who are powerless, hurt and angry and sometimes behave accordingly.

Constructive Social Work by Parton and O'Byrne (2000) offers a useful insight into the importance of the social work process, and the ways in which listening and dialogue can be utilized as tools to affirm young people's experience and feelings, whilst also providing opportunities to ask constructive questions and to develop alternative futures.

Harris and Broad's (2005) discussion of the planning process for young people leaving care, *In My Own Time*, demonstrates a number of ways in which formal requirements can themselves be utilized to give young people a degree of control over outcomes.

10 Towards effective practice

Social work faces a significant challenge

In drawing together the various threads of ideas, policy and practice which have been introduced throughout this book, I will seek to identify some of the key messages and continuing challenges for social work as a form of practice with young people. The task of undertaking effective social work interventions with young people is difficult for a number of substantial reasons. In sum, these are based on the distinctive features of adolescence and the various ways in which youth is identified as problematic, on the one hand; and they are rooted in continuing debates about the appropriate role and functions of social work itself, on the other.

Thus, we can acknowledge that the problems of the young have been the subject of continuing fascinated concern which has, in turn, generated a considerable research effort, as well as ideologically driven attempts to find 'solutions', both within and beyond the social work arena.

In pursuit of understanding, the difficulties identified with the condition of youth have been conceptualized in a number of ways:

- as an inherent feature of adolescent transitions;
- as a product of other people's assumptions and attitudes;
- as a material consequence of social and structural influences;
- as an interacting combination of the above.

Clearly, the preferred form of intervention with young people will depend very much on the starting point (that is, the beliefs and assumptions) of those who work with them. At the same time, however, the approach taken by practitioners will also depend on their understanding of the proper scope, principles, functions and methods of social work itself. Practitioners have to make choices, and these are subject to a number of influences, including their own values and working assumptions, as well as the structural and agency context, and external rules, constraints and incentives which apply to them.

Effective social work practice with young people thus depends on negotiating a series of complex and interlocking questions, both about youth and young people, and about the nature of the professional task. Social work is not simply a technical activity, but depends on the appreciation and application of a number of core values, notably those concerning anti-oppressive practice, where young people are

179

concerned. Indeed, a sense of the place and purposes of the profession itself is an essential starting point for the task of helping young people to negotiate the problems they encounter, and empowering them to achieve positive outcomes in their lives and in their social contexts.

Social work: Its roles and tasks

At the time of writing, social work as a profession is undergoing a review process which is intended to produce a clear and definitive statement of the profession's key 'roles and tasks' (GSCC, 2007). This is perhaps a reflection of the continuing uncertainty of the profession and its governing institutions about just what its essential nature is, and how it should define its relationships with people who use its services. Interestingly, as part of this consultative exercise, the views of service users have been sought out specifically (Beresford, P., 2007), and it seems that there is a growing commitment to putting their ideas and expectations at the heart of the discipline of social work.

Despite the kind of policy changes and practice developments we have identified previously, there remains considerable concern from the service user perspective about the limited evidence of change across the social work spectrum, including the area of practice with young people. Thus, it is argued that much good work on promoting and evaluating 'what works' in participation has not led to consistently improved outcomes for young people, especially those in public care: 'there is still a strong sense at the level of policy, provision and general decision-making that children have very little influence over social work and social care' (Beresford, P., 2007, p. 34). It is acknowledged that this is partly to do with the complexity of the task and the diversity of those groups and individuals with whom social work is likely to engage, but it also appears to indicate a persistent underlying difficulty. This is partly attributed to the barriers young people encounter in expressing their views and aspirations, in contrast to adult user interests which have become quite effective in getting themselves heard, at least (p. 11).

Beresford suggests that it may be productive to think in terms of a 'barriers' model of intervention, drawing on the experiences of the disabled people's movement, in particular. The barriers which prevent people accessing services or achieving their own personal goals are held to be at least as important as any personal characteristics or circumstances, according to this perspective, and should therefore be the starting point for social work. These barriers, in turn, operate in two distinct ways:

> Service users point to two key sets of structural issues affecting social work. These are first the broader barriers and restrictions which oper-ate on them as individuals and second, the nature of the organisations in which social work is provided and the ideologies, values and beliefs operating in them. Clearly these two sets of issues operate in relation to each other. (Beresford, P., 2007, p. 19)

As a result, the starting point for effective intervention to challenge and remove the 'barriers' faced by service users must be a commitment to their 'rights' and entitlements. This is especially so given what we know about the context of disadvantage and discrimination, including poverty, faced by those who turn to social work organizations for help, it would seem (p. 20).

Service users have identified a number of key features of social work, which must be integral to all aspects of practice. These include a commitment to work with service users to tackle the barriers they face; a positive approach to securing and safeguarding 'human rights'; dialogue and participation; meaningful relationships; integrated practice; positive rather than defensive practice; and a commitment to ensuring that service users can take the lead in service planning and provision, both individually and collectively (Beresford, P., 2007). Whilst evidence of positive moves in this direction can be found in some areas of social work with adults, this is much less the case for children and young people, and therefore, specific initiatives must be taken to involve young people (and parents or carers) in designing and leading interventions (p. 50).

In response, the professional regulatory body for social work in England appears to have largely accepted these arguments. Social work, it states: 'is committed to protecting and advancing the human and civil rights of children and adults, and recognises the equal worth of all individuals, regardless of age, gender, race and ability, and no matter how marginalised' (GSCC, 2007, p. 5). 'Good social work', it is stated, puts service users at the heart of practice, transforms lives and draws on a 'wide range' of empowering methods, as well as service user knowledge and expertise (p. 7).

However, operationalizing these principles is likely to be demanding and complex, given the range of situations identified which might demand social work intervention (GSCC, 2007, p. 8). These include, notably, occasions when the individual might put herself or himself at risk of significant harm, or put others 'at risk of harm, distress or loss', in which case practitioners are expected to 'balance' the interests of service users and other people. These aspects of the social work task have particular implications for practice with young people, for instance in the context of self-harm, challenging behaviour or youth offending, as we have already observed. So, what should social workers do in cases where they are expected to 'balance' competing interests (p. 8), or to exercise powers of compulsion over young people? We are reminded that:

> Social work retains considerable powers over people and families – in assessment of risk, removal of certain children or adults, rationing resources, judging eligibility, holding professional and administrative knowledge – and needs well-developed power-sharing strategies with people using services. For these powers to be exercised properly, they should be exercised explicitly, honestly and with full discussion.
>
> (GSCC, 2007, p.11)

Social work should be done 'with' service users, rather than 'to' or 'for' them; nor should social work be used as the 'acceptable face' of refusal to give access to services (p. 13). In the light of this, it is difficult to see, for example, how social work processes can be used to undertake 'age assessments' of young people who seek asylum in order to determine whether or not they should be offered support. This appears to contravene the fundamental principles of a rights-based approach to practice, which should be challenging rather than reinforcing barriers to entitlement.

It is this sort of example which crystallizes the challenge for practitioners in giving substance to general statements of goals or values, when they encounter divergent expectations from their own agencies, or conflicts in professional principles which cannot simply be resolved by 'balancing' alternative interests. Indeed, this uncertainty is reflected in the GSCC's position, with the observation that: 'The emerging public and political debate about the balance of responsibilities between the individual, the family and the State will have a significant bearing on the social work role' (GSCC, 2007, p. 11). It is important to consider the changing shape and expectations of social work in the light of other perspectives which are central to our understanding of what is desirable and what is achievable in terms of delivering good practice.

Rethinking professionalism: The 'committed expert'

Alongside the review of social work's 'roles and tasks', we have seen the continuing development of a distinct, formal, professional identity in the UK, based on the establishment of national occupational standards, key roles and codes of practice. The job title 'social worker' is now protected in law, and entitlement to use this title depends on achieving a degree-level qualification (or higher). These manifestations of professionalism seem to imply a belief in social work as an 'expert' function, which is distinctive and specialized and creates a sense of distance both from other occupational groupings and from the wider community, and of course, people who use services.

Concerns about the nature and meaning of professionalism have led to a number of attempts to reframe the social work task in such a way that it can still lay claim to expertise, whilst not losing its sense of solidarity with and commitment to the interests of service users. In the past the notion of professionalism may have involved assumptions about objective and distinctive forms of knowledge and methods of intervention, associated perhaps with the 'medical' model of diagnosis and treatment, and this has led to problems for social work, creating power and knowledge imbalances between practitioners and service users (Beresford, P., 2007). In order for social work to be able to lay claim to 'expert' status whilst also maintaining its commitment to the core values set out previously, it must undertake the task of redefining the qualities and intervention strategies which constitute a 'professional' approach to practice. Frost (2006) suggests that the process of change and redefinition can be identified in relation to professions in general, in response to a number of wider social trends, such as 'globalisation, informationalism, the emergence of the network society and managerialism' (2006, p. 1). Some of these influences have had a destabilizing effect on established notions of professionalism; for example, the 'information explosion' has resulted in much wider access to legitimate knowledge, whilst the 'expert' cannot possibly hope to have a comprehensive understanding of any given subject: 'The student, the patient or the client we work with can be armed with information that we might not be familiar with' (Frost, 2006, p. 3), and is thus in a position to challenge our authority. For social work, in particular, which has always experienced a degree of insecurity about its own evidence base and standing, this possibility may represent a significant threat.

At the same time, evidence of professional failure, for instance drawing on high-profile cases where things have gone wrong, has undermined professionals' claim to certainty and infallibility across a range of disciplines, including social work of course. Thus, ironically, social work has achieved formal recognition of its professional status at just the point where the broader concept itself has come under sustained challenge in the light of a series of wider social changes. In order to establish itself as having credibility and authority as a discipline, social work must therefore identify and embrace a distinctive rationale for its purposes and practices. This may, indeed, be a positive development to the extent that it enables practitioners to articulate and sustain a set of operating principles consistent with user-centred ideals. Indeed, aspects of social work practice which might previously have been identified as shortcomings, such as its eclecticism, might now be seen as potential strengths, because they are more closely in line with the aspirations of service users: 'Service users value the wide range of social work approaches, including individual, family group and community work . . . They . . . want to see social work which will intervene on their behalf, offer reliable information, support and advocacy and is familiar with their rights and needs' (Beresford, P., 2007, p. 50). Precisely because of the variations in individual circumstances, characteristics and needs, social workers should have access to a wide range of knowledge and a wide repertoire of interventions, according to this argument.

There are other features of social work practice, too, which can be identified as core elements of its distinctive professional identity, and which support a collaborative and empowering approach to intervention.

Networking

It has been recognized for some time, especially amongst those proponents of 'community social work', that a key aspect of the role has been to recognize the connections between people and their 'systems', both formal and informal, and to foster and encourage supportive networks. For example, this may mean developing local knowledge in order to ensure that young unaccompanied asylum seekers are able to draw on appropriate support from familiar cultural, religious or linguistic sources.

Negotiation/advocacy

Social work often has to deal with the consequences of personal and social exclusion, so negotiation and advocacy skills may be central to the process of promoting reintegration or inclusion. This may include mediating between parents or carers and young people over the terms on which they can stay or return home; or it may mean advocating their rights to education or accommodation with colleagues and other agencies who may not be ready or willing to acknowledge their entitlement.

Relationship building

It has been a recurrent theme of this book that disruption and insecurity are common features of the lives of young people with whom social work engages. It thus becomes all the more important that they are able to build secure and stable relationships with significant adults, and this is something which social workers must be prepared to undertake, notwithstanding fears about professional boundaries and the risks of 'getting too close'.

Knowledge generation

Social work's growing commitment to the value of service user perspectives and expertise is significant partly because it changes our approach to what counts as legitimate 'knowledge'. The problem of being categorized and stigmatized by formal, 'official' processes, of which social work may be a part, may be crucial. Practitioners need to be able to work alongside service users to generate alternative forms of knowledge and understanding, in order to challenge oppressive and life-limiting labels.

There are no doubt further elements which could be incorporated in the redefinition of professionalism in social work, but the important point here is that it is possible to maintain the idea of a skilled and knowledgeable workforce which can apply these qualities in support of core principles of support, participation, rights and social justice. Social workers need not feel that they are being deskilled by adopting 'professional' attributes such as these.

The institutional context

Much has been made in recent times of the changing nature of social work agencies, and the perceived constraints that have impacted on the opportunities for positive practice. The concept of 'managerialism' is by now well established, and its associated paraphernalia of targets, quality assurance, performance indicators, league tables and comprehensive procedures are embedded in many areas of practice, particularly in the statutory sector: 'The framework in which we struggle to manage caseloads on a daily basis, or within which we try to create space for new or fresh thinking, is not normally one of our own making, but it is rather imposed from above' (Haines, 2002, p. 142). This point is made specifically in relation to youth justice, but it also holds true in the experience of many practitioners across statutory settings. Webb (2006), for example, is particularly concerned about the emergence of a 'performance culture' in social work, and the way in which this 'shapes the types of relationship that develop' between managers, practitioners and service users (p. 185). Social workers appear, according to him, to have become 'knowledge workers', whose central tasks are to carry out prescribed assessments, calculate risks and allocate provision accordingly.

Indeed, it is somewhat ironic perhaps that opportunities for creative and empowering social work often appear to be more readily available outside the state sector, or in new areas of practice, such as the Connexions Service,[1] which has by and large been implemented without the involvement of social workers. Indeed, when it was introduced, the role of the 'personal adviser' in Connexions was explicitly distinguished from that of the social worker on the grounds that it would be less 'stigmatising' and more acceptable for young people wishing to explore issues of concern (*Guardian*, 4 April 2001).

Similarly, many of the more imaginative, participative and relationship-based interventions with young people 'looked after' have been undertaken by voluntary child care organizations, such as NCH or Barnardo's. The consequences for social work practice in general, though, are problematic, for several reasons. Firstly, interventions are fragmented, and this, in itself, creates potential problems for achieving effective sustained working relationships, where young people are continually being referred on, or where interventions are subdivided amongst a variety of providers. In addition, it seems as if the notion of social work involvement implying some sort of stigma still persists, with the inevitable consequences in terms of engagement and encouraging young people to value the service provided. It is crucial that we do not begin with a negative view of our own involvement as social work professionals. The subdivision of work also creates boundary issues, particularly where some aspects of the overall task are perceived as more highly valued, or more interesting, and this kind of fault line may well have consequences for collaborative working in the interests of young people. Certainly, tensions between residential care and field workers have been recognized as problematic over time.

Apart from reiterating the point that certain professional attributes are important in this context (networking skills and relationship building, for example), it is also important to underline the value of engaging with institutional requirements and inbuilt assumptions, rather than lapsing into routine compliance or cynicism (Jones, C., 2001). Similar processes can, in fact, be informed by different objectives and principles, for example in the area of work with young offenders: 'Critical practice . . . begins from an understanding of the institutional context of youth justice and the implications of the choices that are made within this broader context' (Haines, 2002, p. 143). Haines argues that a professional ethos often stands in opposition to a limited managerial perspective, and that this is important if we are to avoid routinized control in youth justice. However, similar observations can be made in relation to the conduct of social work with young people in general.

Webb (2006), for instance, argues that it is crucial that social workers remain anchored to strong ethical frameworks, and do not allow their practice to become uncritically routinized. A reflective and critical perspective is thus an essential and continuing component of practice, and should be brought to bear on every aspect of the task. In terms of the impact on service users, it is not possible to separate entirely the routinized elements of practice from those which are about establishing relationships and offering care and support. Because of this, it is suggested, we need to think in terms of continuity and consistency in the minutiae of the task as well as the overall aims and objectives of assessment and intervention: 'It is through the constitution of *caring relations* and not *caring actions* that ethical commitment becomes significant in front-line practice. The former is synonymous with reciprocity by entailing inter-subjective concern' (Webb, 2006, p. 216).

In a context of increasing social fragmentation, Webb argues that this is a necessary component of the social work role. Enabling people to feel secure and attached is 'at the heart' of practice (2006, p. 231), and this can be achieved best by working alongside them as they 'work through important life-changes'. We know that young people who experience problems are highly likely to be undergoing significant transitions, so it is crucial to seek to adapt procedures and systems to the currents of change which they are experiencing. The idea of collaborative knowledge generation, touched upon earlier, is consistent with this perspective, and requires a critical approach to standard documentation; for example, space needs to be provided for young people to express wishes and feelings in their own words, and in their own way. The tools available may make this difficult, as we have already noted in the case of the ASSET document (Smith, R., 2007), but given the power of official versions of the 'truth', it is all the more important that practitioners seek to adapt them to include and emphasize what young people think.

Similarly, the fragmentation engendered by service structures may need to be bridged by the practitioner. Notably, for example, where disabled young people move from the remit of children's services to the adult sector, this may involve a major transformation in provision. However, this may also be associated with significant losses, in terms of familiar surroundings, peer networks and educational settings. It is therefore all the more important that practitioners with whom the young person has an established relationship seek to maintain that, at least in the interim, irrespective of the organizational boundaries which might inhibit this. Social work's critical edge must be brought to bear on structures as well as procedures, especially in a context where diversification and change in these arrangements appear to be the norm.

Challenge, change and young people

The preceding discussion has explored some of the issues facing modern-day social work, and in general terms we have considered possible orientations and strategies which may enable practitioners to sustain effective practice in the face of these. At this point, we will turn once again to consider the implications specifically for young people, in the light of the various ways in which the problems they encounter are constituted and experienced.

In focusing on the difficulties faced by young people in this way, some general conclusions for social work practice will be drawn which should be applicable to them both individually and in terms of the various groups which they represent. Young people's needs and aspirations inevitably differ, but there are some aspects of their experience which may be seen as more or less universal, in relation to which optimal intervention strategies can be identified. Adolescence is, for example, a time of 'major emotional, physical and social transformations' (Coleman and Hendry, 1999, p. 225), so issues of 'coping and adjustment' will be encountered by virtually all young people. For those who face particular problems, the question for us must be addressed in terms of how these are defined *for* social work, and the capacities *of* social work to respond effectively.

Dealing with problematic 'transitions'?

Change is recognized as being an unavoidable feature of adolescence. For most young people, of course, it is fairly predictable and can be negotiated without undue difficulty. However, for others, as we have seen, the conventional life changes associated with 'growing up' become problematic for one reason or another. It is at this point that social work comes to have a part to play. However, as we have recognized previously, the form and content of social work intervention may also be subject to a variety of structural and procedural constraints. Given these uncertainties, then, what are the potential elements of effective practice?

Because it appears to be a universal experience, the concept of 'youth transitions', if not entirely unproblematic (MacDonald and Marsh, 2005), may be a helpful starting point for assessment and intervention.

It would, therefore, supersede prior definitions of the young person's 'problem', which might be characterized in terms of 'running away', 'disability' or 'getting into trouble', for example. Immediately, exploration of young people's fears, hopes and dreams is reframed in terms of the issues which are most significant for them, rather than those which are prioritized by others (agencies or families, for example). We could perhaps then draw up a picture of multiple and interlocking transitions, exploring the extent to which they are planned, desired, expected or controlled, as well as their consequences, and what alternatives might be better. It is important to develop an understanding of the connections between different aspects of change in young people's lives. For example, the experience of becoming a parent at an early age will also have consequences for a range of other aspects of the young person's life, including education, living arrangements, and peer and family relationships. Intervention may therefore need to focus not just on issues of health, well-being and parenting, but on a range of other issues, including social networks and opportunities for personal and social development.

To some extent, indeed, this is consistent with the strategic approach espoused by government, and encapsulated in the 'five outcomes' promoted by *Every Child Matters* (DfES, 2003). Even where young people have 'complex' health conditions or impairments, it has been recognized that 'transition' is not just about transferring to adult-oriented services or facilities:

> For successful transition, many young people will also benefit from help in developing skills in communication, decision-making, assertiveness and self-care, helping them to manage social, educational and employment opportunities and challenges and develop the independent living skills which underpin fulfilment and well-being
> (DH, 2006, p. 15)

This reflects what young people themselves say about wanting a more 'adult, future-focused' approach (p. 16), and one which recognizes their autonomy. This is particularly important in this context, where there may be both professional and institutional resistance to the development of inclusive, young-person-centred forms of provision. It is noted that professionals who have a long-standing involvement with young people may, themselves, have difficulty coming to terms with them 'growing up', and seeking personal autonomy (p. 17). This may be especially difficult where young people are identified as vulnerable for whatever reason, and practitioners have to overcome both personal and institutional resistance to risk taking.

A checklist of important principles has thus been established for practitioners in the health sector, specifically in relation to young people who are expected to continue to be provided with adult services. However, most of these are clearly transferable to other contexts for work with young people:

Good transitions – what young people say they want.

- Active management of transition – consider the timing; plan early and prepare for leaving children's services and arriving at the adult service.
- Take into account how attitudes, thinking and behaviour vary between individual young people.
- Involve young people in service design and delivery: provide opportunities for young people to ask questions, express opinions and make decisions.
- Provide accessible information about services; share information between services; ensure multi agency working, co-ordination and accountability across different organisations within the public sector and voluntary organisations.
- Stress the importance of a trusted adult who can challenge and support them, act as advocate and help them to develop self-advocacy skills.
- Establish a shared philosophy between adult and paediatric care.
- Adopt an individualised honest approach.
- Address loss of continuity of care at transition; ensure new relationships are established.
- Train professionals in adolescent health in both paediatric and adult sectors.　　　　　　　　　　　　　　　　(DH, 2006, p. 19)

Importantly, this recognizes some of the challenges for practitioners in assisting young people to negotiate institutional barriers and fault lines, at the same time as recognizing the significance of individual differences and the variable dynamics of personal change. Thus, for example, the central role of a 'trusted adult' who will be available throughout the process is stressed, as is the importance of building good intervention networks between agencies and services. It is also recognized that continuity is often threatened by arbitrary boundaries, and it may be the role of the practitioner to provide the consistent thread which links very different service frameworks and settings. Indeed, social workers (or others in the 'key worker' role) may find themselves having to coordinate a variety of different formal processes which apply different timescales and procedures, which are both confusing in themselves and may cut across the priorities set by the young person and her or his family.

Of course, it is important, too, whatever the 'need' or condition formally identified, that transitions do not become dominated by service priorities at the expense of young people's own goals and aspirations, which may have little to do with these. Indeed, their priorities might be very much about minimizing the consequences of being involved with statutory services and being set apart from peers and 'normal' experiences and relationships. The starting point for intervention should not be determined by the service context, but should seek to focus on the wishes, aspirations and goals of young people. It is important that they are not defined by past experience or current circumstances, as Taylor (2006, p. 179) observes in relation to looked after young people, who 'do not want to be viewed as the "children's home kids" or "care kids", but as individuals in their own right'.

For practitioners, then, the approach to transitions is often very much about 'reframing' or modifying institutional structures and procedures so that they can accommodate and be responsive to the variety and complexity of young people's own, often deeply personal, life changes, and future needs and desires.

Self-fulfilling expectations? Beating the odds

Social work practitioners and young people alike are often bounded by external perceptions. It is perhaps to be expected in the nature of the social work task that the starting point for interventions will be a 'problem' of one sort or another. However, as we have observed, this may be compounded by those processes which tend to highlight the problematic aspects of young people's characteristics or behaviour, and we may find ourselves having to deal with these issues in order to achieve a proper focus on needs and expectations from their own perspective. In other words, it may be part of the social work task to challenge the ways in which young people themselves are problematized.

This has a number of significant implications for practice. Firstly, it may well necessitate taking an 'appreciative' position in relation to young people whose behaviour is viewed as unacceptable or worthy of condemnation, such as those who sexually harm others. It is important to distinguish clearly between behaviour which will not be tolerated and the young person who should none the less be treated with respect and valued.

Indeed, an important part of the social work task may be to work with the young person to deal with the implications of being labelled or defined in purely negative terms. The influence of others' attitudes and characterizations may confirm individuals' perceptions of themselves as having limited self-worth, or being inherently 'bad'. Bandura's (1977) notion of 'social learning' is helpful here, in that it illustrates the process by which individuals begin to internalize ideas and assumptions as accepted knowledge, particularly where these carry the weight of authority. Exposed to the persistent view that they are worthless or wicked, young people may come to accept that as fact, and further-more, to accept that there is little they can do to alter the situation. Associated with this is Seligman's (1975) concept of 'learned helpless-ness', which suggests that people begin to accept over time that there is little they can do to change their circumstances or characteristics. Whilst this perspective might lead at first sight to rather depressing conclusions, it is also pointed out that behaviours and perceptions that are learned can be 'unlearned', and that there is capacity for practition-ers to enable service users to identify possibilities for change (Trevithick, 2005, p. 72).

This suggests that an initial focus for intervention might be the young person's beliefs about herself or himself and the extent to which they may be self-fulfilling. Social workers may need to think in terms of challenging negative beliefs and emphasizing positive attributes, strengths and achievements instead. This might involve a process of 'deconstruction', in Fook's (2002) terms, whereby dominant perspectives are questioned and contradictory evidence and alternative possibilities are explored. In this way, the potential for change can be generated. At this point, a 'strengths' approach would enable the practitioner to 'shift from a problem focus to a concentration on the assets, capacities and positive opportunities' for the young person *and* 'the community' (Bates and Butler, 2004, p. 117).

Whilst the practitioner supports the service user in rethinking her or his self-image and potential in this way, the task is incomplete if it does not also involve an active process of challenging and seeking to change external beliefs and preconceptions about the individual. In other words, the process of development and transformation does not simply take place between the social worker and the young person, but also involves renegotiating social identities. Challenging 'popular perceptions', for example, 'that routinely link children in care with trouble' (Taylor, 2006, p. 180) needs to be seen as a key aspect of the practitioner's role. Recent interest in restorative justice and youth offender panels offers one existing vehicle for reframing views of young people who offend. Making use of the opportunity to engage them in constructive responses to the offence not only takes account of other stakeholders, such as victims, but also emphasizes the capacity of the young person to act responsibly and make a positive contribution. For social work practitioners in the youth justice system, it will be important to utilize restorative interventions to support an alternative view of the young person, and to emphasize her or his capacity to act responsibly.

As we know, the broader context is one in which the problems of youth are often personalized and located firmly with young people. This is problematic because it creates a misleading impression, loading responsibility and blame exclusively onto the young, whilst it also generates potential for specific sub-groups to become the target for discriminatory assumptions and practices. The commitment of social work to anti-oppressive practice requires the profession to adopt a critical view of those attitudes and beliefs which misrepresent young people, both individually and collectively. As Fook (2002) suggests, social work can contribute significantly to this by rethinking the language used to define service users and their problems. It is valuable, for instance, to give accounts of behaviour which contextualize and explain it, rather than treating it as a necessary attribute of the service user. Indeed, she suggests, it may be important to reconsider some of the basic building blocks of problem definition, so that 'knowledge' is not seen as fixed or privileged, and even the idea of a 'problem' may helpfully be reconstituted in terms of 'situations', 'contexts' or 'circumstances' (Fook, 2002, p. 125).

In other words, the aim should be to generate a more open understanding of different and possibly competing accounts of service users and their contexts. Implicit assumptions, such as the distinction between 'deserving' and 'undeserving' cases, should be made explicit, so that they can be questioned and unacknowledged processes of discrimination and selection made clear. Effective practice needs to be self-conscious, and to take an actively critical view of the impact of language and narratives on outcomes for young people: 'We cannot escape language, therefore we need to choose some words instead of others and we need to prioritise information. However, all of us should take time to be critical . . . and to maintain an awareness of the possible subtle effects of our choice of words' (Holland, 2004, p. 144). In this sense it is a continuing task of social workers to test assumptions, including their own, especially where these are linked to popular and powerful beliefs about the young, in general, or certain sub-groups in particular. Indeed, diversity and uncertainty are highly likely to be reflected in much social work practice, and it is therefore important to recognize the validity and value of different 'narratives', especially those which are not routinely acknowledged, or have difficulty in finding a means of expression (Fook, 2002).

Social work, young people and structural oppression

Most problematic, but arguably most crucial for young people, is the question of how social work addresses the third type of problem they encounter, which originates in inequality, discrimination and disadvantage. We know that social work typically engages with service users whose background and experiences often reflect a history of social exclusion, and that this forms the context for any practice intervention. It is therefore crucial that practitioners do not overlook this, or fall prey to 'victim blaming', by applying standards and norms which are simply unrealistic in the light of young people's circumstances.

However, meaningful and progressive social work practice also has to deal with a number of professional uncertainties and institutional constraints, especially for those working in statutory settings. Jones (2001), for example, has captured a real sense of frustration and sometimes despair amongst practitioners who feel that their progressive ideals have been subverted by government diktat, organizational constraints and bureaucratic processes:

> I used to enjoy the freedom of being a social worker to develop relationships with clients, to take a few risks, but now everything is controlled and other people make the key decisions and feed it back to you to implement. It all seems to be about covering people's backs and saving money.
>
> (Social worker quoted in Jones, C., 2001, p. 555)

Despite this observation, it is important to retain a positive view of social work's possibilities, and indeed its achievements in pursuing 'structural' objectives. Dominelli (2002), for example, argues that an anti-oppressive stance is fundamental to social work practice, and that the practice is incomplete if it does not incorporate this element. It is not possible for practitioners to bracket off certain elements of the task from the wider systems and influences which are brought to bear. Failing to challenge inequality and discrimination is effectively to collude with it:

> Facilitating joint (individual and social) responsibility for what happens to people in need also indicates that those representing 'society', namely politicians and social workers, cannot absolve themselves of what is going on, nor can they shunt responsibility for personal well-being onto a marginalised person while maintaining that they support the formation of an inclusive social order. Social workers, as those signifying society's commitment to vulnerable people, are entitled to critique the inadequacy of existing social arrangements and mobilise themselves, clients and others to bring about egalitarian social relations.   (Dominelli, 2002, p. 185)

Accepting this as a core function of social work intervention, we can see therefore that it is not possible simply to adopt a neutral approach to crucial issues such as the over-representation of young black people in the justice system. Social work needs to integrate this knowledge into its actions; for example, practitioners can establish monitoring mechanisms, build support networks, draw on community organizations, incorporate explicit reference to institutional discrimination into their documentation, and engage colleagues in discussion of the issue. This is not an exclusive list, but it illustrates the point that practice need not be stretched far to incorporate anti-discriminatory social action.

We should take encouragement, too, from the recognition of social work's responsibilities in this respect by its professional bodies. The suggestion in the General Social Care Council's 'roles and tasks' document (2007) that social workers should adopt a critical approach to institutional practice is encouraging, even though bounded by contradictory messages. Social work is expected to adopt a commitment to 'human rights' at its core, to pursue social justice and to challenge 'discrimination and exclusion' (GSCC, 2007, p. 7). It 'champions' those who do not have a voice, and supports their efforts to 'overcome barriers'. The structurally ambiguous place of social work appears to have been recognized and its critical voice endorsed.

It might be suggested, indeed, that social work has been at the forefront of promoting service user rights and participative approaches, which are now widely endorsed in respect of work with young people, as we have seen. Practitioners have already played a significant role in demonstrating how to engage with young people and involve them in planning and leading the services provided for them (see Wright et al., 2006, for example). In Hampshire, for example, 'looked after' young people have been able to gain a significant role in determining policies and practice:

> As 'experts' in the care system, we train and give presentations to professionals who work with young people; advise and challenge managers on decisions relating to the services that affect young people; promote the importance of 'true' consultation with young people; and work to change society's stereotype of children in care.
>
> (CAT^2 member, quoted in Wright et al., 2006, p. 53)

We should not over-idealize the impact of progressive social work, or underestimate the scale of the task, given the widespread evidence of inequality and discrimination in our contemporary society. However, it is important to recognize that social work does hold the capacity for positive practice, which links the task of addressing intensely felt individual problems with the equally important job of achieving change in the wider context within which personal difficulties are experienced: 'Working in anti-oppressive ways encompasses working within values that espouse interdependence, reciprocity, equality, democracy, and a sophisticated understanding of the complexities of the social relations that shape an intervention and the dialogical interactions which in turn (re)shape these' (Dominelli, 2002, p. 183). We might indeed argue that social work is uniquely placed to understand and make connections between individual and social needs, and that it is a core element of its 'professionalism' that it takes responsibility for this function.

Almost by definition, the young people who use social work services will be marginalized in one way or another, and sometimes they will experience multiple discriminations. In offering validation for their individual strengths in tandem with support for their collective efforts to gain a voice, social work thus generates mutually reinforcing dynamics. As Dominelli (2002, p. 185) points out, 'an individual's potential for change or taking control of his or her life is never simply a matter of what he or she does or does not want to do'. Practitioners must maintain a continuing awareness of the 'individual in context', recognizing that effective change necessitates a transformation of social relations rather than atomized individuals.

The orientation of social work is therefore necessarily critical. It must be ready to question dominant assumptions and challenge those structures and systems (of which it may be a part) which stereotype and segregate young people, according to pejoratively applied characteristics. Instead, it must pursue dialogue and respectful engagement with young people, irrespective of their background, behaviour or personal attributes.

Concluding thoughts: Social work, young people and social change

In undertaking this review of social work practice with young people, it has become increasingly clear that there is a significant gap between aspirations and reality. There is a widespread acknowledgement now of the importance of involving service users, on the one hand, and the broader principle of young people's participation, on the other. Despite this, and the many examples of good practice available, there persists a recurrent impression that things are not improving quickly enough, and in some cases, they are getting worse. For young people who are asylum seekers, for example, or black young people in the justice system, oppression and harmful treatment appear to be entrenched, whilst young disabled people continue to encounter significant barriers to achieving their personal and social goals. Of course, the root causes of these persistent injustices lie well outside the sphere of social work; however, practitioners often have to deal with the consequences in terms of individual stress and disadvantage. To make a difference, then, social work needs to carry with it a keen sense of social justice, and the rights of young people, as well as their individual hopes and dreams.

Social work also needs to incorporate its own principles of assertiveness and self-worth into the task of articulating its concerns and working alongside disadvantaged young people to promote their interests and challenge injustice. As we have seen, this is not an optional extra but a core component of 'holistic' (Dominelli, 2002, p. 184) and progressive practice, without which the needs and wishes of young people who use social work services cannot be met. Social work and social justice are inseparable.

Chapter summary

Social work with young people is inevitably about helping them to manage complex and problematic transitions. It is often the case that young people themselves are identified as the source of the problem, and their own perceptions and experiences may be devalued or ignored. Social work none the less must seek to establish positive and effective relationships with young people; value them irrespective of what they have done; and utilize its skills and authority to ensure that they are able to exercise control over key decisions about their well-being, their opportunities and their future lives.

Key messages for social work with young people:

- Youth is a period of multiple transitions which will have a significant impact.
- For most young people, these transitions are unsettling but negotiated successfully.
- For some young people, the changes they face are complex and traumatic, for a variety of reasons.
- Social work, by its nature, is likely to engage with young people experiencing difficulties and living complicated lives.
- The ways in which young people and their problems are perceived are significant.
- Social work interventions have to negotiate a number of challenges, including conflicting perceptions, the ambiguity of their role, and the impact of unsettling life experiences.
- The things that matter to young people are not always the issues which lead to social work involvement.
- Social workers must, therefore, base their practice on the need to establish effective and sustained relationships with young people whose lives are subject to substantial uncertainties.
- Interventions must start from 'where young people are' rather than where we want them to be.
- Social work has a significant part to play in helping young people to challenge powerlessness and oppression, and to gain control over what happens to them, as well as a sense of responsibility for what they do.
- Practice must be grounded in acceptance of young people, irrespective of their behaviour, and a commitment to problem-solving, empowerment and achievement.
- Social workers must be prepared to side with young people and advocate for them, even where they are the subject of general disapproval.
- Development is not linear, so inevitably progress towards positive outcomes is not straightforward, especially in the context of problematic transitions.
- Good practice is often about 'holding on', being available, offering support and staying positive.

Notes

CHAPTER 1 WHO ARE WE TALKING ABOUT?

1 The age of criminal responsibility across Europe, for example, varies between 8 in Scotland and 18 in Belgium and Luxembourg (Muncie and Goldson, 2006, p. 200).

CHAPTER 2 WHY ARE YOUNG PEOPLE SEEN AS A SOCIAL PROBLEM?

1 The term 'D/deaf' is used to indicate that some D/deaf people assert their right to a distinctive (Deaf) culture and language, whilst others choose not to make this distinction.

CHAPTER 3 LOOKING AT THINGS FROM YOUNG PEOPLE'S PERSPECTIVE

1 For reasons which are difficult to explain, the post of Children's Commissioner for England is weaker in several crucial respects than the equivalent positions in Scotland, Wales and Northern Ireland, leaving children's rights less well protected as a result.
2 Introduced by the Children (Leaving Care) Act 2000.

CHAPTER 5 CARE OR CONTROL?

1 The 'statutory partners' who must be included in membership of a YOT are: a police officer, social worker, probation officer, education and health workers.

CHAPTER 6 YOUNG PEOPLE'S EXPERIENCES AND EXPECTATIONS OF SOCIAL WORK

1 Quality Protects was launched in September 1998 with eight key objectives which were rapidly extended to eleven (DH, 1999), with a rather typical New Labour battery of sub-objectives, targets and performance indicators appended to these.
2 In writing this, I think I would have to acknowledge having failed to appreciate this point on occasion in my own practice, and an apparently small omission (a missed appointment, say) to me may have had a more significant negative impact on service users than I recognized at the time.

CHAPTER 9 SOCIAL INCLUSION, YOUNG PEOPLE AND THE ROLE OF SOCIAL WORK

1 PACE identifies itself as 'London's leading charity promoting the mental health and emotional wellbeing of the lesbian, gay, bisexual and transgender community'; see http://www.pacehealth.org.uk.

CHAPTER 10 TOWARDS EFFECTIVE PRACTICE

1 Connexions is the generic name for the locally provided, but government-led, advisory, careers, counselling and information service for young people.
2 'The Care Action Team (CAT), established in 1999, is a group of young people who are or have been in care. They work alongside members and officers of Hampshire County Council to improve the services offered to young people in and leaving care' (Wright et al., 2006, p. 52).

References

Aldgate, J. (2006) 'Children, Development and Ecology' in Aldgate, J., Jones, D., Rose, W. and Jeffery, C. (eds) *The Developing World of the Child*, London, Jessica Kingsley, pp. 17–34

Allard, A., Brown, G. and Smith, R. (1995) *The Way it Is*, London, Children's Society

Allen, M. (2003) *Into the Mainstream: Care Leavers Entering Work, Education and Training*, York, Joseph Rowntree Foundation

Arnstein, S. (1967) 'A Ladder of Citizen Participation', *American Institute of Planners Journal*, 35, 4, pp. 216–24

Audit Commission (1996) *Misspent Youth*, London, Audit Commission

Bailey, S. (2006) 'Adolescence and Beyond: Twelve Years Onwards' in Aldgate, J., Jones, D., Rose, W. and Jeffery, C. (eds) *The Developing World of the Child*, London, Jessica Kingsley, pp. 205–25

Bailham, D. and Harper, P. (2004) 'Attachment Theory and Mental Health' in Dwivedi, K. and Harper, P. (eds) *Promoting the Emotional Well-Being of Children and Adolescents and Preventing Their Mental Ill Health*, London, Jessica Kingsley, pp. 49–68

Bandura, A. (1977) *Social Learning Theory*, Englewood Cliffs, Prentice Hall

Banks, S. (2001) *Ethics and Values in Social Work*, Basingstoke, Palgrave

Bannister, A. and Huntington, A. (eds) (2002) *Communicating with Children and Adolescents: Action for Change*, London, Jessica Kingsley

Barn, R. (1993) *Black Children in the Public Care System*, London, Batsford

Barn, R., Andrew, L. and Mantovani, N. (2005) *Life After Care: A Study of the Experiences of Young People from Different Ethnic Groups*, York, Joseph Rowntree Foundation

Bates, P. and Butler, S. (2004) 'Community Connections and Creative Mental Health Practice' in Lymbery, M. and Butler, S. (eds) *Social Work Ideals and Practice Realities*, Basingstoke, Palgrave, pp. 107–32

Batmanghelidjh, C. (2006) *Shattered Lives*, London, Jessica Kingsley

Bebbington, A. and Miles, J. (1989) 'The Background of Children who enter Local Authority Care', *British Journal of Social Work*, 19, pp. 349–68

Beck, U. (1992) *Risk Society*, London, Sage

Beresford, B. (2004) 'On the Road to Nowhere? Young Disabled People and Transition', *Child: Care, Health and Development*, 30, 6, pp. 581–7

Beresford, P. (2007) 'The Changing Roles and Tasks of Social Work from Service Users' Perspectives', http://gscc.org.uk/NR/rdonlyres/0722DD7D6-B915–4F41-B54B-79C62FDB9D95/0/SoLSUliteraturereviewreportMarch07.pdf, accessed 11 February 2008

Berrington, A., Diamond, I., Ingham, R. and Stevenson, J. (2005) *Consequences of Teenage Parenthood: Pathways which Minimise the Long Term Negative Effects of Teenage Childbearing*, Southampton, University of Southampton

Biehal, N. (2005) *Working with Adolescents: Supporting Families, Preventing Breakdown*, London, BAAF

Biehal, N. and Wade, J. (2002) *Children Who Go Missing: Research, Policy and Practice*, London, Department of Health

Biestek, F. (1961) *The Casework Relationship*, London, Allen and Unwin

Boeck, T., Fleming, J. and Kemshall, H. (2006) 'The Context of Risk Decisions: Does Social Capital Make a Difference?', *Forum Qualitative Research*, 7, 1, www.qualitative-research.net/fqs/fqs-e/inhalt1–06-e.htm, accessed 11 February 2008

Bonell, C. (2004) 'Why is Teenage Pregnancy Conceptualized as a Social Problem? A Review of Quantitative Research from the USA and UK', *Culture, Health and Sexuality*, 6, 3, pp. 255–72

Bottoms, A. (1977) 'Reflections on the Renaissance of Dangerousness', *Howard Journal of Criminal Justice*, 16, pp. 70–96

Bracknell Forest Borough Council (2006) *Independent Reviewing Officer Service Annual Report*, Bracknell, Bracknell Forest Borough Council

Broad, B. (1998) *Young People Leaving Care: Life after the Children Act 1989*, London, Jessica Kingsley

Brogan, D. (2005) *Anti-Social Behaviour Orders*, London, Youth Justice Board

Burnett, R. and Appleton, C. (2004) *Joined-Up Youth Justice*, Lyme Regis, Russell House

Butler, I. and Drakeford, M. (2005) *Scandal, Social Work and Social Welfare*, Bristol, Policy Press

Bywaters, P. and Rolfe, A. (2002) *Look Beyond the Scars*, London, NCH

Cambridgeshire County Council Children and Young People's Services (2006) *Good Practice Examples in Cambridgeshire*, Cambridge, Cambridgeshire County Council

Cameron, L. and Murphy, J. (2002) 'Enabling Young People with a Learning Disability to Make Choices at a Time of Transition', *British Journal of Learning Disabilities*, 30, pp. 105–12

Cemlyn, S. and Briskman, L. (2003) 'Asylum, Children's Rights and Social Work', *Child and Family Social Work*, 8, pp. 163–78

Cherry, S. (2005) *Transforming Behaviour: Pro-Social Modelling in Practice*, Cullompton, Willan

Coleman, J. and Hendry, L. (1999) *The Nature of Adolescence* (3rd edition), Hove, Routledge

Consortium for Street Children (2003) *Street Children in the United Kingdom*, http://www.streetchildren.org.uk/Reports/CSC%20Briefing%20Paper-%20Street CHildren%20in%20the%20UK%205.03%20FULL.doc

Corby, B. (2004) 'The Mistreatment of Young People' in Roche, J., Tucker, S., Thomson, R. and Flynn, R. (eds) *Youth in Society* (2nd edition), London, Sage, pp. 207–17

Crawford, A. and Newburn, T. (2003) *Youth Offending and Restorative Justice*, Cullompton, Willan

Creighton, S. (2004) *Child Protection Statistics 1. Child Protection in the Community*, http://www.nspcc.org.uk/Inform/OnlineResources/Statistics/CPStats/1Community_pdf_gf25474.pdf, accessed 14 August 2007

CYPU (Children and Young People's Unit) (2001) *Learning to Listen: Core Principles for the Involvement of Children and Young People*, London, CYPU

DCFS (Department for Children, Families and Schools) (2007) *Youth Transitions Research Overview*, London, DCFS

Dean, H. (1997) 'Underclassed or Undermined? Young People and Social Citizenship' in MacDonald, R. (ed.) *Youth, the 'Underclass' and Social Exclusion*, London, Routledge, pp. 55–69

DfES (Department for Education and Skills) (2003) *Every Child Matters*, London, Stationery Office

DfES (Department for Education and Skills) (2005a) *Youth Matters*, London, Stationery Office

DfES (Department for Education and Skills) (2005b) *Statutory Guidance on the Duty on Local Authorities to Promote the Educational Achievement of Looked After Children under Section 52 of the Children Act 2004*, London, DfES

DfES (Department for Education and Skills) (2006a) *Teenage Pregnancy: Working Towards 2010*, London, DfES

DfES (Department for Education and Skills) (2006b) *Care Matters: Transforming the Lives of Children and Young People in Care*, London, DfES

DfES (Department for Education and Skills) (2006c) *Teenage Pregnancy Next Steps: Guidance for Local Authorities and Primary Care Trusts on Effective Delivery of Local Strategies*, London, DfES

DfES (Department for Education and Skills) (2006d) *The Lead Professional: Practitioner's Guide*, London, DfES

DfES (Department for Education and Skills) (2006e) *Information Sharing: Practitioners' Guide*, London, DfES

DfES (Department for Education and Skills) (2006f) *Youth Matters: Next Steps*, London, DfES

DfES (Department for Education and Skills) (2006g) *Common Assessment Framework*, London, DfES

DfES (Department for Education and Skills) (2007a) *Care Matters: Young People's Responses*, London, DfES

DfES (Department for Education and Skills) (2007b) *Care Matters: Time for Change*, London, DfES

DH (Department of Health) (1999) *The Government's Objectives for Children's Social Services*, London, Department of Health

DH (Department of Health) (2000a) *Framework for the Assessment of Children in Need and their Families*, London, Stationery Office

DH (Department of Health) (2000b) *Assessing Children in Need and their Families: Practice Guidance*, London, Stationery Office

DH (Department of Health) (2000c) *Safeguarding Children Involved in Prostitution*, London, Department of Health

DH (Department of Health) (2001) *Children (Leaving Care) Act 2000: Regulations and Guidance*, London, Stationery Office

DH (Department of Health) (2002) *Children's Homes National Minimum Standards: Children's Homes Regulations*, London, Stationery Office

DH (Department of Health) (2003a) *Pathway Plan: Version 1*, London, Department of Health

DH (Department of Health) (2003b) *Outcome Indicators for Looked after Children: Twelve Months to September 2002*, London, Department of Health

DH (Department of Health) (2006) *Transition: Getting it Right for Young People*, London, Department of Health

Dominelli, L. (2002) *Anti-Oppressive Social Work Theory and Practice*, Basingstoke, Palgrave

Downes, C. (1988) 'Foster Families for Adolescents: The Healing Potential of Time-Limited Placements', *British Journal of Social Work*, 18, pp. 473–87

Duncan, S. (2005) *What's the Problem? Teenage Parents: A Critical Review*, London, London South Bank University

Durant, C., Thomas, R. and Manning, R. (2005) *Each One, Teach One! Returning Young Parents to Education, Employment or Training (RYPEET)*, Leicester, Connexions

Edebalk, P. (2005) 'Children Looked After and Their Right to Participation in Accordance with the UN Convention on the Rights of the Child, Article 12', *Childhoods 2005 Conference*, Oslo, July

Emerson, E. and Hatton, C. (2007) *The Mental Health of Children and Adolescents with Learning Disabilities in Britain*, Lancaster, Lancaster University

Erikson, E. (1963) *Childhood and Society*, London, Vintage

Fahlberg, V. (1994) *A Child's Journey Through Placement*, London, BAAF

Farrington, D. (2002) 'Understanding and Preventing Youth Crime' in Muncie, J., Hughes, G. and McLaughlin, E. (eds) *Youth Justice: Critical Readings*, London, Sage, pp. 425–30

Fergusson, D., Horwood, J. and Lynskey, M. (1997) 'Childhood Sexual Abuse, Adolescent Behaviours and Sexual Revictimization', *Child Abuse and Neglect*, 21, 8, pp. 789–803

Fish, J. (2006) *Heterosexism in Health and Social Care*, Basingstoke, Palgrave Macmillan

Fletcher-Campbell, F. and Archer, T. (2003) *Achievement at Key Stage 4 of Young People in Public Care*, Slough, National Foundation for Educational Research

Folgheraiter, F. (2004) *Relational Social Work*, London, Jessica Kingsley

Fook, J. (2002) *Critical Social Work*, London, Sage

Foucault, M. (1979) *Discipline and Punish*, Harmondsworth, Penguin

Foundation for People with Learning Difficulties (2007) 'Statistics about People with Learning Difficulties', http://www.learningdisabilities.org.uk/information/learning-disabilities-statistics, accessed 14 August 2007

Fox Harding, L. (1997) *Perspectives in Child Care Policy* (2nd edition), Harlow, Addison Wesley Longman

Franklin, A. and Sloper, P. (2004) 'Participation of Disabled Children and Young People in Decision-Making within Social Services Departments in England', *Research Works*, York, Social Policy Research Unit

Franklin, B. (2002a) 'Children's Rights: An Introduction' in Franklin, B. (ed.) *The New Handbook of Children's Rights*, London, Routledge, pp. 1–11

Franklin, B. (ed.) (2002b) *The New Handbook of Children's Rights*, London, Routledge

French, S. and Swain, J. (2004) 'Young Disabled People' in Roche, J., Tucker, S., Thomson, R. and Flynn, R. (eds) *Youth in Society* (2nd edition), London, Sage, pp. 199–206

Frost, N. (2006) 'Professionalism and Social Change – The Implications of Social Change for the "Reflective Practitioner" ', http://www.leeds.ac.uk/medicine/meu/lifelong06/papers/P_NickFrost.pdf, accessed 11 February 2008

Furlong, A. and Cartmel, F. (2001) *Young People and Social Change*, Buckingham, Open University Press

Garland, D. (2001) *The Culture of Control*, Oxford, Oxford University Press

Garland, D. (2006) 'Concepts of Culture in the Sociology of Punishment', *Theoretical Criminology*, 10, 4, pp. 419–47

Gibson, S. (2006) 'Beyond a "Culture of Silence": Inclusive Education and the Liberation of "Voice" ' *Disability and Society*, 21, 4, pp. 315–29

Giddens, A. (1991) *Modernity and Self-Identity*, Cambridge, Polity

Goyder, E., Blank, L. and Peters, J. (2003) *Supporting Teenage Parents: The Potential Contribution*, Sheffield, Sheffield Hallam University

Graber, J. and Brooks-Gunn, J. (1996) 'Transitions and Turning Points: Navigating the Passage from Childhood through Adolescence', *Developmental Psychology*, 32, pp. 768–76

Graham, J. and Bowling, B. (1995) *Young People and Crime*, London, Home Office

Gray, P. (2005) 'The Politics of Risk and Young Offenders' Experiences of Social Exclusion and Restorative Justice', *British Journal of Criminology*, 45, 6, pp. 938–57

Griffin, C. (1993) *Representations of Youth*, Cambridge, Polity

GSCC (General Social Care Council) (2002) *Codes of Practice for Social Care Workers*, London, GSCC

GSCC (General Social Care Council) (2007) *Roles and Tasks of Social Work in England*, London, GSCC

Gunn, R. (2005) 'Young People's Participation in Social Services Policy Making', *Research, Policy and Planning*, 23, 3, pp. 127–37

Haines, K. (2002) 'Youth Justice and Young Offenders' in Adams, R., Dominelli, L. and Payne, M. (eds) *Critical Practice in Social Work*, Basingstoke, Palgrave, pp. 137–48

Harris, J. and Broad, B. (2005) *In My Own Time: Achieving Positive Outcomes for Young People Leaving Care*, Leicester, De Montfort University

Hart, R. (1992) *Children's Participation from Tokenism to Citizenship*, Geneva, UNICEF

Hart, R. (1997) *Children's Participation in Sustainable Development*, London, Earthscan

Hawton, K. and James, A. (2005) 'Suicide and Deliberate Self-Harm in Young People', *British Medical Journal*, 330, pp. 891–4

Hendrick, H. (2003) *Child Welfare*, Bristol, Policy Press

Herrenkohl, E., Herrenkohl, R., Egolf, B. and Rosso, M. (1998) 'The Relationship between Early Maltreatment and Teenage Parenthood', *Journal of Adolescence*, 21, pp. 291–303

Hewitt, P. (2003) *The Looked After Kid*, Edinburgh, Mainstream

Hind, T. (2004) *Being Real: Promoting the Emotional Health and Mental Well-Being of Lesbian, Gay and Bisexual Young People Accessing PACE Youth Work Services*, London, PACE

Hine, J. (2004) *Children and Citizenship*, London, Home Office

Hirst, J., Formby, E. and Owen, J. (2006) *Pathways into Parenthood: Reflections from Three Generations of Teenage Mothers and Fathers*, Sheffield, Sheffield Hallam University

HM Government (2006) *Working Together to Safeguard Children*, London, Stationery Office

Hogeveen, B. (2006) 'Unsettling Youth Justice and Cultural Norms: The Youth Restorative Action Project', *Journal of Youth Studies*, 9, 1, pp. 47–66

Holland, S. (2004) *Child and Family Assessment in Social Work Practice*, London, Sage

Home Office (1997) *No More Excuses*, London, Home Office

Howarth, D. (2000) *Discourse*, Buckingham, Open University Press

Howe, D. (1995) *Attachment Theory for Social Work Practice*, Basingstoke, Macmillan

Howe, D. (2001) 'Attachment' in Horwath, J. (ed.) *The Child's World*, London, Jessica Kingsley, pp. 194–206

Howe, D., Schofield, G., Brandon, M. and Hinings, D. (1999) *Attachment Theory, Child Maltreatment and Family Support: A Practice and Assessment Model*, Basingstoke, Palgrave Macmillan

Humphries, B. (2004) 'An Unacceptable Role for Social Work: Implementing Asylum Policy', *British Journal of Social Work*, 34, pp. 93–107

Hussain, Y., Atkin, K. and Ahmad, W. (2002) 'South Asian Young Disabled People and Their Families', *Findings*, 742, York, Joseph Rowntree Foundation

Jigsaw (2003) *Consultation with Disabled Children in Sutton 2003*, Mitcham, Jigsaw

Joint Chief Inspectors (2005) *Report on Arrangements to Safeguard Children*, London, Commission for Social Care Inspection

Jones, C. (2001) 'Voices from the Front Line: State Social Workers and New Labour', *British Journal of Social Work*, 31, pp. 547–62

Jones, G. (1997) 'Youth Homelessness and the "Underclass"' in Macdonald, R. (ed.) *Youth, the 'Underclass' and Social Exclusion*, London, Routledge, pp. 96–112

Kelly, R. (2005) 'Foreword' in DfES *Youth Matters*, London, Stationery Office

Kirkwood, A. (1993) *The Leicestershire Inquiry 1992*, Leicester, Leicestershire County Council

Knight, A., Clark, A., Petrie, P. and Statham, J. (2006) *The Views of Children and Young People with Learning Disabilities about the Support they Receive from Social Services: A Review of Consultations and Methods*, London, Thomas Coram Research Unit

Kohli, R. and Mather, R. (2003) 'Promoting Psychosocial Well-Being in Unaccompanied Asylum Seeking Young People in the United Kingdom', *Child and Family Social Work*, 8, pp. 201–12

Kurtz, A. (2002) 'What Works for Delinquency? The Effectiveness of Interventions for Teenage Offending Behaviour', *Journal of Forensic Psychiatry*, 13, 3, pp. 671–92

Lancashire Area Child Protection Committee (n.d.) *Protocol: Working with Sexually Active Young People Under the Age of 18*, Lancaster, Lancashire ACPC

Levy, A. and Kahan, B. (1991) *The Pindown Experience and the Protection of Children*, Stafford, Staffordshire County Council

Lister, R., Smith, N., Middleton, S. and Cox, L. (2005) 'Young People and Citizenship' in: Barry, M. (ed.) *Youth Policy and Social Inclusion: Critical Debate with Young People*, London, Routledge, pp. 33–51

Logan, J. (2001) 'Sexuality, Child Care and Social Work Education', *Social Work Education*, 20, 5, pp. 563–75

Lupton, D. (1999) *Risk*, London, Routledge

Macaskill, C. (2006) *Beyond Refuge: Supporting Young Runaways*, London, NSPCC

McCrystal, P., Percy, A. and Higgins, K. (2007) 'Exclusion and Marginalisation in Adolescence: The Experience of School Exclusion on Drug Use and Antisocial Behaviour', *Journal of Youth Studies*, 10, 1, pp. 35–54

MacDonald, R. and Marsh, J. (2005) *Disconnected Youth? Growing Up in Britain's Poor Neighbourhoods*, Basingstoke, Palgrave

Marchant, R. (2001) 'The Assessment of Children with Complex Needs' in Horwath, J. (ed.) *The Child's World*, London, Jessica Kingsley, pp. 207–20

Marchant, R. and Jones, M. (2000) 'Assessing the Needs of Disabled Children and Their Families' in Department of Health (ed.) *Assessing Children in Need and Their Families: Practice Guidance*, London, Stationery Office

Margo, J. and Dixon, M. (2006) *Freedom's Orphans: Raising Youth in a Changing World*, London, Institute for Public Policy Research

Marshall, H. and Stenner, P. (2004) 'Friends and Lovers' in Roche, J., Tucker, S., Thomson, R. and Flynn, R. (eds) *Youth in Society* (2nd edition), London, Sage, pp. 184–90

Mason, J. and Fattore, T. (eds) (2005) *Children Taken Seriously*, London, Jessica Kingsley

Mayall, B. (2002) *Towards a Sociology for Childhood*, Buckingham, Open University Press

Meltzer, H., Gatward, R., Corbin, T., Goodman, R. and Ford, T. (2003) *The Mental Health of Young People Looked After by Local Authorities in England*, London, Stationery Office

Merton, B., Comfort, H. and Payne, M. (2007) 'Recognising and Recording the Impact of Youth Work' in Harrison, R., Benjamin, C., Curran, S. and Hunter, R. (eds) *Leading Work with Young People*, London, Sage, pp. 271–84

Middleton, L. (1999) *Disabled Children: Challenging Social Exclusion*, Oxford, Blackwell

Morgan, R. (2006) *Running Away: A Children's Views Report*, Newcastle, Office of the Children's Rights Director

MORI (2002) *Youth Survey 2002*, London, YJB

Morris, J. (2002) 'Young Disabled People Moving into Adulthood', *Foundations*, 512, York, Joseph Rowntree Foundation

Mullender, A. (2002) 'Persistent Oppressions: The Example of Domestic Violence' in Adams, R., Dominelli, L. and Mullender, A. (eds) *Critical Practice in Social Work*, Basingstoke, Palgrave, pp. 63–71

Muncie, J. and Goldson, B. (2006) 'States of Transition: Convergence and Diversity in International Youth Justice' in Muncie, J. and Goldson, B. (eds) *Comparative Youth Justice*, London, Sage, pp. 196–218

Munro, E. (2001) 'Empowering Looked After Children', *Child and Family Social Work*, 6, pp. 129–37

NCSR/NFER (2006) *Drug Use, Smoking and Drinking among Young People in England in 2005: Headline Figures*, http://www.ic.nhs.uk/webfiles/publications/drugsmokedrinkyoungeng2005/DrugSMokingDrinkingYoungPeople240306_PDF.pdf, accessed 3 July 2007

Nessa, N. (2004) 'Disability' in Office for National Statistics (ed.) *The Health of Children and Young People*, London, Stationery Office, pp. 3–20

Netcare (2007) 'Working Together to Find Solutions . . . ', http://www.netcare.ni.com/services/solutions/viewdetails.asp?serviceID=3, accessed 11 February 2008

Newburn, T. (2007) *Criminology*, Cullompton, Willan

Norman, C. and Wilks, S. (1993) *A Fit State for Motherhood?*, London, The Children's Society

NSPCC (National Society for Prevention of Cruelty to Children) (2006a) 'The Prevalence and Incidence of Abuse and Neglect: Topline Data', http://www.nspcc.org.uk/Inform/OnlineResources/Statistics/KeyCPStats/1_asp_ifega26453.html, accessed 14 August 2007

NSPCC (National Society for Prevention of Cruelty to Children) (2006b) 'Runaways', http://nspcc.org.uk/Inform/OnlineResources/Statistics/KeyCPStats/14_asp_ifega26460.html, accessed 14 August 2007

Office for National Statistics (2003) *The Mental Health of Young People Looked After by Local Authorities in England*, London, Stationery Office

Oliver, M. (1990) *The Politics of Disablement*, Basingstoke, Macmillan

Packman, J. (1981) *The Child's Generation* (2nd edition), Oxford, Blackwell and Martin Robertson

Packman, J. and Hall, C. (1998) *From Care to Accommodation*, London, Stationery Office

Packman, J. with Randall, J. and Jacques, N. (1986) *Who Needs Care?*, Oxford, Blackwell

Park, A., Phillips, M. and Johnson, M. (2004) *Young People in Britain: The Attitudes and Experiences of 12 to 19 Year Olds*, London, DfES

Participation Works (2007) *Participation Charter*, http://www.participationworks.org.uk/AboutUs/Charter/tabid/68/Default.aspx, accessed 8 February 2008

Parton, N. and O'Byrne, P. (2000) *Constructive Social Work: Towards a New Practice*, Basingstoke, Palgrave

PAT (Policy Action Team) 12 (2000) *Young People*, London, Social Exclusion Unit

Pearce, J. (2003) 'The Choice and Opportunity Project: Young Women and Sexual Exploitation', *Findings*, 513, York, Joseph Rowntree Foundation

Pearson, G. (1983) *Hooligan: A History of Respectable Fears*, Macmillan, Basingstoke

Pearson, G. (2002) 'Youth Crime and Moral Decline: Permissiveness and Tradition' in Muncie, J., Hughes, G. and McLaughlin, E. (eds) *Youth Justice: Critical Readings*, London, Sage, pp. 45–9

Perkins, M. (2006) 'Genetic and Biological Influences' in Aldgate, J., Jones, D., Rose, W. and Jeffery, C. (eds) *The Developing World of the Child*, London, Jessica Kingsley, pp. 55–66

Peterson, C., Maier, S. and Seligman, M. (1993) *Learned Helplessness: A Theory for the Age of Personal Control*, New York, Oxford University Press

Phoenix, J. (2007) 'Doing Youth Justice: Research Report', http://esrcsociety today.ac.uk/ESRCInfoCentre/ViewAwardPage.aspx?awardnumber=RES-000–23–5015, accessed 11 February 2008

Piaget, J. (1959) *The Language and Thought of the Child* (3rd edition), London, Routledge

Plant, B. and McFeely, S. (2004) *Working with Young People: 'Real Life Stuff'*, Salisbury, APS

Prime Minister's Strategy Unit (2005) *Improving the Life Chances of Disabled People*, London, Prime Minister's Strategy Unit

Quilgars, D. (2002) 'The Mental Health of Children' in Bradshaw, J. (ed.) *The Well-Being of Children in the UK*, London, Save the Children, pp. 346–62

Rabiee, P., Sloper, P. and Beresford, B. (2005) 'Doing Research with Children and Young People Who Do Not Use Speech for Communication', *Children and Society*, 19, pp. 385–96

Reder, P., Duncan, S. and Gray, M. (1993) *Beyond Blame: Child Abuse Tragedies Revisited*, London, Routledge

Richardson, C. (2006) *The Truth about Self-Harm*, London, Mental Health Foundation

Robinson, G. (2005) 'What Works in Offender Management?', *Howard Journal*, 44, 3, pp. 307–18

Roche, J. (2002) 'The Children Act 1989 and Children's Rights: A Critical Reassessment' in Franklin, B. (ed.) *The New Handbook of Children's Rights*, London, Routledge, pp. 60–80

Rose, N. (1999) *Governing the Soul* (2nd edition), London, Free Association Books

Roy, A., Wattam, C. and Young, F. (2002) 'Looking after Children and Young People' in Adams, R., Dominelli, L. and Payne, M. (eds) *Critical Practice in Social Work*, Basingstoke, Palgrave, pp. 116–25

Royal College of Psychiatrists (1998) *Managing Deliberate Self-Harm in Young People*, London, Royal College of Psychiatrists

Rutherford, A. (1995) *Growing Out of Crime* (2nd edition), Winchester, Waterside Press

Rutter, M., Giller, H. and Hagell, A. (1998) *Antisocial Behaviour by Young People*, Manchester, Fields Press

Sampson, R. and Laub, J. (1990) 'Crime and Deviance Over the Life Course: The Salience of Adult Social Bonds', *American Sociological Review*, 55, pp. 609–27

Schofield, G. and Brown, K. (1999) 'Being There: A Family Centre Worker's Role as a Secure Base for Adolescent Girls in Crisis', *Child and Family Social Work*, 4, pp. 21–31

Scottish Executive (2003) *Vulnerable Children and Young People: Young Runaways*, Edinburgh, Scottish Executive

Scottish Executive (2005) *Restorative Justice Services in the Children's Hearings System*, Edinburgh, Scottish Executive

Self, A. and Zealey, L. (eds) (2007) *Social Trends No. 37*, Basingstoke, Palgrave

Seligman, M. (1975) *Helplessness: On Depression, Development and Death*, San Francisco, Freeman

SEU (Social Exclusion Unit) (1999) *Teenage Pregnancy*, London, SEU

SEU (Social Exclusion Unit) (2002) *Young Runaways*, London, SEU

SEU (Social Exclusion Unit) (2005) *Transitions: Young Adults with Complex Needs*, London, Office of the Deputy Prime Minister

Sharland, E. (2006) 'Young People, Risk Taking and Risk Making: Some Thoughts for Social Work', *British Journal of Social Work*, 38, 2, pp. 247–65

Sherrard, J., Tonge, B. and Ozanne-Smith, J. (2002) 'Injury Risk in Young People with Intellectual Disability', *Journal of Intellectual Disability Research*, 46, 1, pp. 6–16

Sinclair, R. (1998) 'Involving Children in Planning Their Care', *Child and Family Social Work*, 3, pp. 137–42

Sinclair, R. (2000) 'Young People's Participation', *Quality Protects Research Briefing No. 3*, London, Department of Health

Smeaton, E. and Rees, G. (2004) *Running Away in South Yorkshire*, London, Children's Society

Smith, M. (2007) 'Family Change and Child Well-Being', ESRC/DfES Public Policy Seminar, London, 19 March

Smith, R. (2000) 'Order and Disorder: The Contradictions of Childhood', *Children and Society*, 14, 1, pp. 3–10

Smith, R. (2003) *Youth Justice: Ideas, Policy, Practice*, Cullompton, Willan

Smith, R. (2005) *Values and Practice in Children's Services*, Basingstoke, Palgrave

Smith, R. (2007) *Youth Justice: Ideas, Policy, Practice* (2nd edition), Cullompton, Willan

Souter, A. and Kraemer, S. (2004) ' "Given Up Hope of Dying": A Child Protection Approach to Deliberate Self-Harm in Adolescents Admitted to a Paediatric Ward', *Child and Family Social Work*, 9, pp. 259–64

Spicer, N. and Evans, R. (2006) 'Developing Children and Young People's Participation in Strategic Processes: The Experience of the Children's Fund Initiative', *Social Policy and Society*, 5, 2, pp.177–88

Stainton Rogers, R. (2004) 'The Making and Moulding of Modern Youth: A Short History' in Roche, J., Tucker, S., Thomson, R. and Flynn, R. (eds) *Youth in Society* (2nd edition), London, Sage, pp. 1–9

Stalker, K.(2002) 'Young Disabled People Moving into Adulthood in Scotland', *Foundations*, n42, York, Joseph Rowntree Foundation

Stein, M. (2005) *Resilience and Young People Leaving Care*, York, Joseph Rowntree Foundation

Stein, M. and Carey, K. (1986) *Leaving Care*, Oxford, Blackwell

Swann, C., Bowe, K., McCormick, G. and Kosmin, M. (2003) *Teenage Pregnancy and Parenthood: A Review of Reviews*, London, Health Development Agency

Taylor, C. (2006) *Young People in Care and Criminal Behaviour*, London, Jessica Kingsley

Teenage Pregnancy Unit (2004) *Enabling Young People to Access Contraceptive and Sexual Health Information and Advice*, London, DfES

Thomas, N. (2005) *Social Work with Young People in Care*, Basingstoke, Palgrave

Thomas, N. and O'Kane, C. (1999) 'Children's Participation in Reviews and Planning Meetings When They Are "Looked After" in Middle Childhood', *Child and Family Social Work*, 4, pp. 221–30

Thompson, N. (2003) *Communication and Language: A Handbook of Theory and Practice*, Basingstoke, Palgrave

Timimi, S. (2005) *Naughty Boys*, Basingstoke, Palgrave

Trevithick, P. (2005) *Social Work Skills: A Practice Handbook* (2nd edition), Maidenhead, Open University Press

Trotter, C. (2006) *Working with Involuntary Clients* (2nd edition), London, Sage

Tucker, S. (2004) 'Youth Working: Professional Identities Given, Received or Contested?' in Roche, J., Tucker, S., Thomson, R. and Flynn, R. (eds) *Youth in Society* (2nd edition), pp. 81–9

Turner, C. and Jagusz, S. (n.d.) *Feedback from Young People on the SEU Recommendations for Young Runaways – Report for the Social Exclusion Unit*, London, Barnardo's

United Nations (1989) *Convention on the Rights of the Child*, Geneva, United Nations

Utting, W. (1997) *People Like Us*, London, Stationery Office

Valentine, G. and Skelton, T. (2007) 'Re-Defining Norms: D/deaf Young People's Transitions to Independence', *Sociological Review*, 55, 1, pp. 104–23

Viewpoint (2006) *Looked After Children Report 2006*, Bridgend, Viewpoint

Wade, J. (2003) *Leaving Care*, Quality Protects Research Briefing, 7, Dartington, Department of Health/Research in Practice/Making Research Count.

Ward, A. (2004) 'Working with Young People in Residential Settings' in Roche, J., Tucker, S., Thomson, R. and Flynn, R. (eds) *Youth in Society* (2nd edition), Buckingham, Open University Press, pp. 235–44

Ward, H., Skuse, T. and Munro, E. (2005) ' "The Best of Times, the Worst of Times": Young People's Views of Care and Accommodation' *Adoption and Fostering Journal*, 29, 1, pp. 8–17

Ward, L., Mallett, R., Heslop, P. and Simons, K. (2003) 'Transition Planning: How Well Does it Work for Young People with Learning Disabilities and their Families', *British Journal of Special Education*, 30, 3, pp. 132–7

Waterhouse, R. (2000) *Lost in Care*, London, Stationery Office

Webb, S. (2006) *Social Work in a Risk Society*, Basingstoke, Palgrave

White, S. (1997) 'Beyond Retroduction? Hermeneutics, Reflexivity and Social Work Practice', *British Journal of Social Work*, 27, 5, pp. 739–53

Whitehurst, T. (2006) 'Liberating Silent Voices – Perspectives of Children with Profound and Complex Learning Needs on Inclusion', *British Journal of Learning Disabilities*, 35, pp. 55–61

Wiggins, M., Oakley, A., Sawtell, M., Austerberry, H., Clemens, F. and Elboune, D. (2005) *Teenage Parenthood and Social Exclusion: A Multi-Method Study*, London, Social Science Research Unit

Williamson, H. (1997) 'Status Zer0 Youth and the "Underclass": Some Considerations' in MacDonald, R. (ed.) *Youth, the 'Underclass' and Social Exclusion*, London, Routledge, pp. 70–82

Willow, C. (1996) *Children's Rights and Participation in Residential Care*, London, National Children's Bureau

Wood, M. (2005) *Perceptions and Experience of Antisocial Behaviour: Findings from the 2003/2004 British Crime Survey*, London, Home Office

Wright, P., Turner, C., Clay, D. and Mills, H. (2006) *The Participation of Children and Young People in Developing Social Care*, London, SCIE

Yeo, M. and Sawyer, S. (2005) 'Chronic Illness and Disability', *British Medical Journal*, 330, pp. 721–3

Youth Justice Board (n.d.) *ASSET*, London, YJB

Index